THE PREACHER'S HEBREW/GREEK COMPANION SERIES

General Editor / Old Testament Editor

Jonathan G. Kline, PhD
Senior Editor
Hendrickson Publishers

New Testament Editor

Sean M. McDonough, PhD
Professor of New Testament
Gordon-Conwell Theological Seminary

The Preacher's Hebrew Companion Series

Isaiah 1–39

THE PREACHER'S HEBREW COMPANION TO

Isaiah 1–39

A Selective Commentary for
Meditation and Sermon Preparation

Bryan Murawski

HENDRICKSON
ACADEMIC

an imprint of Hendrickson Publishing Group

The Preacher's Hebrew Companion to Isaiah 1–39:
A Selective Commentary for Meditation and Sermon Preparation

Published by Hendrickson Academic
an imprint of Hendrickson Publishing Group
Hendrickson Publishers, LLC
P. O. Box 3473
Peabody, Massachusetts 01961-3473
www.hendricksonpublishers.com

ISBN 979-8-4005-0034-3

First Printing — August 2024

Library of Congress Control Number: 2024931056

CONTENTS

ISAIAH 6:1–13

Isaiah's Commissioning

51

ISAIAH 7:10–17

The Sign of Immanuel

87

ISAIAH 8:23–9:6 [9:1–7]

A Child Is Born

107

ISAIAH 11:1–10

The Messiah's Kingdom

133

ISAIAH 14:12–20c

The Fall of the King of Babylon

157

ISAIAH 27:1–13

A Pleasant Vineyard

179

ISAIAH 28:1–13

Woes upon the Leadership

213

SERIES EDITORS' PREFACE

Overview

Like many preachers, you may wish you could use the biblical languages in your sermon preparation, but the task seems daunting. Perhaps you lack confidence in your language skills—especially if it's been a long time since you studied Greek or Hebrew—and when you turn to technical commentaries, you feel overwhelmed. Or perhaps you simply don't have the time to do the laborious work of digging into the original-language texts. To help you overcome these challenges, we designed this series, the Preacher's Hebrew Companion (as well as its New Testament counterpart series, the Preacher's Greek Companion). In collaboration with the series authors, our goal as series editors is to gently guide you, the busy preacher, through the Hebrew text of select biblical passages in a way that will empower you to integrate original-language exegesis and homiletics. Our prayer is that you will find this book and the other volumes in this series spiritually and intellectually encouraging as well as pleasant to use. We hope your use of the series will make your sermon preparation a more profound and satisfying process and will invigorate your preaching.

Structure

Each volume in this series includes the following three features for a given biblical book (or portion of a book):

- **a curated selection of passages** we believe many preachers would likely choose to preach on from the biblical book (or portion of the book) in question; **or, for shorter biblical books, the entire book**, broken up into manageable passages
- all the basic **lexical and grammatical tools** you need (whatever your Hebrew skill level may be) **to work through and meditate on the Hebrew text** of these passages in a way that strengthens your sermon preparation and empowers you to preach more effectively
- **succinct, select comments** intended to help you responsibly and effectively bridge the gap between reading the Hebrew text and delivering a sermon on it

The Preacher's Hebrew Companion is not a traditional commentary series, as is reflected in its title and subtitle: "*Companion*" (not "Commentary") and "*Selected* Passages for *Meditation* and *Sermon Preparation*." That is, we conceived this series as a *supplement* to the wealth of fine commentaries that already exist, not as a replacement for any of them. We recommend using this series alongside traditional commentaries, which by design include helpful information that is not covered in ours.

The Selection of Passages

Each volume in the Preacher's Hebrew Companion series provides the Hebrew text of **approximately ten to twelve passages** from a particular biblical book (or portion thereof):

- In addition to having expertise in Hebrew and exegesis, our series authors typically have extensive preaching experience or are full-time preachers by vocation. Unless the biblical book in question is short enough to be included in full, they chose **passages** they think **preachers would most likely desire to preach**. In order to encourage preaching through the biblical book in an "expository" rather than a thematic manner, these passages are presented in canonical order. That said, for longer books (such as Isaiah or Matthew), we encouraged authors to choose passages that highlight or represent important themes found in the book; for such books, however, the chosen passages are still presented in canonical order. The curated, limited number of passages in each series volume allows you, if you wish, to use the passages as the basis for a "ready-made" sermon series of whatever length suits your schedule (e.g., for a series consisting of, say, four, seven, ten, or twelve sermons). Alternatively, you might choose to preach a series using some of the passages in a volume and then supplement these with passages from the biblical book in question that are not found in the volume.

- The aims of the series guided our decisions about passage length. On the one hand, we encouraged authors to choose **passages that are not too long**, so that the portions of text won't be daunting to you if your Hebrew skills are rudimentary; nor do we want you to be overwhelmed by wading through dozens of verses in Hebrew. For this reason, our ideal length for most passages has been approximately ten verses. On the other hand, in order to do justice to the natural boundaries of longer passages, we have taken care not to artificially truncate such texts. Consider, for example, the account of the crossing of the Red Sea (Exod 14–15) or the story of the raising of Lazarus (John 11). Although these texts are far too long to be included in full in a volume in this series, each constituent part of these texts is vital to understanding their narrative development and message. For such passages, we asked authors to focus—as a preacher might typically do when delivering a sermon on a lengthy passage—on what they consider to be the most salient verses from the passage. Accordingly, we have provided the Hebrew text for only these verses, with the author summarizing the other verses (in English).

- Finally, when authors deemed it helpful (especially for longer biblical books), they have indicated, on the first page devoted to each passage, the **larger literary unit to which the passage belongs**,[1] thus helping you see the passage in question as part of a larger whole rather than as an isolated pericope. In cases where this larger literary context is indicated, we encourage you to pick up a Bible and read and dwell on this context while using this volume to work through the passage.

The Presentation of Each Passage

This volume helps you work through each passage it contains by presenting the Hebrew text of the passage along with the lexical and grammatical information you need in order to dig into this original-language text. Designed to be highly accessible, this format is intended (1) to enable you to work through the text in manageable chunks and according to your abilities, regardless of your skill level in Hebrew; (2) to simultaneously facilitate both study and devotion; and (3) in conjunction with the author's commentary, to help you bridge the gap, as easily and seamlessly as possible, between the original-language text and preaching.

More specifically, this volume contains the following five sections for each passage:

- A **brief introduction** to the passage—typically comprising only a few sentences—is included in order to set the stage for the passage and highlight its important themes.

- For ease of reading and to encourage you to slow down and contemplate the text, the passage is typically divided into subunits. For each of these subunits, we provide the **Hebrew text** of each clause or phrase, along

1. Occasionally, such a literary unit is coterminous with the passage itself.

with **transliteration** (as a pronunciation help for those whose Hebrew is at a rudimentary level) and the author's **translation**.[2]

- Next, each clause or phrase from the subunit is presented in an interlinear fashion, notably with **a contextual gloss (or multiple contextual glosses) and parsing for each word**.[3] For example:

1a	בְּרֵאשִׁית בָּרָא אֱלֹהִים		
	In the beginning, God created		
בְּרֵאשִׁית רֵאשִׁית	in beginning of/ when . . . began *bə·rē'·**šîṯ***	CST W/ PREP בְּ	noun
בָּרָא ברא	(he) created *bā·**rā'***	QAL PF 3MS	verb
אֱלֹהִים אֱלֹהִים	God *'ĕ·lō·**hîm***	ABS	noun

This formatting allows you to easily analyze each word in the clause or phrase (by helping you on the level of semantics and morphology) and to perceive how the words work together as a whole (by helping you on the level of syntax).

- A key feature of each volume in this series is the inclusion of **concise comments** to accompany some clauses and phrases. These have two primary goals: (1) to enable you to understand and exegete the text more deeply than might be possible from reading it in English, and (2) to equip

2. The Hebrew text used in this series has been taken from the Michigan-Claremont-Westminster Electronic Hebrew Bible, a popular electronic version based on the BHS that has been revised by its creators on the basis of comparison with the Leningrad Codex. This electronic text is in the public domain and has been made available courtesy of the J. Alan Groves Center for Advanced Biblical Research. For simplicity's sake, whenever there is a *ketiv-qere*, only the *qere* has been presented (without being marked as such). Interested readers should feel free to consult critical editions, such as the BHS, to see where instances of *ketiv-qere* or other text-critical issues occur.

3. The glosses are the author's own and intentionally err on the "literal" end of the spectrum, in order to help you apprehend the basic meaning(s) of each word in context. The parsings have been supplied by the team at Hendrickson. Naturally, some words can plausibly be parsed more than one way in context; in such cases, the parsing provided is the one we deemed to make the most sense, but other parsings could have been listed instead.

you with insights into the original-language text that will be of direct value for your preaching. To help you focus and not become overwhelmed with too much information, we encouraged our authors to comment only on those clauses and phrases for which they thought doing so would accomplish these two goals. In addition, because the volumes in this series are not only language aids but—ultimately and more importantly—preaching aids, we asked authors to highlight those features in the Hebrew text that bring out key themes, rhetorical and theological emphasis, narrative development, character development, connections with other biblical texts, and the like. Although noting various other features in the Hebrew text may have been intrinsically interesting from a grammatical perspective or helpful for strengthening your language skills, authors have generally refrained from commenting on such features when doing so would not be likely to aid you in moving from text to sermon in any substantial way.[4] In short, an author's brief, select comments are intended—in conjunction with the volume's language aids—to provide you both with *focus* and with *space* to slow down, meditate, wonder, and mature in your understanding and experience of the text, as you form your own judgments on it and prepare to proclaim the divine word to your hearers. The author's comments are not intended to circumscribe the possible interpretive options with one single answer (especially for texts whose interpretation is the particular subject of debate among Christian believers). Rather, they are meant to stimulate your thinking, to help you see features of the text (and connections with other texts) that you may not have perceived before, and to prompt you to ask questions that may not have previously occurred to you.

Each passage ends with a brief section titled **"From Text to Sermon,"** in which our authors, building on their comments, suggest ways you can move from working through the Hebrew text to the task of homiletics, highlighting potential points of emphasis or particular insights you may wish to share with your audience. In this way, the authors provide you with possible ways to bring the text to life for your audience (e.g., types

4. Another way we have kept the presentation streamlined and uncluttered, so that you can achieve maximum focus, is by intentionally keeping source citations to a minimum. Authors' comments on a given passage are the fruit of their scholarly research on the passage, their personal reflection on it, and their experience preaching and teaching it. They cite secondary sources only when they draw a specific insight from one particular source or wish to point you to a particularly helpful resource for further reading. As stated above, we naturally encourage you to also use traditional commentaries (which typically provide more documentation) in your study and sermon preparation.

of illustrations you might use). Because individual preachers (and each of our series authors) bring their own particular skills, perspectives, backgrounds, and oratorial approaches to bear on the homiletical task, and because every biblical text has its own unique features, we encouraged our authors to structure the "From Text to Sermon" section as a free-form series of short paragraphs whose content and emphases are guided by their own personal judgment about what is most helpful for a variety of preachers in different places, cultures, and times. The remarks in this section are always grouped according to rubrics (in the form of inline headers); but rather than restrict authors with a "one-size-fits-all" set of rubrics, we allowed them to create their own rubrics and even, if helpful, to vary these rubrics across passages within their volume in light of the unique features and emphases of each passage.[5] We view the resulting diversity of approaches and emphases across this series (and even within a given volume) as a strength, and we hope this aspect of the series will encourage you to use your own judgment about how to preach each passage in a way that best suits you and your listeners, being sensitive to the promptings and guidance of the Spirit of God.

Audience and Theological Perspective

Since our hope is that many different kinds of people will find the volumes in this series useful, we have designed the Preacher's Hebrew Companion to be helpful to a broad spectrum of Christian preachers:

- Our intention is that the series will be **useful and accessible to a large and diverse group of preachers serving a variety of communities throughout the world**. For this reason, we encouraged authors to exercise sensitivity and broad-mindedness in their comments and particularly when writing the "From Text to Sermon" section, in which they could run the risk of being too culturally specific. In particular, we asked authors that any sermon illustrations they included in this section generally be as universal as possible or that, instead of providing specific illustrations, they point to themes from the passage you may wish to illustrate in one way or another. That said, because specificity is essential for good communication, we also allowed authors to suggest—when they deemed

5. That said, we suggested the following possible rubrics to authors as starting points to consider: theological themes, themes for application and illustration, integrating the broader historical and literary context, learning from the language, and (as deemed helpful and not reductionistic) "the big idea" of the passage.

it particularly helpful—concrete, culturally specific examples as springboards to help you think about examples that will be relevant for your own context.

- We asked our authors to express any **theological perspectives** in a way that is **consistent with the beliefs stated in the Apostles' Creed**. Because this series aims to meet the needs of Christian preachers of various theological viewpoints, we encouraged a diversity of theological perspectives within these bounds across the volumes in the series. In addition, because the series has a joint focus on exegesis (close attention to what a specific text says) and homiletics (how to preach said text), we advised authors when making any theological comments to let these flow naturally from the text at hand, rather than using the text as a springboard to discuss issues that would more properly fall under the rubric of systematic theology. Although we asked authors to avoid reading any given passage through the lens of a theological system grounded in other biblical texts, we also strongly encouraged them to discuss allusions to other biblical passages or other innerbiblical literary connections if they felt that doing so would help you understand the message of the text at hand and know how to preach it more effectively.

Acknowledgments

We would like to offer our heartfelt gratitude to the following individuals, who have played a central role in the creation of this series:

- Arley Kangas, Marco Resendes, and Tyler Comer, for their excellent work on various aspects of the making of these volumes, especially transliterating, proofreading, and generating the indexes.
- Phil Frank, for his expert typesetting and for patiently working with us, in our capacity as series editors, to achieve the desired formatting and aesthetic for these volumes.
- The series authors, for joining us in this unique project and for sharing our vision and lending their considerable skills to the task. These volumes are the result of a fruitful collaboration between the Hendrickson team and the series authors (with both parties contributing to the content). We are truly grateful for the opportunity to have worked on this project together.

All of us—the series editors, the series authors, and the team at Hendrickson—pray that the volume you now hold in your hands will empower and encourage you to work through the Hebrew text of the Bible in order to deepen your sermon preparation and strengthen your proclamation of the word of God. We nurture a deep respect and appreciation for the challenging work that you as a preacher do on the "front lines," and we recognize the many challenges (logistical, mental, emotional, spiritual, and more) that you encounter on a weekly, indeed a daily, basis. We are honored to come alongside you and support you in your important labors, and we pray that your use of this book will bear much fruit for the kingdom of God.

JONATHAN G. KLINE
SEAN M. MCDONOUGH

AUTHOR'S INTRODUCTION

The book of Isaiah has profoundly impacted God's people from its very beginning. Though longevity of ministry does not automatically indicate success, in the prophet Isaiah's case it attests to the endurance and stability of the divine message during one of the most tumultuous times of Judah's history. With a ministry stretching from the death of King Uzziah in approximately 739 BC (Isa 6:1) until a few years into the reign of King Manasseh, Hezekiah's notorious son (ca. 681 BC), Isaiah preaches to God's people for nearly six decades.

And what a message he preaches! Deftly mixing stern warnings of impending judgment with promises of restoration and hope for a Messiah and his coming kingdom, Isaiah gives the people something to look forward to, for better or worse. The historical context, namely the Assyrian threat against Judah, sets the background for the book, with the shadow of Babylon's future invasion ever darkening the picture. However, the cross of Calvary emerges larger than any potential threat, providing a hope that will be fulfilled in the messianic Davidic king, the suffering servant, the herald of a new creation, the one who reigns with perfect justice and righteousness for all eternity.

Isaiah's message, most of it coming to us in poetic form, needs to be heard in its original voice. English versions, as good as they are, lose much in translation. This commentary seeks to give the language of the text center stage, highlighting its beauty, force, and often-hidden poetic features, which all serve to amplify Isaiah's voice for the contemporary audience.

In writing this work, I purposefully leaned on minimal secondary resources in order to show the preacher and student of the Bible what can be learned when engaging the Hebrew text directly. In selecting the passages for this volume, I chose at least one passage from each of the major divisions of the text (e.g., The Oracles of the Nations [Isa 13–23]; Isaiah's Little Apocalypse [24–27]; etc.). In this way, the preacher will have a sampling from every area of Isaiah. Also, at the forefront of my consideration was addressing passages I think many preachers would be drawn to if preaching a limited series on the book (e.g., Isa 9:1–7).

Though we are 2,700 years removed from the prophet, God's words enjoy an enduring quality (40:8; 55:11). We come to the text expecting it to convict us and encourage us. We taste eternity future and experience the gospel of our present redemption. Like Isaiah, we will behold the glory of God and be forever changed by it.

I preached my first sermon for an expository series in Isaiah on May 23, 2021, in Belleville, Michigan. Members of Redemption Bible Church endured (and hopefully enjoyed) many sermons throughout the book, chapter by chapter, verse by verse. Sometime around Isaiah 28, the Lord unexpectedly moved me from my pastorate to teach as an Old Testament professor at Cairn University in Langhorne, Pennsylvania. Still, the message of Isaiah continued to find influence in my ministry—in the classroom, in chapel, and at various churches in the area, including Emmanuel Community Church in Bayville, New Jersey, and New Monmouth Baptist Church in New Monmouth, New Jersey. Even more than through the sermons, the message of Isaiah continues to impact me in my own personal studies as I submit myself to its magnificent words.

I am grateful for Jonathan Kline's invitation to this series back in the early days of its inception. How thrilled I was to hear of a commentary written for preachers, firmly rooted in the Hebrew text (as all Old Testament sermons should be)! Additionally, Karen D. Lavery's careful work as an editor helped improve the quality of this manuscript in innumerable ways. I am also grateful for Lauren Raab, one of the student workers for Cairn University's divinity department, who carefully checked all my references, corrected my poor grammar, and made many insightful comments and suggestions. Any mistakes that remain are my own. Finally, my family's patience with me as I worked on this volume does not escape my notice. I am blessed indeed to have a supportive and faithful bride and four children who love both Dad and the Lord.

I dedicate this book to my parents, Frank and Kim, who patiently and eagerly supported me from the very earliest days of my ministry aspirations. More importantly, they modeled godliness and love, creating a spiritual greenhouse in their home for their children.

LIST OF ABBREVIATIONS

1	first person	indef	indefinite
2	second person	INF	infinitive
3	third person	INTERR/interr	interrogative
ABS	absolute	JUSS	jussive
adj	adjective	M	masculine
adv	adverb	NIPH	Niphal
ATTR	attributive	P	plural
C	common	PASS	passive
COHORT	cohortative	PF	perfect
CONJ/conj	conjunction	PRED	predicative
CST	construct	PREP/prep	preposition
DEF. ART.	definite article	PRON/pron	pronoun
demonstr	demonstrative	PTCP	participle
F	feminine	S	singular
HIPH	Hiphil	SUBST	substantive
HITH	Hithpael	SX	suffix
HOPH	Hophal	w/	with
IMPF	imperfect	WAYY	wayyiqtol
IMPV	imperative		

NOTE: All verse numbers in this volume refer to the Hebrew text; when the English verse numbering differs, it is listed in brackets following the Hebrew numbering.

ISAIAH 1:10–20

THE CONSEQUENCES OF RELIGIOUS HYPOCRISY

Isaiah's ministry extended many decades, according to the biblical records. These were not easy times for the prophet, nor were they especially godly times for the people of Israel. By offering regular sacrifices and observing all the proper spiritual ceremonies, the people appeared religious on the outside. But their hearts were far from the Lord. Isaiah warned the people that their prayers fell on deaf ears due to this empty show of religiousness. Even more concerning, judgment was just around the corner should they continue to lack heartfelt devotion.

LARGER LITERARY CONTEXT › 1:1–31

1:10–11

10a שִׁמְעוּ דְבַר־יְהוָה

šim'û dəvar-YHWH

Listen to YHWH's word,

10b קְצִינֵי סְדֹם

qəṣînê sədōm

O chiefs of Sodom!

10c הַאֲזִינוּ תּוֹרַת אֱלֹהֵינוּ

ha'ăzînû tôrat 'ĕlōhênû

Pay attention to our God's instruction,

10d עַם עֲמֹרָה׃

'am 'ămōrâ.

O people of Gomorrah!

11a לָמָּה־לִּי רֹב־זִבְחֵיכֶם

lāmmâ-lî rōv-zivḥêkem

"Why should I care about your many sacrifices?"

11b יֹאמַר יְהוָה

yō'mar YHWH

says YHWH.

11c שָׂבַעְתִּי עֹלוֹת אֵילִים וְחֵלֶב מְרִיאִים

śāva'tî 'ōlôt 'êlîm wəḥēlev mərî'îm

"I feel stuffed with the burnt offerings of rams and the fat of fattened calves.

11d וְדַם פָּרִים וּכְבָשִׂים וְעַתּוּדִים לֹא חָפָצְתִּי׃

wədam pārîm ûkəvāśîm wə'attûdîm lō' ḥāfāṣtî.

and I will not be pleased with the blood of bulls and lambs and goats."

10a	שִׁמְעוּ דְבַר־יְהוָה

Listen to YHWH's word,

שִׁמְעוּ שׁמע	hear/listen *šim·ʿû*	QAL IMPV MP	verb
דְּבַר־ דָּבָר	word/speech *də·var-*	CST	noun
יְהוָה יהוה	the Lord *YHWH*	ABS	noun

Isaiah uses the same two roots in v. 10 that he used in v. 2: שׁמע ("listen") and אזן ("pay attention"). Earlier, he commanded the heavens and the earth to listen. Here, he narrows down his focus to the people of Israel. These commands are specific to God's people; therefore, preachers should keep believers in mind as the primary audience of the sermon.

10b	קְצִינֵי סְדֹם

O chiefs of Sodom!

קְצִינֵי קָצִין	chiefs/rulers *qə·ṣî·nê*	CST	noun
סְדֹם סְדֹם	Sodom *sə·dōm*	ABS	noun

By calling the people of Jerusalem "Sodom" and "Gomorrah," Isaiah indicates that God's people behave like these sinful cities of old (Gen 19). Where we would expect the preposition כְּ, which would indicate a simile ("you are *like* Sodom"), Isaiah's language is much stronger, *equating* the Israelites with the sinful cities without the distance of comparison. Isaiah implies that judgment is also coming for Jerusalem as it did for Sodom and Gomorrah. This unflattering comparison would have offended and shocked the original readers, as many biblical authors use these cities as examples par excellence of God's judgment upon the wicked (e.g., Jer 23:14; Lam 4:6; Ezek 16:46).

10c	הַאֲזִ֛ינוּ תּוֹרַ֥ת אֱלֹהֵ֖ינוּ

Pay attention to our God's instruction,

הַאֲזִ֛ינוּ אזן	hear/listen/give ear *ha·ʾă·**zî**·nû*	HIPH IMPV MP	verb
תּוֹרַ֥ת תּוֹרָה	law/instruction *tô·**rat***	CST	noun
אֱלֹהֵ֖ינוּ אֱלֹהִים	our God *ʾĕ·lō·**hê**·nû*	CST W/ 1CP SX	noun

Isaiah's use of the imperative הַאֲזִינוּ ("hear!") may recall Moses' words to the Israelites in Deut 32:1—"Give ear, O heavens, and I will speak, and let the earth hear the words of my mouth" (ESV), especially considering the use of this verb with the close association of שָׁמַיִם ("heavens") from Isa 1:2. If this echo is intentional, then it frames the current words of the prophet in the covenantal context of Deuteronomy. God holds Israel to such a standard because he and they are in covenantal relationship with each other, and Israel has failed to uphold her end of the stipulations.

10d	עַ֥ם עֲמֹרָֽה׃

O people of Gomorrah!

עַ֥ם עַם	people/nation *ʿ**am***	CST	noun
עֲמֹרָֽה׃ עֲמֹרָה	Gomorrah *ʿă·mō·**râ***	ABS	noun

Note the tight synonymous parallelism in v. 10. "Listen to" parallels "Pay attention to," "YHWH's word" parallels "our God's instruction," "O chiefs of Sodom" parallels "O people of Gomorrah." It is one of the finest examples of synonymous parallelism in Isaiah. Isaiah also employs alliteration here between the two words עַם ("people") and עֲמֹרָה ("Gomorrah").

11a	לָ֣מָּה־לִּ֤י רֹֽב־זִבְחֵיכֶם֙

"Why should I care about your many sacrifices?"

Hebrew	Gloss	Parsing	POS
לָ֣מָּה־ לָ֫מָּה	why *lām·mâ-*	---	adv
לִּ֤י לְ	to me ***lî***	--- W/ 1CS SX	prep
רֹֽב־ רֹב	many/multitude/ abundant *rōv-*	CST	noun
זִבְחֵיכֶם֙ זֶ֫בַח	your sacrifices *ziv·ḥê·**kem***	CST W/ 2MP SX	noun

God does not reject the cultic practices themselves. After all, he set up these institutions! As will become clearer as Isaiah's thought progresses, God instead rejects the condition of the Israelites' hearts that makes these religious ceremonies and sacrifices hollow and worthless. Without the heart, the hands don't matter. This kind of indictment is not uncommon in biblical literature (cf. 1 Sam 15:22; Ps 40:7 [6]; 51:16–17; Prov 21:3; Eccl 5:1; Hos 6:6; Mic 6:6–8).

11b	יֹאמַ֣ר יְהוָ֑ה

says YHWH.

Hebrew	Gloss	Parsing	POS
יֹאמַ֣ר אמר	(he) says *yō'·**mar***	QAL IMPF 3MS	verb
יְהוָ֑ה יהוה	the Lord *YHWH*	ABS	noun

11c	שָׂבַ֛עְתִּי עֹל֥וֹת אֵילִ֖ים וְחֵ֣לֶב מְרִיאִ֑ים

"I feel stuffed with the burnt offerings of rams and the fat of fattened calves.

Hebrew	Gloss	Parsing	POS
שָׂבַ֛עְתִּי שׂבע	I am full/satisfied *śā·va'·**tî***	QAL PF 1CS	verb

עֹלוֹת עֹלָה	burnt offerings *ʿō·**lôt***	CST	noun
אֵילִים אַיִל	rams *ʾê·**lîm***	ABS	noun
וְחֵלֶב חֵלֶב	and fat *wə·**ḥē**·lev*	CST W/ CONJ וְ	noun
מְרִיאִים מְרִיא	fatlings/fattened calves *mə·rî·**ʾîm***	ABS	noun

Though rams are mentioned in association with burnt offerings (e.g., Lev 8:18), the Levitical law does not specifically mention fattened calves (though cf. 2 Sam 6:13; 1 Kgs 1:9, 19, 25; Amos 5:22). This may be an example of step parallelism, which takes a pattern of "A, but what's more, B." The Israelites were even offering the choicest of animals not specifically required in the law, yet God still did not accept these sacrifices.

11d וְדַם פָּרִים וּכְבָשִׂים וְעַתּוּדִים לֹא חָפָצְתִּי׃

and I will not be pleased with the blood
of bulls and lambs and goats."

וְדַם דָּם	and blood *wə·**dam***	CST W/ CONJ וְ	noun
פָּרִים פַּר	bulls/young bulls/steers *pā·**rîm***	ABS	noun
וּכְבָשִׂים כֶּבֶשׂ	and lambs *û·ḵə·vā·**śîm***	ABS W/ CONJ וְ	noun
וְעַתּוּדִים עַתּוּד	and goats/male goats *wə·ʿat·tû·**dîm***	ABS W/ CONJ וְ	noun
לֹא לֹא	not ***lōʾ***	---	particle
חָפָצְתִּי׃ חפץ	I will delight/take pleasure in/be pleased with *ḥā·**fāṣ**·tî*	QAL PF 1CS	verb

Verbs enclose these last two phrases, forming a rough chiasm. The effect puts emphasis on the verbs שָׂבַעְתִּי ("I am full") and לֹא חָפָצְתִּי ("I will not be pleased").

12a כִּ֤י תָבֹ֙אוּ֙ לֵרָא֖וֹת פָּנָ֑י

*kî tā**vō**ʾû lērāʾ**ôt** pā**nāy***

When you come to worship before me,

12b מִֽי־בִקֵּ֥שׁ זֹ֛את מִיֶּדְכֶ֖ם

*mî-viq**qēš** **zōʾt** miyyed**ḵem***

who asked this of you,

12c רְמֹ֥ס חֲצֵרָֽי׃

*rə**mōs** ḥăṣē**rāy**.*

to trample my courts?

13a לֹ֣א תוֹסִ֗יפוּ הָבִיא֙ מִנְחַת־שָׁ֔וְא

***lōʾ** tô**sî**fû hā**vîʾ** minḥat-**šāw**ʾ*

Do not continue to bring a hollow offering;

13b קְטֹ֥רֶת תּוֹעֵבָ֛ה הִ֖יא לִ֑י

*qə**ṭō**ret tôʿē**vâ** **hîʾ** **lî***

incense is an abominable stench to me.

13c חֹ֤דֶשׁ וְשַׁבָּת֙ קְרֹ֣א מִקְרָ֔א

ḥō**deš wəšab**bāt** qə**rōʾ** miq**rāʾ

New Moon celebrations and Sabbath,
the calling of a religious ceremony—

13d לֹא־אוּכַ֥ל אָ֖וֶן וַעֲצָרָֽה׃

*lōʾ-ʾû**ḵal** **ʾā**wen waʿăṣā**râ**.*

I can't even!—wickedness and religious assembly.

14a חָדְשֵׁיכֶ֤ם וּמוֹעֲדֵיכֶם֙ שָֽׂנְאָ֣ה נַפְשִׁ֔י

*ḥodšê**ḵem** ûmôʿădê**ḵem** śānə**ʾâ** naf**šî***

My very soul despises your New Moon celebrations
and your special feasts.

14b הָֽיוּ עָלַ֖י לָטֹ֑רַח

*hāy**û** ʿā**lay** lā**ṭō**raḥ*

They have become a great weight upon my shoulders.

14c נִלְאֵ֖יתִי נְשֹֽׂא׃

*nil'**ê**tî nə**śō**'.*

I am tired of carrying this burden.

15a וּבְפָֽרִשְׂכֶ֣ם כַּפֵּיכֶ֗ם

*ûvəfāriś**ḵem** kappê**ḵem***

And when you stretch out your hands,

15b אַעְלִ֤ים עֵינַי֙ מִכֶּ֔ם

*'a'**lîm** ʿê**nay** mik**kem***

I will shut my eyes to you.

15c גַּ֛ם כִּֽי־תַרְבּ֥וּ תְפִלָּ֖ה

gam kî** tar**bû** təfil**lâ

Even when you increase your prayers,

15d אֵינֶ֣נִּי שֹׁמֵ֑עַ

*'ê**nen**nî šō**mē**aʿ*

I won't be listening.

15e יְדֵיכֶ֖ם דָּמִ֥ים מָלֵֽאוּ׃

*yədê**ḵem** dā**mîm** mā**lē**'û.*

Those hands you stretched out are full of blood.

12a	כִּ֣י תָבֹ֔אוּ לֵרָא֖וֹת פָּנָ֑י

When you come to worship before me,

כִּ֣י	when	---	conj
כִּי	*kî*		
תָבֹ֔אוּ	you come	QAL IMPF 2MP	verb
בוא	*tā·**vō**·ʾû*		
לֵרָא֖וֹת	to appear/be seen	NIPH INF CST W/ PREP לְ	verb
ראה	*lē·rā·**ʾôt***		
פָּנָ֑י	before me/before my face	CST W/ 1CS SX	noun
פָּנֶה	*pā·**nāy***		

The infinitive לֵרָאוֹת ("to appear/be seen") refers here in the sense of appearing before God for worship.

12b	מִֽי־בִקֵּ֥שׁ זֹ֖את מִיֶּדְכֶ֑ם

who asked this of you,

מִֽי־	who	---	interr pron
מִי	*mî-*		
בִקֵּ֥שׁ	(he) seeks	PIEL PF 3MS	verb
בקשׁ	*viq·**qēš***		
זֹ֖את	this	---	demonstr pron
זאת	***zōʾt***		
מִיֶּדְכֶ֑ם	from your hand	CST W/ PREP מִן + 2MP SX	noun
יָד	*miy·yed·**ḵem***		

Several phrases in this verse, including תָבֹאוּ לֵרָאוֹת פָּנָי ("coming to appear before [God]") and מִיֶּדְכֶם ("from your hand") imply a gathering at the temple to worship. Worshipers gathered at the central place of worship (the temple) and brought sacrifices and offerings (something "in their hands") in order to please God. This is akin to saying a Christian comes to church bringing his/her offering.

12c	רְמֹס חֲצֵרָי׃

to trample my courts?

רְמֹס רמס	to trample *rə·mōs*	QAL INF CST	verb
חֲצֵרָי׃ חָצֵר	my courts *ḥă·ṣē·rāy*	CST W/ 1CS SX	noun

The imagery here is intentionally violent and shocking. Elsewhere, the root רמס ("trample") describes trampling someone to death (2 Kgs 7:17, 20; 9:33), a beast trampling its prey (Mic 5:7), and an army wreaking devastation (Isa 16:4). This imagery falls right in line with the other shocking imagery of this chapter.

13a	לֹא תוֹסִיפוּ הָבִיא מִנְחַת־שָׁוְא

Do not continue to bring a hollow offering;

לֹא לֹא	not *lō'*	---	particle
תוֹסִיפוּ יסף	(you) continue/add *tô·sî·fû*	HIPH IMPF 2MP	verb
הָבִיא בוא	to bring *hā·vî'*	HIPH INF CST	verb
מִנְחַת־ מִנְחָה	offering/gift/tribute *min·ḥat-*	CST	noun
שָׁוְא שָׁוְא	worthlessness *šā·w'*	ABS	noun

The imperfect תוֹסִיפוּ ("continue") implies the Israelites had a habit of worshiping God with empty, hollow hearts. Their offerings were consistent, but worthless due to their lack of inward humility. Elsewhere, the noun שָׁוְא ("empty/vain") can refer to worthless idols (Ps 31:7), deception (Prov 30:8), and is used twice in the Ten Commandments (Deut 5:11, 20).

13b	קְטֹ֫רֶת תּוֹעֵבָ֥ה הִ֖יא לִ֑י

incense is an abominable stench to me.

קְטֹ֫רֶת קְטֹרֶת	incense/smoke *qə · ṭō · ret*	ABS	noun
תּוֹעֵבָ֥ה תּוֹעֵבָה	abomination *tô · ʿē · vâ*	ABS	noun
הִ֖יא הִיא	it *hîʾ*	---	personal pron
לִ֑י לְ	to me *lî*	--- W/ 1CS SX	prep

Isaiah uses one of the strongest words possible—תּוֹעֵבָה ("abomination"). This word was usually reserved for pagan sacrifices (e.g., 2 Kgs 23:13) or especially heinous sins (e.g., Lev 18:29–30; Prov 15:8; 28:9). The incense of the Israelites should have been a sweet-smelling aroma to God's nostrils; instead, it was a foul stench, repulsing him.

13c	חֹ֤דֶשׁ וְשַׁבָּת֙ קְרֹ֣א מִקְרָ֔א

New Moon celebrations and Sabbath,
the calling of a religious ceremony—

חֹ֤דֶשׁ חֹדֶשׁ	New Moon *ḥō · deš*	ABS	noun
וְשַׁבָּת֙ שַׁבָּת	and Sabbath *wə · šab · bāt*	ABS W/ CONJ וְ	noun
קְרֹ֣א קרא	calling *qə · rōʾ*	QAL INF CST	verb
מִקְרָ֔א מִקְרָא	convocation/assembly *miq · rāʾ*	ABS	noun

Readers should keep in mind that God originally instituted the very sacrifices and assemblies he here condemns (cf. 1 Chr 23:31). A Christian analogy might be God chiding the church for observing the Lord's Supper. The fact that these observances were originally implemented by God and now God complains that he can't stand them adds to the shock value of the passage.

13d לֹא־אוּכַ֥ל אָ֖וֶן וַעֲצָרָֽה׃

I can't even!—wickedness and religious assembly.

לֹא־	not	---	particle
לֹא	*lō*ʾ-		
אוּכַ֥ל	I am able	QAL IMPF 1CS	verb
יכל	*ʾû·**ḵal***		
אָ֖וֶן	wickedness/sorrow	ABS	noun
אָ֫וֶן	*ʾā·wen*		
וַעֲצָרָֽה׃	and assembly/solemn assembly	ABS W/ CONJ וַ	noun
עֲצָרָה	*wa·ʿă·ṣā·**râ***		

The Hebrew here is especially terse. English translations tend to smooth it out. God's language is strong, and he appears so exasperated that he cannot even properly finish his sentence. This phrase also works as a summary for this entire unit. Religious ceremonies and sinful iniquity should not mix. God cannot bear it.

14a חָדְשֵׁיכֶ֤ם וּמוֹעֲדֵיכֶם֙ שָׂנְאָ֣ה נַפְשִׁ֔י

My very soul despises your New Moon celebrations and your special feasts.

חָדְשֵׁיכֶ֤ם	your New Moons	CST W/ 2MP SX	noun
חֹ֫דֶשׁ	*ḥod·šê·**ḵem***		
וּמוֹעֲדֵיכֶם֙	and your appointed times/meetings	CST W/ CONJ וּ + 2MP SX	noun
מוֹעֵד	*û·mô·ʿă·dê·**ḵem***		
שָׂנְאָ֣ה	(it) hates/despises	QAL PF 3FS	verb
שׂנא	*śā·nə·ʾ**â***		
נַפְשִׁ֔י	my soul	CST W/ 1CS SX	noun
נֶ֫פֶשׁ	*naf·**šî***		

Notice again the strength of the language. God could have spoken his thoughts with a first-person verb. The addition of the superfluous נַפְשִׁי ("my soul") adds emphasis—from the very being of God bubbles up this hatred for hollow religious festivals.

14b **הָ֥יוּ עָלַ֖י לָטֹ֑רַח**

They have become a great weight upon my shoulders.

הָ֥יוּ היה	they have become *hā · yû*	QAL PF 3CP	verb
עָלַ֖י עַל	upon me *ʿā · lay*	--- W/ 1CS SX	prep
לָטֹ֑רַח טֹרַח	to/as a burden *lā · ṭō · raḥ*	ABS W/ PREP לְ	noun

Consider the weight (pun intended) of this metaphor—the omnipotent God feels burdened by the vast sins of the Israelites! Isaiah may intentionally imply another pun with the word טֹרַח ("burden"): All these commands were prescribed by God in the Torah, but now they have become *ṭōraḥ* (טֹרַח) to him!

14c **נִלְאֵ֖יתִי נְשֹֽׂא׃**

I am tired of carrying this burden.

נִלְאֵ֖יתִי לאה	I am tired/worn out *nil · ʾê · tî*	NIPH PF 1CS	verb
נְשֹֽׂא׃ נשׂא	to lift/carry *nə · śōʾ*	QAL INF CST	verb

Once again, the word נִלְאֵיתִי ("I am worn out") comes as a surprise when we consider the source—the all-powerful God of the universe. The sin must be heavy indeed if it can wear out the omnipotent God of the universe! Preachers should carefully explain the anthropomorphic imagery here, ensuring that listeners do not take it literally but still feel the weight of the figurative language.

15a **וּבְפָרִשְׂכֶ֣ם כַּפֵּיכֶ֗ם**

And when you stretch out your hands,

וּבְפָרִשְׂכֶ֣ם + פרשׂ	and when you spread out/stretch out *û · və · fā · riś · ḵem*	PIEL INF CST W/ CONJ וְ + PREP בְּ + 2MP SX	verb

כַּפֵּיכֶם כַּף	your palms/hands *kap·pê·**ḵem***	CST W/ 2MP SX	noun

15b אַעְלִ֤ים עֵינַי֙ מִכֶּ֔ם

I will shut my eyes to you.

אַעְלִ֤ים עלם	I will conceal/hide *'a‘·**lîm***	HIPH IMPF 1CS	verb
עֵינַי֙ עַ֫יִן	my eyes *‘ê·**nay***	CST W/ 1CS SX	noun
מִכֶּ֔ם מִן	from you *mik·**kem***	--- W/ 2MP SX	prep

The verb עלם ("I will conceal/hide") is not the normal word for shutting one's eyes. The force of this expression shows that God does not merely close his eyes but rather more dramatically covers his eyes (like a blindfold, or perhaps even through blinding) to avoid seeing the people's worship.

15c גַּ֥ם כִּֽי־תַרְבּ֖וּ תְפִלָּ֑ה

Even when you increase your prayers,

גַּ֥ם גַּם	even ***gam***	---	adv
כִּֽי־ כִּי	when/if ***kî***	---	conj
תַרְבּ֖וּ רבה	you make many/abundant *tar·**bû***	HIPH IMPF 2MP	verb
תְפִלָּ֑ה תְּפִלָּה	prayer *tə·fil·**lâ***	ABS	noun

15d	אֵינֶ֣נִּי שֹׁמֵ֑עַ

I won't be listening.

אֵינֶ֣נִּי אַיִן	I am/will not *ʾê·**nen**·nî*	--- W/ 1CS SX	particle
שֹׁמֵ֑עַ שׁמע	listening/hearing *šō·**mē**·aʿ*	QAL PTCP MS	verb

These phrases in v. 15 are in parallelism and should be understood together. God has blinded himself and deafened his ears to the prayers of his people. These statements highlight the magnitude of the offense against God.

15e	יְדֵיכֶ֖ם דָּמִ֥ים מָלֵֽאוּ׃

Those hands you stretched out are full of blood.

יְדֵיכֶ֖ם יָד	your hands *yə·dê·**ḵem***	CST W/ 2MP SX	noun
דָּמִ֥ים דָּם	blood *dā·**mîm***	ABS	noun
מָלֵֽאוּ׃ מלא	(they) are full/filled *mā·**lē**·ʾû*	QAL PF 3CP	verb

Hands filled or defiled with blood is Bible-speak for "guilty of murder" (cf. 59:3; Ps 106:38; Ezek 23:37). For example, God uses the phrase when accusing Cain of murdering Abel (Gen 4:10–11). By using this strong language, Isaiah accuses the Israelites of being just as guilty as murderers such as Cain. Whether God is being literal or speaking metaphorically here, we cannot be sure; perhaps the answer is a mix of both.

1:16–17

16a רַחֲצוּ הִזַּכּוּ

*raḥă**ṣû** hizzak**kû***

Wash up! Get clean!

16b הָסִירוּ רֹעַ מַעַלְלֵיכֶם מִנֶּגֶד עֵינָי

*hā**sî**rû **rō**a‘ ma‘aləlê**ḵem** min**ne**ged ‘ê**nāy***

Throw out your evil deeds from my sight!

16c חִדְלוּ הָרֵעַ׃

*ḥid**lû** hā**rē**a‘.*

Quit your evil!

17a לִמְדוּ הֵיטֵב

*lim**dû** hê**ṭēv***

Study up on good!

17b דִּרְשׁוּ מִשְׁפָּט

*dir**šû** miš**pāṭ***

Pursue justice!

17c אַשְּׁרוּ חָמוֹץ

*’aššə**rû** ḥā**môṣ***

Reprove the ruthless!

17d שִׁפְטוּ יָתוֹם

*šif**ṭû** yā**tôm***

Bring justice to orphans!

17e רִיבוּ אַלְמָנָה׃

***rî**vû ’almā**nâ**.*

Stand up for widows!

16a רַחֲצוּ הִזַּכּוּ

Wash up! Get clean!

רַחֲצוּ רחץ	Wash yourselves *ra·ḥă·**ṣû***	QAL IMPV MP	verb
הִזַּכּוּ זכה	Make yourselves clean *hiz·zak·**kû***	HITH IMPV MP	verb

Verse 16 begins a series of nine imperatives, all meant to forcefully rouse the Israelites from their spiritual defilement.

16b הָסִירוּ רֹעַ מַעַלְלֵיכֶם מִנֶּגֶד עֵינָי

Throw out your evil deeds from my sight!

הָסִירוּ סור	take away/remove *hā·**sî**·rû*	HIPH IMPV MP	verb
רֹעַ רֹעַ	bad/evil ***rō**·aʿ*	CST	noun
מַעַלְלֵיכֶם מַעֲלָל	your deeds/works *ma·ʿa·lə·lê·**ḵem***	CST W/ 2MP SX	noun
מִנֶּגֶד נֶגֶד	from before *min·**ne**·ged*	--- W/ PREP מִן	prep
עֵינָי עַיִן	my eyes *ʿê·**nāy***	CST W/ 1CS SX	noun

Notice how עֵינָי ("my eyes") recalls God's declaration "I will shut my eyes to you" in the previous verse. Keeping the metaphors tied together, Israel has committed so much sin that her iniquity has blinded God's vision. Removing the sin will give God a clearer line of sight to "see" Israel's prayers.

16c חִדְלוּ הָרֵעַ׃

Quit your evil!

חִדְלוּ חדל	Cease *ḥid·**lû***	QAL IMPV MP	verb
הָרֵעַ׃ רעע	to do evil/bad *hā·**rē**·aʿ*	HIPH INF CST	verb

17a	לִמְדוּ הֵיטֵב		
	Study up on good!		
לִמְדוּ למד	Learn *lim·**dû***	QAL IMPV MP	verb
הֵיטֵב יטב	to do good *hê·**ṭēv***	HIPH INF ABS	verb

The verb למד ("learn") occurs seventeen times in Deuteronomy, most often associated with "teaching" the next generation or "learning" how to fear God or "learning" his laws and judgments. It is also used plentifully in Ps 119 (13x), connected with devotion to the word of God. God ironically excoriates the Israelites to learn something they should already know how to do.

17b	דִּרְשׁוּ מִשְׁפָּט		
	Pursue justice!		
דִּרְשׁוּ דרשׁ	seek/pursue *dir·**šû***	QAL IMPV MP	verb
מִשְׁפָּט מִשְׁפָּט	justice/judgment *miš·**pāṭ***	ABS	noun

This imperative functions as a heading for the next three imperatives. How should Israel "pursue justice?" Negatively, they "reprove the ruthless," or correct those causing injustice. Positively, they stand up for orphans and widows, those most inclined to suffer for lack of justice. This becomes a recurring theme in Scripture: standing up for the vulnerable in society is an indication of heart change and true religion (Jas 1:27; cf. Ps 146:7). If the Israelites truly change internally, their external behavior will show it by loving those most in need of care. In addition to these theological observations, the expositor may also notice the preponderance of courtroom (legal) language in these final four imperatives.

17c **אַשְּׁרוּ חָמוֹץ**

Reprove the ruthless!

אַשְּׁרוּ אשׁר	Reprove *ʾaš·šə·**rû***	PIEL IMPV MP	verb
חָמוֹץ חָמוֹץ	the ruthless/oppressor *ḥā·**môṣ***	ABS	noun

17d **שִׁפְטוּ יָתוֹם**

Bring justice to orphans!

שִׁפְטוּ שׁפט	judge/defend *šif·**ṭû***	QAL IMPV MP	verb
יָתוֹם יָתוֹם	orphan *yā·**tôm***	ABS	noun

17e **רִיבוּ אַלְמָנָה׃**

Stand up for widows!

רִיבוּ ריב	contend/strive ***rî**·vû*	QAL IMPV MP	verb
אַלְמָנָה׃ אַלְמָנָה	widow *ʾal·mā·**nâ***	ABS	noun

1:18–20

18a לְכוּ־נָ֥א וְנִוָּכְחָ֖ה יֹאמַ֣ר יְהוָ֑ה

*lǝḵû-**nāʾ** wǝniwwāḵǝ**ḥâ** yōʾ**mar** YHWH*

"Please, come for a walk and let us reason together," says YHWH.

18b אִם־יִהְי֨וּ חֲטָאֵיכֶ֤ם כַּשָּׁנִים֙ כַּשֶּׁ֣לֶג יַלְבִּ֔ינוּ

*ʾim-yih**yû** ḥăṭāʾē**ḵem** kaššā**nîm** kaššeleg yal**bînû***

"Even though right now your sins are as red as scarlet, they will be made as white as snow.

18c אִם־יַאְדִּ֥ימוּ כַתּוֹלָ֖ע כַּצֶּ֥מֶר יִהְיֽוּ׃

*ʾim-yaʾ**dîmû** ḵattô**lāʿ** kaṣṣemer yih**yû**.*

Even though they are as red as crimson, they will be as white wool.

19a אִם־תֹּאב֖וּ וּשְׁמַעְתֶּ֑ם

*ʾim-tōʾ**vû** ûšǝmaʿ**tem***

If you would just be willing to listen,

19b ט֥וּב הָאָ֖רֶץ תֹּאכֵֽלוּ׃

***ṭûv** hāʾāreṣ tōʾ**ḵē**lû.*

you will eat the good stuff of the land.

20a וְאִם־תְּמָאֲנ֖וּ וּמְרִיתֶ֑ם

*wǝʾim-tǝmāʾă**nû** ûmǝrî**tem***

But if you refuse and disobey,

20b חֶ֣רֶב תְּאֻכְּל֔וּ

*ḥerev tǝʾukkǝ**lû***

you'll be eaten by a sword instead!"

20c כִּ֛י פִּ֥י יְהוָ֖ה דִּבֵּֽר׃

***kî pî** YHWH dib**bēr**.*

For the mouth of YHWH has spoken.

18a **לְכוּ־נָ֛א וְנִוָּכְחָ֖ה יֹאמַ֣ר יְהוָ֑ה**

"Please, come for a walk and let us reason together," says YHWH.

לְכוּ־ הלך	Come/walk *lə·ḵû-*	QAL IMPV MP	verb
נָ֛א נָא	I pray/now ***nā'***	---	particle
וְנִוָּכְחָ֖ה יכח	and let us argue/reason *wə·niw·wā·ḵə·**ḥâ***	NIPH COHORT 1CP W/ CONJ וְ	verb
יֹאמַ֣ר אמר	(he) says *yō'·**mar***	QAL IMPF 3MS	verb
יְהוָ֑ה יהוה	the LORD *YHWH*	ABS	noun

God offers Israel an invitation here with the words לְכוּ־נָא וְנִוָּכְחָה ("Please, come for a walk and let us reason together"). The latter word is again courtroom language. God wants to spell out for Israel the two ways this trial can go.

18b **אִם־יִהְי֨וּ חֲטָאֵיכֶ֤ם כַּשָּׁנִים֙ כַּשֶּׁ֣לֶג יַלְבִּ֔ינוּ**

"Even though right now your sins are as red as scarlet, they will be made as white as snow.

אִם־ אִם	if/when/though *'im-*	---	conj
יִהְי֨וּ היה	(they) will be/are *yih·**yû***	QAL IMPF 3MP	verb
חֲטָאֵיכֶ֤ם חֵטְא	your sins *ḥă·ṭā·'ê·**ḵem***	CST W/ 2MP SX	noun
כַּשָּׁנִים֙ שָׁנִי	as the scarlet *kaš·šā·**nîm***	ABS W/ PREP כְּ + DEF. ART.	noun
כַּשֶּׁ֣לֶג שֶׁלֶג	as the snow *kaš·**še**·leg*	ABS W/ PREP כְּ + DEF. ART.	noun

יַלְבִּינוּ לבן	they will be made white *yal·**bî**·nû*	HIPH IMPF 3MP	verb

Though English translations often separate them, the words כַּשָּׁנִים ("scarlet") and כַּשֶּׁלֶג ("snow") are adjacent in the Hebrew text. This heightens the deliberate contrast between them. The same observation can be made with the latter part of the verse, where "red" and "scarlet" sit adjacent to "wool." The words here likely purposefully invoke David's words of repentance in Ps 51:9 [7]: "Purge me with hyssop, and I shall be clean; wash me, and I shall be whiter than snow" (ESV).

18c **אִם־יַאְדִּימוּ כַתּוֹלָע כַּצֶּמֶר יִהְיוּ׃**

Even though they are as red as crimson,
they will be as white wool.

אִם־ אם	if/when/though *ʾim-*	---	conj
יַאְדִּימוּ אדם	they will be/are red *ya'·**dî**·mû*	HIPH IMPF 3MP	verb
כַתּוֹלָע תּוֹלָע	as the scarlet *ḵat·tô·**lā**ʿ*	ABS W/ PREP כְּ + DEF. ART.	noun
כַּצֶּמֶר צֶמֶר	as the wool *kaṣ·**ṣe**·mer*	ABS W/ PREP כְּ + DEF. ART.	noun
יִהְיוּ׃ היה	they will be/are *yih·**yû***	QAL IMPF 3MP	verb

The Hebrew here elides the word "white." "Wool" implies "white." One is meant to think of the white fleece of a sheep.

19a **אִם־תֹּאבוּ וּשְׁמַעְתֶּם**

If you would just be willing to listen,

אִם־ אם	if/when *ʾim-*	---	conj
תֹּאבוּ אבה	you will be willing *tō'·**vû***	QAL IMPF 2MP	verb

וּשְׁמַעְתֶּם שמע	and you will hear/listen *û·šə·maʿ·**tem***	QAL WEQATAL 2MP	verb

Once again, the verb וּשְׁמַעְתֶּם ("listen") appears (cf. 1:2, 10, 15). It is the driving verb of this passage. The preacher may want to strongly emphasize this imperative throughout the sermon.

19b טוּב הָאָרֶץ תֹּאכֵלוּ׃

you will eat the good stuff of the land.

טוּב טוּב	good *ṭûv*	CST	noun
הָאָרֶץ אֶרֶץ	the land/earth *hā·ʾā·reṣ*	ABS W/ DEF. ART.	noun
תֹּאכֵלוּ׃ אכל	you will eat *tō'·**ḵē**·lû.*	QAL IMPF 2MP	verb

This sounds like the covenantal blessings promised in texts like Lev 25:19 and Deut 11:15. The Israelites would enjoy blessings when obedient and curses when disobedient. Clearly, in keeping with the context of this passage, the obedience God searched for was not merely external ritual, but internal commitment overflowing with love for the destitute.

20a וְאִם־תְּמָאֲנוּ וּמְרִיתֶם

But if you refuse and disobey,

וְאִם־ אִם	and if *wə·ʾim-*	--- W/ CONJ וְ	conj
תְּמָאֲנוּ מאן	you refuse *tə·mā·ʾă·**nû***	PIEL IMPF 2MP	verb
וּמְרִיתֶם מרה	and you will be disobedient *û·mə·rî·**tem***	QAL WEQATAL 2MP	verb

Since "refusal" and "disobedience" are the two wrong choices, they contrast with the imperative "hear/listen." This indicates that God does not mean for Israel to "hear" only in an *auditory* sense. Hearing means obedience and following God's commands (cf. Matt 7:24–27).

20b	חֶ֖רֶב תְּאֻכְּל֑וּ

you'll be eaten by a sword instead!"

חֶ֖רֶב חֶ֫רֶב	sword *ḥe·rev*	ABS	noun
תְּאֻכְּל֑וּ אכל	you will be consumed *tə·ʾuk·kə·**lû***	PUAL IMPF 2MP	verb

Note the two metaphorical paths offered here: obey and "eat" (תֹּאכֵלוּ) the good of the land, or disobey and "be eaten" (תְּאֻכְּלוּ) by a sword instead (a figure of speech indicating death at the hands of an enemy).

20c	כִּ֛י פִּ֥י יְהוָ֖ה דִּבֵּֽר׃

For the mouth of YHWH has spoken.

כִּ֛י כִּי	for/truly *kî*	---	conj
פִּ֥י פֶּה	mouth *pî*	CST	noun
יְהוָ֖ה יהוה	the LORD *YHWH*	ABS	noun
דִּבֵּֽר׃ דבר	(he) has spoken *dib·**bēr***	PIEL PF 3MS	verb

From Text to Sermon

Big Idea. External ritual is meaningless without internal righteousness.

Avenues for Illustration and Application. Isaiah 1 offers many stark pictures of Israel's sin. Calling Jerusalem "Sodom" and "Gomorrah" must have had a pretty shocking effect. You may want to contextualize this for modern listeners. If your kid does well in his football game, you might say, "Nice game, Tom Brady!" If your child does not do so well, maybe you would tease him by substituting the name of one of the Detroit Lions.

Modern listeners will likely not know much about ancient Israelite religious festivals such as New Moon. Don't assume they are familiar with burnt offerings and burning incense. You can bridge the gap of knowledge by simply explaining that these were methods of worship and religious holidays for the Jewish people. You may even want to offer a rewording of this passage, not to replace the Scripture, but as an illustration of what it might sound like to our ears:

"What is all this money you put in the offering plates?" says the Lord. "I have had enough of your offerings. I don't delight in your spiritual gifts! When you come to appear before me on a Sunday morning, it's like you trample over anything that is holy. Your worship songs are vain to me. Communion is an abomination to me. I cannot endure your Sunday morning services. My soul hates Christmas and Easter. Your religious holidays are a burden to me, and I'm tired of having to endure them. When you pray, I blind myself so I don't have to watch you, and I make myself deaf so I don't have to hear you. You think yourself a prayer warrior, but you're really a bunch of murderers."

You will also want to really lean into God's exasperated tone in vv. 13–15. Consider the weight of all the emotional phrases when read together: "I cannot endure . . . my soul hates . . . they have become a burden to me . . . I am weary of bearing them . . . I will hide my eyes from you . . . I will not listen" (ESV). Encourage your church to imagine God saying these things to *them*.

But do not leave the congregation in despair. Verses 16–17 provide built-in applications for the passage. These nine imperatives should give preachers a place to land in the sermon. Make sure to spell out what it means to "wash yourselves" (hint: it's not a physical bath!). Help readers know what it looks like to "seek justice" in different spheres of life—in the workplace, in the city streets, in school, at home. Religious ritual must be connected with ethical living and the enactment of justice; otherwise, it is a "dead" faith (Jas 2:17–26). How does a modern Christian help the socially disadvantaged and vulnerable in society? Be specific. Give ways for congregants to help the unborn child, the immigrant, the literal orphans and widows. In Isaiah's day, people were really good at putting on religious services. Speaking anachronistically, their offerings were huge; their pews were filled; their programs were buzzing with excitement. Meanwhile, orphans and widows starved around them. Perhaps consider how you can lead your church to avoid similar religious hypocrisy and make a lasting impact among the needy in your community.

Near the end of the sermon, use Isaiah's language to call for action. Consider the repetition of the verb שׁמע ("hear/listen"; 1:10, 15, 19; cf. 1:2). Preachers would do well to recognize that even though their congregation might "hear" them audibly, their hearts may not "hear" them in the biblical sense. Their actions will betray whether they have truly heard the word of God. Isaiah also ends this passage with a call to two possible paths: eat or be eaten (1:19–20). Hear/obey and eat the good of the land, or refuse/rebel and be eaten by the sword. Encourage modern listeners to understand that a similar choice stands before them, depending on their response to the text (Matt 7:13–14).

New Testament Connections. Isaiah 1 shows how easy it is for religious behaviors to become cheap substitutes for righteous hearts. Jesus preached quite a bit about the same kind of sinful tendencies. In his words, the people of Jerusalem were whitewashed tombs (Matt 23:27). They were cups that looked clean on the outside but were filthy on the inside (23:25–26). They were the church of Laodicea—famous, rich, mega, yet lukewarm and spiritually dead (Rev 3:15–18). They were the Old Testament version of the Pharisees and Sadducees.

When applying the imperatives in vv. 16–17, you may want to lean on New Testament passages like Heb 9:14: "how much more will the blood of Christ, who through the eternal Spirit offered himself without blemish to God, purify our conscience from dead works to serve the living God" (ESV, cf. 10:22). The gospel enables believers to live out the imperatives for inward cleansing and social change. Root these imperatives in the gospel of Jesus Christ in order to rightly orient the church in her mission. The blood of Christ provides hope for all people, even those struggling with religious hypocrisy.

ISAIAH 5:1–7

THE SONG OF THE VINEYARD

Everyone loves a good song. Everyone also loves a good story, especially one with a twist ending. Isaiah 5 has both. After several chapters where the prophet condemns the pride, idolatry, and religious hypocrisy of the people of Judah and Jerusalem, Isaiah now switches his tactic to get the message across. He sings a beautiful song about a vineyard, a song that tells a story. But the story has a moral point, and that point packs a punch: Judah has produced bad fruit and has therefore invoked God's judgment. If Isaiah sings the story correctly, his audience will find themselves agreeing to their own condemnation—and likewise, the modern preacher can similarly draw in modern listeners to help them recognize their own sin and wickedness.

LARGER LITERARY CONTEXT › 5:1–30

5:1–2

1a אָשִׁ֤ירָה נָּא֙ לִֽידִידִ֔י

*ʾā**šî**râ **nā**ʾ lîdî**dî***

Please let me sing for my beloved!

1b שִׁירַ֥ת דּוֹדִ֖י לְכַרְמ֑וֹ

*šî**rat** dô**dî** ləḵar**mô***

A song of my beloved, about his vineyard:

1c כֶּ֛רֶם הָיָ֥ה לִֽידִידִ֖י

ke**rem hā**yâ** lîdî**dî

My beloved had a vineyard

1d בְּקֶ֥רֶן בֶּן־שָֽׁמֶן׃

*bə**qe**ren bən-**šā**men.*

on a fertile hill.

2a וַיְעַזְּקֵ֣הוּ וַֽיְסַקְּלֵ֗הוּ

*wayʿazzə**qē**hû waysaqqə**lē**hû*

First, he dug it all out. Then he removed its stones.

2b וַיִּטָּעֵ֙הוּ֙ שֹׂרֵ֔ק

*wayyiṭṭā**ʿē**hû śō**rēq***

Next, he planted it with the best grapes.

2c וַיִּ֤בֶן מִגְדָּל֙ בְּתוֹכ֔וֹ

*way**yi**ven mig**dāl** bətô**ḵô***

Then he built a tower right in the center of it,

2d וְגַם־יֶ֖קֶב חָצֵ֣ב בּ֑וֹ

*wəgam-**ye**qev ḥā**ṣēv** **bô***

and he even carved out a wine vat in it!

2e וַיְקַו לַעֲשׂוֹת עֲנָבִים

*way**qaw** la'ăśôt 'ănā**vîm***

Finally, he waited for it to produce grapes,

2f וַיַּעַשׂ בְּאֻשִׁים׃

*way**ya**'aś bə'u**šîm**.*

but it produced stink fruit!

1a אָשִׁירָה נָּא לִידִידִי

Please let me sing for my beloved!

אָשִׁירָה שִׁיר	Let me sing *'ā·**šî**râ*	QAL COHORT 1CS	verb
נָּא נָא	please/I pray ***nā'***	---	particle
לִידִידִי יָדִיד	for my beloved *lî·dî·**dî***	CST W/ PREP לְ + 1CS SX	noun

By using לִידִידִי ("beloved"), Isaiah intentionally sets up his listeners to assume that *they* are the "beloved" in this song. After all, Scripture uses the term regularly for the people of Israel (e.g., Deut 33:12; Pss 60:7 [5]; 108:7 [6]; 127:2; Jer 11:15).

1b שִׁירַת דּוֹדִי לְכַרְמוֹ

A song of my beloved, about his vineyard:

שִׁירַת שִׁירָה	song *šî·**rat***	CST	noun
דּוֹדִי דּוֹד	my beloved *dô·**dî***	CST W/ 1CS SX	noun
לְכַרְמוֹ כֶּרֶם	about his vineyard *lə·kar·**mô***	CST W/ PREP לְ + 3MS SX	noun

שִׁירַת ("song") may have evoked thoughts akin to the Song of Solomon, especially when combined with the vineyard imagery of this poem. This is another of Isaiah's tactics in setting up the Israelites to identify with the positive elements of the song. Though vineyards were also used in Scripture metaphorically for God's people (even within Isaiah; cf. 1:8; 3:14), the element of "my beloved" was introduced first and would likely have a deeper draw for the listeners, especially in light of the negative comments to come.

1c **כֶּ֥רֶם הָיָ֖ה לִֽידִידִ֑י**

My beloved had a vineyard

כֶּ֥רֶם כֶּרֶם	vineyard *ke·rem*	ABS	noun
הָיָ֖ה היה	(he) has *hā·yâ*	QAL PF 3MS	verb
לִֽידִידִ֑י יָדִיד	to/for my beloved *lî·dî·dî*	CST W/ PREP לְ + 1CS SX	noun

1d **בְּקֶ֥רֶן בֶּן־שָֽׁמֶן׃**

on a fertile hill.

בְּקֶ֥רֶן קֶרֶן	hill/hillside *bə·qe·ren*	ABS W/ PREP בְּ	noun
בֶּן־ בֵּן	son of *bən-*	CST	noun
שָֽׁמֶן׃ שֶׁמֶן	fat/oil *šā·men.*	ABS	noun

Notice the alliteration with the preponderance of *b* and *en* sounds. If your Hebrew is proficient enough, reciting these lines aloud may give modern listeners a feel for the hymnic nature of the song. The text here uses שָׁמֶן ("oil") to describe the lush hill, which may directly relate to the production of olive oil. The picture describes a hill so ready to produce vines that it practically already leaks olive oil from its soil.

2a **וַיְעַזְּקֵהוּ וַיְסַקְּלֵהוּ**

First, he dug it all out. Then he removed its stones.

וַיְעַזְּקֵהוּ עזק	and he dug about/ around it *way·ʿaz·zə·**qē**·hû*	PIEL WAYY 3MS W/ 3MS SX	verb
וַיְסַקְּלֵהוּ סקל	and he destoned it *way·saq·qə·**lē**·hû*	PIEL WAYY 3MS W/ 3MS SX	verb

Several *wayyiqtol* verbs move the song along at a fast pace, demonstrating the hard-working activity of the farmer. Preachers will want to explain each of these steps in the process, as modern listeners will likely have little familiarity with ancient horticultural practices. Fields needed to be cleared of stones and debris in order for vines to grow unhindered.

2b **וַיִּטָּעֵהוּ שֹׂרֵק**

Next, he planted it with the best grapes.

וַיִּטָּעֵהוּ נטע	and he planted it *way·yiṭ·ṭā·**ʿē**·hû*	QAL WAYY 3MS W/ 3MS SX	verb
שֹׂרֵק שֹׂרֵק	choice grapes *śō·**rēq***	ABS	noun

The noun שֹׂרֵק ("choice grapes") denotes a finer quality fruit. Preachers will want to emphasize that the farmer began with the best possible product. The fault in this vineyard was not the result the farmer's shoddy efforts.

2c **וַיִּבֶן מִגְדָּל בְּתוֹכוֹ**

Then he built a tower right in the center of it,

וַיִּבֶן בנה	and he built *way·**yi**·ven*	QAL WAYY 3MS	verb
מִגְדָּל מִגְדָּל	tower *mig·**dāl***	ABS	noun
בְּתוֹכוֹ בְּתוֹךְ	in its midst *bə·tô·**ḵô***	--- W/ 3MS SX	prep

A tower might have been built in order to provide a lookout for intruders or potential threats to the garden (e.g., wild animals). Again, preachers should help congregations understand the care taken here to do everything possible for the garden to produce.

2d	וְגַם־יֶ֫קֶב חָצֵ֣ב בּ֑וֹ		
	and he even carved out a wine vat in it!		
וְגַם־ גַּם	and even *wə·gam-*	--- W/ CONJ וְ	adv
יֶ֫קֶב יֶ֫קֶב	wine vat *ye·qev*	ABS	noun
חָצֵ֣ב חצב	he hewed/carved *ḥā·ṣēv*	QAL PF 3MS	verb
בּ֑וֹ בְּ	in it *bô*	--- W/ 3MS SX	prep

The adverb גַּם ("even") indicates that this was an extra step not normally taken by other farmers. The beloved certainly went the extra mile to tend to his product. The sermon should similarly emphasize the care of the farmer, as it will heighten the contrast to come.

2e	וַיְקַ֥ו לַעֲשׂ֖וֹת עֲנָבִ֑ים		
	Finally, he waited for it to produce grapes,		
וַיְקַ֥ו קוה	and he waited for *way·qaw*	PIEL WAYY 3MS	verb
לַעֲשׂ֖וֹת עשׂה	to do/make *la·ʿă·śôt*	QAL INF CST W/ PREP לְ	verb
עֲנָבִ֑ים עֵנָב	grapes *ʿă·nā·vîm*	ABS	noun

2f וַיַּ֖עַשׂ בְּאֻשִֽׁים

but it produced stink fruit!

וַיַּ֖עַשׂ עשׂה	and it made/did *way·ya·ʿaś*	QAL WAYY 3MS	verb
בְּאֻשִֽׁים׃ בְּאֻשִׁים	stinking/worthless things/ wild grapes *bə·ʾu·šîm*	ABS	noun

Notice the back-to-back uses of the verb עשׂה ("to do/make"). The farmer expected the vine to "produce" grapes, but on the contrary, it "produced" stink fruit. This verb will appear five more times in this pericope: four times in v. 4 (see below) and once in v. 5 (the verb also appears twice in 5:10). The word בְּאֻשִׁים ("stink fruit") is difficult to translate (the LXX typically translates it ἄκανθα, "thorns"), but however one emphasizes it, the word should contrast sharply (and offensively) with the choice grapes the farmer expected. Isaiah's word choice evokes shock and disgust in his listeners, setting up the coming gut-punch of the song's twist.

5:3–4

3a וְעַתָּ֛ה יוֹשֵׁ֥ב יְרוּשָׁלִַ֖ם וְאִ֣ישׁ יְהוּדָ֑ה

*wəʿ**attâ** yô**šēv** yərûšā**laim** wə**ʾîš** yəhû**dâ***

And now, O dwellers of Jerusalem and men of Judah,

3b שִׁפְטוּ־נָ֕א בֵּינִ֖י וּבֵ֥ין כַּרְמִֽי׃

*šifṭû-**nāʾ** bê**nî** ûvên kar**mî**.*

please judge between me and between my vineyard.

4a מַה־לַּעֲשׂ֥וֹת עוֹד֙ לְכַרְמִ֔י

*ma-laʿă**śôt** **ʿôd** ləḵar**mî***

What else can I possibly do for my vineyard

4b וְלֹ֥א עָשִׂ֖יתִי בּ֑וֹ

*wə**lōʾ** ʿā**śî**tî **bô***

that I haven't already done with it?

4c מַדּ֧וּעַ קִוֵּ֛יתִי לַעֲשׂ֥וֹת עֲנָבִ֖ים

*mad**dûa**ʿ qiw**wê**tî laʿă**śôt** ʿănā**vîm***

Why, when I looked for it to produce grapes,

4d וַיַּ֥עַשׂ בְּאֻשִֽׁים׃

*way**ya**ʿaś bəʾu**šîm**.*

did it produce stink fruit?

3a	וְעַתָּ֛ה יוֹשֵׁ֥ב יְרוּשָׁלִַ֖ם וְאִ֣ישׁ יְהוּדָ֑ה

And now, O dwellers of Jerusalem and men of Judah,

וְעַתָּה עַתָּה	and now *wə·ʿat·**tâ***	--- W/ CONJ וְ	adv
יוֹשֵׁב ישׁב	inhabitants/dwellers *yô·**šēv***	Q (CST) PTCP MS	verb
יְרוּשָׁלִַם יְרוּשָׁלַ֫ם	Jerusalem *yə·rû·šā·**laim***	ABS	noun
וְאִישׁ אִישׁ	and man *wə·**ʾîš***	CST W/ CONJ וְ	noun
יְהוּדָה יְהוּדָה	Judah *yə·hû·**dâ***	ABS	noun

The opening וְעַתָּה ("and now"), combined with the change to direct address, highlights a change in the song's stanza. It should also highlight a shift in the sermon outline.

3b	שִׁפְטוּ־נָ֕א בֵּינִ֖י וּבֵ֥ין כַּרְמִֽי׃

please judge between me and between my vineyard.

שִׁפְטוּ־ שׁפט	judge *šif·ṭû-*	QAL IMPV MP	verb
נָ֕א נָא	please/I pray ***nāʾ***	---	particle
בֵּינִי בֵּין	between me *bê·**nî***	--- W/ 1CS SX	prep
וּבֵין בֵּין	and between *û·**vên***	--- W/ CONJ וְ	prep
כַּרְמִי׃ כֶּרֶם	my vineyard *kar·**mî***	CST W/ 1CS SX	noun

At this point, the song begins to disorient careful listeners. The singer began by speaking about his beloved who had a vineyard. Israelites might have initially assumed *they* were the beloved. Yet here, God implies that they should associate *him* with the beloved. Israelites should now wonder: if God is the beloved, then who is the vineyard? The ambiguity will not be solved until the end of v. 6.

4a	מַה־לַּעֲשׂוֹת עוֹד לְכַרְמִי

What else can I possibly do for my vineyard

מַה־ מָה	what? why? *ma-*	---	interr pron
לַעֲשׂוֹת עשׂה	to do/make *la·ʿă·**śôt***	QAL INF CST W/ PREP לְ	verb
עוֹד עוֹד	yet/again/still ***ʿôd***	---	adv
לְכַרְמִי כֶּרֶם	for my vineyard *lə·ḵar·**mî***	CST W/ PREP לְ + 1CS SX	noun

4b	וְלֹא עָשִׂיתִי בּוֹ

that I haven't already done with it?

וְלֹא לֹא	and not *wə·**lōʾ***	--- W/ CONJ וְ	particle
עָשִׂיתִי עשׂה	I do/make *ʿā·**śî**·tî*	QAL PF 1CS	verb
בּוֹ בְּ	in/with/by it ***bô***	--- W/ 3MS SX	prep

Just as the rhetorical question drew in the original readers in a participatory fashion, the preacher may want to use this invitation to engage the modern listener. Asking rhetorical questions of a church can be a great tool to engage their attention and get them "agreeing" with the text itself. "Whose fault is it that the grapes didn't grow? What more could a vine dresser possibly do? What more do you do for your gardens? Have you ever been similarly frustrated with a garden for not producing any fruit?"

4c	מַדּוּעַ קִוֵּיתִי לַעֲשׂוֹת עֲנָבִים

Why, when I looked for it to produce grapes,

מַדּוּעַ מַדּוּעַ	why? for what reason? *mad·**dû**·aʿ*	---	adv

קִוִּיתִי קוה	I waited for *qiw·**wê**·tî*	PIEL PF 1CS	verb
לַעֲשׂוֹת עשׂה	to do/make *la·ʿă·**śôt***	QAL INF CST W/ PREP לְ	verb
עֲנָבִים עֵנָב	grapes *ʿă·nā·**vîm***	ABS	noun

4d	וַיַּעַשׂ בְּאֻשִׁים׃

did it produce stink fruit?

וַיַּעַשׂ עשׂה	and it did/made *way·**ya**·ʿaś*	QAL WAYY 3MS	verb
בְּאֻשִׁים׃ בְּאֻשִׁים	stinking/worthless things/ wild grapes *bə·ʾu·**šîm***	ABS	noun

The second half of v. 4 summarizes the story of the song so far. The preacher can also use the opportunity to summarize and recap to make sure the listeners follow closely. Allow the pace and storytelling of the prophet to impact the pace and storytelling of the sermon.

5:5–7

5a וְעַתָּה֙ אוֹדִֽיעָה־נָּ֣א אֶתְכֶ֔ם

*wəʿat**tâ** ʾô**dî**ʿâ-**nāʾ** ʾet**ḵem***

So now, I will let you know

5b אֵ֛ת אֲשֶׁר־אֲנִ֥י עֹשֶׂ֖ה לְכַרְמִ֑י

ʾēt** ʾăšer-ʾă**nî** ʿō**śe** ləḵar**mî

what I will do to my vineyard:

5c הָסֵ֤ר מְשׂוּכָּתוֹ֙ וְהָיָ֣ה לְבָעֵ֔ר

*hā**sēr** məśûkkā**tô** wəhā**yâ** ləvā**ʿēr***

I will get rid of its hedge and burn it up;

5d פָּרֹ֥ץ גְּדֵר֖וֹ וְהָיָ֥ה לְמִרְמָֽס׃

*pā**rôṣ** gədē**rô** wəhā**yâ** ləmir**mās**.*

I will break down its wall and it will become a trampling ground.

6a וַאֲשִׁיתֵ֣הוּ בָתָ֗ה

*waʾăšî**tē**hû vā**tâ***

So I will set it on a path for destruction.

6b לֹ֤א יִזָּמֵר֙ וְלֹ֣א יֵעָדֵ֔ר

lōʾ** yizzā**mēr** wə**lōʾ** yēʿā**dēr

It will not be pruned and it will not be hoed.

6c וְעָלָ֥ה שָׁמִ֖יר וָשָׁ֑יִת

*wəʿā**lâ** šā**mîr** wā**šā**yit*

Instead, thorn and thornbush will grow up.

6d וְעַ֤ל הֶֽעָבִים֙ אֲצַוֶּ֔ה

*wə**ʿal** heʿā**vîm** ʾăṣa**wwe***

I will have control over whether the thunderclouds

6e מֵהַמְטִיר עָלָיו מָטָר:

mēhamṭîr ʿālāyw māṭār.

rain any rain upon it.

7a כִּי כֶרֶם יְהוָה צְבָאוֹת בֵּית יִשְׂרָאֵל

kî kerem YHWH ṣəvāʾôt bêt yiśrāʾēl

For the vineyard of YHWH of hosts is the house of Israel,

7b וְאִישׁ יְהוּדָה נְטַע שַׁעֲשׁוּעָיו

wəʾîš yəhûdâ nəṭaʿ šaʿăšûʿāyw

and the people of Judah is his delightful plant.

7c וַיְקַו לְמִשְׁפָּט וְהִנֵּה מִשְׂפָּח

wayqaw ləmišpāṭ wəhinnē miśpāḥ

And he waited for justice, but behold—just blood!

7d לִצְדָקָה וְהִנֵּה צְעָקָה:

liṣdāqâ wəhinnē ṣəʿāqâ.

for blamelessness, but behold!—blabbering!

5a	וְעַתָּה אוֹדִיעָה־נָּא אֶתְכֶם		
	So now, I will let you know		
וְעַתָּה עַתָּה	and now *wə·ʿat·tâ*	--- W/ CONJ וְ	adv
אוֹדִיעָה־ ידע	I will declare/make known *ʾô·dî·ʿâ-*	HIPH COHORT 1CS	verb
נָּא נָא	please/I pray *nāʾ*	---	particle
אֶתְכֶם אֵת	you *ʾet·kem*	--- W/ 2MP SX	particle

Once more, Isaiah uses וְעַתָּה ("so now") and a switch back to first person as a transitional marker for the song. The preacher can wisely follow Isaiah's lead in the sermon outline.

5b	אֵת אֲשֶׁר־אֲנִי עֹשֶׂה לְכַרְמִי		
	what I will do to my vineyard:		
אֵת אֵת	*(direct object marker)* *ʾēt*	---	particle
אֲשֶׁר־ אֲשֶׁר	that/which *ʾă·šer-*	---	relative pron
אֲנִי אֲנִי	I *ʾă·nî*	---	personal pron
עֹשֶׂה עשׂה	am doing *ʿō·śe*	QAL PTCP MS	verb
לְכַרְמִי כֶּרֶם	to my vineyard *lə·kar·mî*	CST W/ PREP לְ + 1CS SX	noun

This is the final occurrence of the verb עשׂה ("to do") in this poem, used for dramatic effect here. Twice in v. 2 the prophet uses the verb, hoping the seeds will "produce" good grapes, but instead they "produce" bad. Four times in v. 4 he uses it, twice in similar fashion to v. 2, then twice to ask what the farmer should "do" about what the vine has "done." Here, the usage culminates with the rhetorical question of what the farmer should "do" to the vineyard. The answer follows in a series of commanding verbs.

5c	הָסֵר מְשׂוּכָּתוֹ וְהָיָה לְבָעֵר		
	I will get rid of its hedge and burn it up;		
הָסֵר סור	to take away/remove *hā·sēr*	HIPH INF ABS	verb
מְשׂוּכָּתוֹ מְשֻׂכָּה	its hedge *mə·śûk·kā·tô*	CST W/ 3MS SX	noun
וְהָיָה היה	and it will be *wə·hā·yâ*	QAL WEQATAL 3MS	verb
לְבָעֵר בער	to burn/consume *lə·vā·ʿēr*	PIEL INF CST W/ PREP לְ	verb

5d	פָּרֹ֥ץ גְּדֵר֖וֹ וְהָיָ֥ה לְמִרְמָֽס׃

I will break down its wall and it will become a trampling ground.

פָּרֹ֥ץ פרץ	to break through *pā·rôṣ*	QAL INF ABS	verb
גְּדֵר֖וֹ גָּדֵר	its wall *gə·dē·rô*	CST W/ 3MS SX	noun
וְהָיָ֥ה היה	and it will be *wə·hā·yâ*	QAL WEQATAL 3MS	verb
לְמִרְמָֽס׃ מִרְמָס	for a trampling ground *lə·mir·mās*	ABS W/ PREP לְ	noun

This entire phrase enjoys perfect synonymous parallelism with the phrase before it (5c). This indicates the strength of the narrator's fury: he could have just said it once, but he chooses to further the imagery by emphasizing it again.

6a	וַאֲשִׁיתֵ֣הוּ בָתָ֔ה

So I will set it on a path for destruction.

וַאֲשִׁיתֵ֣הוּ שית	I will put/set it *wa·ʾă·šî·tē·hû*	QAL IMPF 1CS W/ CONJ וְ + 3MS SX	verb
בָתָ֔ה בָּתָה	end/destruction *vā·tâ*	ABS	noun

The preacher would do well to match the intensity of the sermon with the intensity of the poem, in pace, volume, and verbiage. The farmer does not pull his punches here, so to speak. If this song were set to music, this would be the hard rock section. Notice also that this line in the poem ends abruptly, unbalanced from the previous two lines, quite literally ending on a note of "destruction."

6b	לֹ֤א יִזָּמֵר֙ וְלֹ֣א יֵעָדֵ֔ר

It will not be pruned and it will not be hoed.

לֹ֤א לֹא	no/not *lōʾ*	---	particle

יִזָּמֵר זמר	it will be pruned *yiz·zā·**mēr***	NIPH IMPF 3MS	verb
וְלֹא לֹא	and no/not *wə·**lō'***	--- W/ CONJ וְ	particle
יֵעָדֵר עדר	it will be hoed *yē·'ā·**dēr***	NIPH IMPF 3MS	verb

6c

וְעָלָה שָׁמִיר וָשַׁיִת

Instead, thorn and thornbush will grow up.

וְעָלָה עלה	and it will go up *wə·'ā·**lâ***	QAL WEQATAL 3MS	verb
שָׁמִיר שָׁמִיר	thorn *šā·**mîr***	ABS	noun
וָשַׁיִת שַׁיִת	thornbush *wā·**šā**·yit*	ABS W/ CONJ וְ	noun

What was once expected to produce good fruit instead produced "stink fruit," and now as a result of the farmer's destruction, only thorns and thornbushes will grow. The addition of these two nouns side-by-side heightens the ugly result of this unfruitful garden.

6d

וְעַל הֶעָבִים אֲצַוֶּה

I will have control over whether the thunderclouds

וְעַל עַל	and over/above *wə·**'al***	--- W/ CONJ וְ	prep
הֶעָבִים עָב	the clouds/dark clouds *he·'ā·**vîm***	ABS W/ DEF. ART.	noun
אֲצַוֶּה צוה	I will command *'ă·ṣaw·**we***	PIEL IMPF 1CS	verb

6e	מֵהַמְטִ֥יר עָלָ֖יו מָטָֽר׃
	rain any rain upon it.

מֵהַמְטִ֥יר מטר	to rain *mē·ham·ṭîr*	HIPH INF CST W/ PREP מִן	verb
עָלָ֖יו עַל	upon/over it *ʿā·lāyw*	--- W/ 3MS SX	prep
מָטָֽר׃ מָטָר	rain *mā·ṭār*	ABS	noun

It is at this point that the Israelite listeners may sense something is amiss in their assumptions. Previously, they likely would have identified with the "beloved" and have been as incensed against the vine as the song intends. Here, however, the beloved indicates he has control over the weather. No human commands the weather; this is surely God! But if this is God, then who is the vine in this analogy? Readers might imagine a collective *gulp* from the original listeners as realization slowly dawns upon them.

7a	כִּ֠י כֶ֣רֶם יְהוָ֤ה צְבָאוֹת֙ בֵּ֣ית יִשְׂרָאֵ֔ל
	For the vineyard of YHWH of hosts is the house of Israel,

כִּ֠י כִּי	for/since/because *kî*	---	conj
כֶ֣רֶם כֶּרֶם	vineyard *ke·rem*	CST	noun
יְהוָ֤ה יהוה	the LORD *YHWH*	ABS	noun
צְבָאוֹת֙ צָבָא	hosts/armies *ṣə·vā·ʾôt*	ABS	noun
בֵּ֣ית בַּיִת	house *bêt*	CST	noun
יִשְׂרָאֵ֔ל יִשְׂרָאֵל	Israel *yiś·rā·ʾēl*	ABS	noun

The כִּי ("for") indicates another transition, this one offering an explanation of the song. This is the "aha!" moment for Isaiah's audience, who likely would have identified with the "beloved" in the opening portions of the poem. This revelation would have caused listeners to think through the song once more from a different, more sober perspective. By holding the "house of Israel" to the end of the phrase, it magnifies the surprise reveal of who the poem actually addresses. The word צְבָאוֹת ("hosts") is commonly used of the Lord's heavenly armies (angelic hosts). The word has military connotations, often denoting the literal armies of Israel (2 Sam 3:23) and the like. When used of the Lord's heavenly armies, it conveys his sovereignty and power as king and general of the most powerful forces in the universe.

7b **וְאִ֣ישׁ יְהוּדָ֔ה נְטַ֖ע שַֽׁעֲשׁוּעָ֑יו**

and the people of Judah is his delightful plant.

וְאִ֣ישׁ אִישׁ	and man *wə·ʾîš*	CST W/ CONJ וְ	noun
יְהוּדָ֔ה יְהוּדָה	Judah *yə·hû·dâ*	ABS	noun
נְטַ֖ע נֶ֫טַע	plant *nə·ṭaʿ*	CST	noun
שַֽׁעֲשׁוּעָ֑יו שַׁעֲשֻׁעִים	his delights *ša·ʿă·šû·ʿāyw*	CST W/ 3MS SX	noun

The noun שַֽׁעֲשׁוּעָיו ("his delights") takes a plural form here, likely a plural of intensity, which elevates the original glory of the plant/Israel, effectively also heightening the contrast with the final outcome as well. Israel enjoyed the best of conditions with the greatest potential for growth, yet in the end, she only rebelled against the Lord and produced bad fruit.

7c **וַיְקַ֤ו לְמִשְׁפָּט֙ וְהִנֵּ֣ה מִשְׂפָּ֔ח**

And he waited for justice, but behold—just blood!

וַיְקַ֤ו קוה	and he waited *way·qaw*	PIEL WAYY 3MS	verb
לְמִשְׁפָּט֙ מִשְׁפָּט	for justice/judgment *lə·miš·pāṭ*	ABS W/ PREP לְ	noun
וְהִנֵּ֣ה הִנֵּה	and behold *wə·hin·nē*	--- W/ CONJ וְ	particle

מִשְׁפָּח מִשְׁפָּח	bloodshed *miś·pāḥ*	ABS	noun

This is the third time the verb קוה ("to wait") appears in this song. In vv. 2, 4, the farmer "waits" for the good grapes, but only worthless grapes appear. This waiting now comes to fruition when Isaiah applies it to the Lord, who is "waiting" for justice but only gets bloodshed. The preacher may want to highlight this link to further strengthen the connection between the song and its application. See below (7d) for the alliteration in this line.

7d לִצְדָקָה וְהִנֵּה צְעָקָה׃

for blamelessness, but behold—blabbering!

לִצְדָקָה צְדָקָה	for righteousness *liṣ·dā·qâ*	ABS W/ PREP לְ	noun
וְהִנֵּה הִנֵּה	and behold *wə·hin·nē*	--- W/ CONJ וְ	particle
צְעָקָה׃ צְעָקָה	cry/outcry *ṣə·ʿā·qâ*	ABS	noun

The Hebrew text rhymes לְמִשְׁפָּט with מִשְׁפָּח in v. 7c and לִצְדָקָה with צְעָקָה here. If your Hebrew pronunciation is proficient, speak these lines aloud, as they will have a powerful effect on the ear. Many attempts have been made to bring the rhyme into English (including my own humble efforts), but none match the perfection of the original.

From Text to Sermon

Big Idea. From choice grapes to stink fruit: God will judge Israel's sin.

Avenues for Illustration and Application. One of the most important (and sometimes most neglected) rhetorical devices for preachers is *anticipation* and *surprise*. Isaiah utilizes tension perfectly, not letting on until the last moments of the song that the vineyard in the analogy represents Israel. Preachers would do well to mimic and learn from this rhetorical technique. Be careful not to reveal the true identity of the vine until Isaiah himself does. It may even be prudent not to read the passage in full until the great revelation in the sermon. This will hold the modern audience in tension and potentially even hit them with the surprise, just as Isaiah's original listeners would have experienced.

Isaiah gives several structural markers in the text, which lend preachers potential structural divisions in the sermon. Two וְעַתָּה ("and now"; vv. 3 and 5) separate vv. 1–2, 3–4, and 5–6, and the explanatory כִּי ("for") sets off v. 7 from the rest. Preachers may want to organize the sermon according to this natural structure. The sermon's outline may look something like this:

5:1a — Introduction to the Song

A 5:1b–2 — The Disappointment of the Farmer

B 5:3–4 — Engagement with the Listeners

A′ 5:5–6 — The Judgment of the Vineyard

B′ 5:7 — Application of the Song

Preachers may want to draw attention to the alliteration in the final verse. The Hebrew is meant to be *heard*, not just translated. If your Hebrew is rusty, consider contacting a local Bible professor or another pastor who can help you with pronunciation. Or, consider paraphrasing the verse with your own rhyming translation. When I preached Isa 5, I used a translation from a commentary (giving credit where credit was due). One does not need to be extra creative; one only needs to know where to look.

The text also relies heavily on farming analogies. Depending on whether your audience dwells in a rural or urban setting, they will have varying levels of familiarity with Isaiah's analogy. The church could potentially miss the entire point of the passage if the preacher fails to build a proper contextual bridge between listener and ancient setting. Unless you preach or teach in a small, rural setting, it would be best to assume that no one has knowledge of viticulture. You will need to explain why stones would need to be removed from the field, why the farmer would erect a tower in the middle (for protection, most likely—a lookout station), what a "wine vat" even is. If possible, use common source pictures to illustrate some of these elements, ideally of ancient setups (though modern viticulture has evolved surprisingly little from ancient methods). If the preacher can take care to bring the church along with each step of the farmer's process, the listeners will have a better appreciation for the hard work and labor of love that went into the farmer's efforts. This will in turn heighten the shock when the vine fails to yield productive fruit.

When moving towards application, help listeners identify with the grapes. This will not be an easy task, for listeners will most likely desire to identify with the farmer in the song. This is purposeful, as Isaiah begins without letting the audience in on the ultimate meaning of the poem. But in order to successfully drive home the same kind of application the prophet was aiming for, listeners must ultimately realize that *they too* are the stink fruit. This point will be offensive (as it was for Isaiah's original readers), but do not shy away from making it.

Modern listeners need to understand that the application of this text can invade their personal spaces, not just their church. Ask a series of increasingly personal questions to draw people into the application: When God looks in our *church*, does he see justice or division? Does he see righteousness or bitterness? When God looks in our *homes*, does he see justice or abuse? Does he see righteousness or tears? When God looks at your *life*, does he see justice or anger? Does he see righteousness or ungodliness?

If preachers choose to extend the sermon to the end of Isa 5, the six "woes" of 5:8–30 provide additional application. Why is God angry at his vineyard? It is not only because of bloodshed and an outcry of the oppressed. God is also angry at the greedy rich people (5:8–10), the wealthy drunk people (5:11–14), and the moral autonomy of the Israelites (5:15–25). Each woe is followed by a declaration of coming judgment, making for an easy extended sermon outline:

- Woe #1: Greedy Rich People (5:8)
    - Judgment: Removal of Wealth (5:9–10)
- Woe #2: Wealthy Drunk People (5:11–12)
    - Judgment: Starvation in Exile (5:13–17)
- Woes #3–6: Morally Autonomous People (5:18–23)
    - Judgment: Death by Earthquake (5:24–25)
    - Final Judgment: Foreign Invaders (5:26–30)

New Testament Connections. One cannot help but wonder if Jesus had Isa 5 in mind when he preached the parable of the wicked tenants in Matt 21:33–46 (// Mark 12:1–12). Consider especially how he opens the parable and how similar it sounds to Isa 5: "Hear another parable. There was a master of a house who planted a vineyard and put a fence around it and dug a winepress in it and built a tower and leased it to tenants, and went into another country" (Matt 21:33 ESV). Though the point of Jesus' parable as compared to Isaiah's song is very different, the same care can be seen by both farmers in tending the field and vine. This should not surprise us, as the farmer in both cases is God.

More to the point, preachers may want to consider texts such as Matt 7:15–20:

> Beware of false prophets, who come to you in sheep's clothing but inwardly are ravenous wolves. You will recognize them by their fruits. Are grapes gathered from thornbushes, or figs from thistles? So, every healthy tree bears good fruit, but the diseased tree bears bad fruit. A healthy tree cannot bear bad fruit, nor can a diseased tree bear good fruit. Every tree that does not bear good fruit is cut down and thrown into the fire. Thus you will recognize them by their fruits. (ESV)

The true nature of the Israelites in Isa 5 was revealed by their "fruit," or their actions. The New Testament applies fruit analogies in similar ways for false prophets and even the words of a believer (Jas 3:6–12). Based on these applications, preachers may want to challenge listeners to consider their own "fruit," or consider how their deeds reflect their character. Would the Lord look upon them as "good fruit" or "bad fruit"? This may also point the way for gospel application, as the only true remedy for a rotten heart is total transformation through the blood of Jesus Christ (2 Cor 5:17; cf. Deut 30:6; Ps 51:10; Ezek 11:19).

ISAIAH 6:1–13

ISAIAH'S COMMISSIONING

Most pastors and preachers claim to discern a specific "call" to the ministry. Few, however, have as dramatic and awe-inspiring a call as the prophet Isaiah. In the same year that King Uzziah died—a king that enjoyed a reign of over half a century—Isaiah receives a vision of the King of kings, who has reigned and will reign forever. The Lord's commissioning of Isaiah does not come without its challenges. Isaiah recognizes the stark contrast between his sinfulness and YHWH's holiness. Nevertheless, God mercifully offers cleansing for his sin and sends him to minister to a people who are destined to reject his message. Though the Lord offers the prophet and his people hope, the overall message is still starkly grim. Isaiah's call might be clear, but the people's rejection of that call is just as explicit. This chapter gives hope to the struggling minister. Success in ministry does not depend on the church's response to one's message, but rather the faithfulness of the messenger himself to communicate God's word.

LARGER LITERARY CONTEXT › 6:1–13

6:1–5

1a בִּשְׁנַת־מוֹת הַמֶּלֶךְ עֻזִּיָּהוּ

*bišnat-**môt** ham**me**leḵ uzziy**yā**hû*

In the same year that King Uzziah died,

1b וָאֶרְאֶה אֶת־אֲדֹנָי יֹשֵׁב עַל־כִּסֵּא

*wāʾer**ʾe** ʾet-ʾădō**nāy** yō**šēv** ʿal-kis**sē**ʾ*

I saw the Lord sitting upon a throne,

1c רָם וְנִשָּׂא

***rām** wəniś**śā**ʾ*

lofty and elevated,

1d וְשׁוּלָיו מְלֵאִים אֶת־הַהֵיכָל:

*wəšû**lāyw** məlē**ʾîm** ʾet-hahê**ḵāl**.*

and his robe's skirt filled the temple.

2a שְׂרָפִים עֹמְדִים | מִמַּעַל לוֹ

*śərā**fîm** ʿōmə**dîm** mim**ma**ʿal **lô***

Fiery ones stood above him.

2b שֵׁשׁ כְּנָפַיִם שֵׁשׁ כְּנָפַיִם לְאֶחָד

šēš** kənā**fa**yim **šēš** kənā**fa**yim ləʾe**ḥād

Each one of them had six wings:

2c בִּשְׁתַּיִם | יְכַסֶּה פָנָיו

*biš**ta**yim yəḵas**se** fā**nāyw***

with two wings he would cover his face,

2d וּבִשְׁתַּיִם יְכַסֶּה רַגְלָיו

*ûviš**ta**yim yəḵas**se** rag**lāyw***

and with two wings he would cover his feet,

2e וּבִשְׁתַּ֖יִם יְעוֹפֵֽף׃

*ûviš**ta**yim yəʿô**fēf**.*

and with two wings he would fly all around.

3a וְקָרָ֨א זֶ֤ה אֶל־זֶה֙

*wəqā**rāʾ** **ze** ʾel-**ze***

And each one would call out to another,

3b וְאָמַ֗ר קָד֧וֹשׁ ׀ קָד֛וֹשׁ קָד֖וֹשׁ יְהוָ֣ה צְבָא֑וֹת

*wəʾā**mar** qā**dôš** qā**dôš** qā**dôš** YHWH ṣəvā**ʾôt***

**and they would repeat, "Holy, holy, holy
is YHWH of the heavenly armies!**

3c מְלֹ֥א כָל־הָאָ֖רֶץ כְּבוֹדֽוֹ׃

*mə**lōʾ** ḵol-hā**ʾā**reṣ kəvô**dô**.*

The fullness of the entire earth is his glory!"

4a וַיָּנֻ֙עוּ֙ אַמּ֣וֹת הַסִּפִּ֔ים מִקּ֖וֹל הַקּוֹרֵ֑א

*wayyā**nū**ʿû ʾam**môt** hassip**pîm** miq**qôl** haqqô**rē**ʾ*

**And the pivots of the thresholds shook
from the sound of the one who proclaimed,**

4b וְהַבַּ֖יִת יִמָּלֵ֥א עָשָֽׁן׃

*wəha**ba**yit yimmā**lēʾ** ʿā**šān**.*

and the temple was filled up with smoke.

5a וָאֹמַ֞ר אוֹי־לִ֣י

*wāʾō**mar** ʾ**ôy**-**lî***

And I said, "Woe to me,

5b כִּֽי־נִדְמֵ֗יתִי

***ḵî**-nid**mê**tî*

for I am like a dead man,

5c כִּ֣י אִ֤ישׁ טְמֵא־שְׂפָתַ֙יִם֙ אָנֹ֔כִי

kî ʾîš ṭəmē-śəfātayim ʾānōḵî

for I am a man of unclean lips,

5d וּבְתוֹךְ֙ עַם־טְמֵ֣א שְׂפָתַ֔יִם אָנֹכִ֖י יוֹשֵׁ֑ב

ûvətôḵ ʿam-ṭəmēʾ śəfātayim ʾānōḵî yôšēv

and in the middle of a people of unclean lips—
that's where I live,

5e כִּ֠י אֶת־הַמֶּ֛לֶךְ יְהוָ֥ה צְבָא֖וֹת רָא֥וּ עֵינָֽי׃

kî ʾet-hammeleḵ YHWH *ṣəvāʾôt rāʾû ʿênāy.*

for my eyes have seen the king, YHWH of hosts!"

1a בִּשְׁנַת־מוֹת֙ הַמֶּ֣לֶךְ עֻזִּיָּ֔הוּ

In the same year that King Uzziah died,

בִּשְׁנַת־ / שָׁנָה	in the year / *biš·nat-*	CST W/ PREP בְּ	noun
מוֹת / מָוֶת	death / ***môt***	CST	noun
הַמֶּלֶךְ / מֶלֶךְ	the king / *ham·**me**·leḵ*	ABS W/ DEF. ART.	noun
עֻזִּיָּהוּ / עֻזִּיָּהוּ	Uzziah / *uz·ziy·**yā**·hû*	ABS	noun

Isaiah 1:1 tells readers that the prophet ministered during the reign of four Judean kings: Uzziah (a.k.a. Azariah), Jotham, Ahaz, and Hezekiah (cf. 7:1; 14:28; 36–39). The Lord judged Uzziah's ministry mostly favorably (2 Chr 26:4–5), though he did stumble morally in the end (26:16–21). Most sources place his death ca. 739 BC. It is important to recognize the longevity of Uzziah's reign: according to the Chronicler, he began his reign at sixteen years old and ruled for fifty-two years (2 Chr 26:3).

1b	וָאֶרְאֶ֧ה אֶת־אֲדֹנָ֛י יֹשֵׁ֥ב עַל־כִּסֵּ֖א

I saw the Lord sitting upon a throne,

וָאֶרְאֶ֧ה ראה	And I saw *wā·ʾer·**ʾe***	QAL WAYY 1CS	verb
אֶת־ אֵת	*(direct object marker)* *ʾet-*	---	particle
אֲדֹנָ֛י אֲדֹנָי	the Lord *ʾă·dō·**nāy***	ABS	noun
יֹשֵׁ֥ב ישׁב	sitting *yō·**šēv***	QAL PTCP MS	verb
עַל־ עַל	upon *ʿal-*	---	prep
כִּסֵּ֖א כִּסֵּא	throne *kis·**sēʾ***	ABS	noun

Notice the contrast between the death of Uzziah—one of the longest reigning kings of Judah—and the Lord, eternally reigning upon his throne. The use of the participle יֹשֵׁ֥ב ("sitting") draws attention to the durative nature of the Lord's unending reign. Note also the discussion below on John's use of this chapter in John 12:41.

1c	רָ֣ם וְנִשָּׂ֑א

lofty and elevated,

רָ֣ם רום	high/lifted ***rām***	QAL PTCP MS	verb
וְנִשָּׂ֑א נשׂא	and exalted/lifted up *wə·niś·**śāʾ***	NIPH PTCP MS W/ CONJ וְ	verb

These two participles may modify "the Lord" (NIV) or "throne" (NET; NLT). Their position in the sentence favors the latter, but the Masoretic punctuation favors the former. Either decision does not make much of a functional difference in meaning.

1d	וְשׁוּלָ֣יו מְלֵאִ֣ים אֶת־הַהֵיכָֽל׃

and his robe's skirt filled the temple.

וְשׁוּלָיו שׁוּל	and his skirt/train *wə·šû·**lāyw***	CST W/ CONJ וְ + 3MS SX	noun
מְלֵאִים מלא	filled *mə·lē·**ʾîm***	QAL PTCP MP	verb
אֶת־ אֵת	*(direct object marker)* *ʾet-*	---	particle
הַהֵיכָל׃ הֵיכָל	the temple/palace *ha·hê·**ḵāl***	ABS W/ DEF. ART.	noun

Much discussion centers on the noun שׁוּל. Commentators have pointed out that ancient Near Eastern iconography lacks evidence that robes had trains (Oswalt 1986:170; Roberts 2015:94–95). "Skirt" or "hem" may be more accurate translations. The robe's enormity reflects the Lord's magnificent grandeur.

2a	שְׂרָפִ֨ים עֹמְדִ֤ים ׀ מִמַּ֙עַל֙ ל֔וֹ

Fiery ones stood above him.

שְׂרָפִים שָׂרָף	seraphim/fiery ones *śə·rā·**fîm***	ABS	noun
עֹמְדִים ׀ עמד	standing *ʿō·mə·**dîm***	QAL PTCP MP	verb
מִמַּעַל מַעַל	from above *mim·**ma**·ʿal*	--- W/ PREP מִן	prep
לוֹ לְ	to him ***lô***	--- W/ 3MS SX	prep

The traditional translation "seraphim" is not a translation at all; rather, it is a transliteration of the Hebrew. The word literally means "fiery ones" or "burning ones." This may reflect a fiery appearance. Elsewhere, the word is used of the snakes that bit the Israelites in the wilderness (Num 21:6; cf. Deut 8:15). The word enhances the terror-inducing vision Isaiah receives.

2b	שֵׁשׁ כְּנָפַיִם שֵׁשׁ כְּנָפַיִם לְאֶחָד

Each one of them had six wings:

שֵׁשׁ שֵׁשׁ	six *šēš*	ABS	cardinal number
כְּנָפַיִם כָּנָף	wings *kə·nā·**fa**·yim*	ABS	noun
שֵׁשׁ שֵׁשׁ	six *šēš*	ABS	cardinal number
כְּנָפַיִם כָּנָף	wings *kə·nā·**fa**·yim*	ABS	noun
לְאֶחָד אֶחָד	to another/one *lə·ʾe·**ḥād***	ABS W/ PREP לְ	cardinal number

If the seraphim are serpentine, they are snakes that also fly, once again adding to the terror of the experience (cf. Isa 14:29; 30:6). Isaiah 6 is the only place in Scripture that mentions these angelic beings.

2c	בִּשְׁתַּיִם ׀ יְכַסֶּה פָנָיו

with two wings he would cover his face,

בִּשְׁתַּיִם ׀ שְׁנַיִם	and with two *biš·**ta**·yim*	ABS W/ PREP בְּ	cardinal number
יְכַסֶּה כסה	he would cover *yə·ḵas·**se***	PIEL IMPF 3MS	verb
פָנָיו פָּנֶה	his face *fā·**nāyw***	CST W/ 3MS SX	noun

The unusual use of the first pair of wings has been attributed to the angelic beings attempting to avoid seeing God's glory, or perhaps as an expression of humility (cf. Ezek 1:11, 23). The imperfects in this sentence indicate that this activity of covering is ongoing.

2d וּבִשְׁתַּיִם יְכַסֶּה רַגְלָיו

and with two wings he would cover his feet,

וּבִשְׁתַּיִם שְׁנַיִם	and with two *û·viš·**ta**·yim*	ABS W/ CONJ וְ + PREP בְּ	cardinal number
יְכַסֶּה כסה	he would cover *yə·ḵas·**se***	PIEL IMPF 3MS	verb
רַגְלָיו רֶגֶל	his feet *rag·**lāyw***	CST W/ 3MS SX	noun

Some think "feet" may be euphemistic for the genitals, but this imagery is not appropriate for angelic beings. The text does not care to explain the meaning behind the imagery; the wise preacher should take similar cautions.

2e וּבִשְׁתַּיִם יְעוֹפֵף׃

and with two wings he would fly all around.

וּבִשְׁתַּיִם שְׁנַיִם	and with two *û·viš·**ta**·yim*	ABS W/ CONJ וְ + PREP בְּ	cardinal number
יְעוֹפֵף׃ עוף	he would fly about *yə·ʿô·**fēf***	POLEL IMPF 3MS	verb

The Polel stem is a variation of the Piel. Besides its occurrences in this form in Isaiah (6:2; 14:29; 30:6), this verb and form also appear in Gen 1:20 to describe the birds flying above the earth during creation.

3a וְקָרָא זֶה אֶל־זֶה

And each one would call out to another,

וְקָרָא קרא	and (it) would call/ proclaim *wə·qā·**rā**ʾ*	QAL WEQATAL 3MS	verb
זֶה זֶה	this (one) ***ze***	---	demonstr pron
אֶל־ אֶל	to *ʾel-*	---	prep

זֶה זֶה	this (one) *ze*	---	demonstr pron

Readers should understand the Hebrew here to idiomatically refer to antiphonal call and response. The seraphim call back and forth to one another, praising the Lord for his holiness. Preachers may want to consider a responsive reading during the service to reflect the angelic chorus in the text.

3b וְאָמַר קָדוֹשׁ | קָדוֹשׁ קָדוֹשׁ יְהוָה צְבָאוֹת

and they would repeat, "Holy, holy, holy
is YHWH of the heavenly armies!

וְאָמַר אמר	and it would say *wə·'ā·**mar***	QAL WEQATAL 3MS	verb
קָדוֹשׁ | קָדוֹשׁ	holy *qā·**dôš***	MS PRED	adj
קָדוֹשׁ קָדוֹשׁ	holy *qā·**dôš***	MS PRED	adj
קָדוֹשׁ קָדוֹשׁ	holy *qā·**dôš***	MS PRED	adj
יְהוָה יהוה	the Lord of *YHWH*	CST	noun
צְבָאוֹת צָבָא	hosts/armies *ṣə·vā·**'ôt***	ABS	noun

Only a few other places in Scripture have a threefold repetition like this (e.g., Jer 7:4; 22:29; Ezek 21:32 [27]). The only other place in the Bible where a threefold "Holy! Holy! Holy!" is used is Rev 4:8, a clear allusion to this passage in Isaiah. It seems that after some 700 years between Isaiah and Revelation, the seraphim have not stopped their chorus.

3c מְלֹא כָל־הָאָרֶץ כְּבוֹדוֹ׃

The fullness of the entire earth is his glory!"

מְלֹא מְלֹא	fullness *mə·**lō'***	CST	noun

כָּל־ כֹּל	all *kol-*	CST	noun
הָאָ֑רֶץ אֶ֫רֶץ	the earth *hā·ʾā·reṣ*	ABS W/ DEF. ART.	noun
כְּבוֹדֽוֹ׃ כָּבוֹד	his glory/honor *kə·vô·dô*	CST W/ 3MS SX	noun

The verbless clause puts a certain emphasis on "his glory." Just as a work of art testifies to the genius of the artist, so the earth (and all creation) testifies to the glory of the Creator.

4a וַיָּנֻ֙עוּ֙ אַמּ֣וֹת הַסִּפִּ֔ים מִקּ֖וֹל הַקּוֹרֵ֑א

And the pivots of the thresholds shook
from the sound of the one who proclaimed,

וַיָּנֻ֙עוּ֙ נוע	and (they) tottered/ shook *way·yā·nū·ʿû*	QAL WAYY 3MP	verb
אַמּ֣וֹת אַמָּה	cubits/pivots *ʾam·môt*	CST	noun
הַסִּפִּ֔ים סַף	the thresholds *has·sip·pîm*	ABS W/ DEF. ART.	noun
מִקּ֖וֹל קוֹל	from sound/voice *miq·qôl*	CST W/ PREP מִן	noun
הַקּוֹרֵ֑א קרא	he who proclaimed/ called out *haq·qô·rēʾ*	QAL PTCP MS W/ DEF. ART.	verb

The Hebrew text directly attributes the shaking to the voice(s) of the one(s) proclaiming. Congregants who complain that the music is too loud in church should take note: the word אַמּוֹת ("cubits/pivots") is obscure and may refer to the pivots in the doorways; thus, the very supports of the structure were shaking with the power of the voices.

4b	וְהַבַּ֫יִת יִמָּלֵ֥א עָשָֽׁן׃

and the temple was filled up with smoke.

וְהַבַּ֫יִת בַּ֫יִת	and the house/temple *wə·ha·**ba**·yit*	ABS W/ CONJ וְ + DEF. ART.	noun
יִמָּלֵ֥א מלא	(it) was filled *yim·mā·**lē**ʾ*	NIPH IMPF 3MS	verb
עָשָֽׁן׃ עָשָׁן	smoke *ʿā·**šān***	ABS	noun

The passage is packed with “fullness” language (מלא/מְלֹא): the train of the King’s robe “filled” the temple (v. 1); the whole earth is “full” of God’s glory (v. 3); here, the temple is now “filled” with smoke. The effect of all this filling magnifies the overwhelming glorious presence of God. In addition, the smoke recalls other times in the Old Testament where smoky haze blocks the unholy sinner from directly viewing the presence of God (e.g., the incense altar in the Tabernacle/Temple in Exod 40:5; the smoke and violent trembling that accompanied the appearance of God on Mt. Sinai in Exod 19:18; indeed, Isa 6 may directly allude to the latter with the trembling threshold and smoke).

5a	וָאֹמַ֞ר אֽוֹי־לִ֣י

And I said, “Woe to me,

וָאֹמַ֞ר אמר	and I said *wā·ʾō·**mar***	QAL WAYY 1CS	verb
אֽוֹי־ אוֹי	woe ***ʾôy**-*	---	particle
לִ֣י לְ	to me ***lî***	--- W/ 1CS SX	prep

In Isa 5, the prophet calls out six “woes” (הוֹי) against the wicked Judeans (5:8, 11, 18, 20–22). Here, after encountering the awesome holiness of God, the prophet calls “woe” upon himself, switching to אוֹי (“woe”), a related word. The difference between the two words is slight and may be negligible in the present context. The word הוֹי from Isa 5 is used fifty-one times in Scripture. It is most often used in contexts of warning or mourning (or both), but can appear as a general summons without either of these implications (e.g., Isa 55:1; cf. Harman 1997:1032). The word אוֹי (24x in Scripture) is almost always used in prophetic contexts for expressions of grief due to impending judgment.

5b	כִּֽי־נִדְמֵ֗יתִי
	for I am like a dead man,

כִּֽי־ כִּי	for/because *ḵî-*	---	conj
נִדְמֵ֗יתִי דמה	I am cut off *nid·mê·tî*	NIPH PF 1CS	verb

A survey of English versions would indicate that this phrase presents challenges for translation (NASB: "I am ruined!"; ESV: "I am lost"; KJV: "I am undone"; NET: "I am destroyed"; NLT: "It's all over! I am doomed."). The options come from confusion over whether the word derives from דָּמָה ("be destroyed/cut off") or another word from the root דמה ("be silenced"), a biform of דמם (Roberts 2015:99). Both fit the context, as the death of unholy sinners in the presence of the holy God is not unknown in the Old Testament (e.g., Nadab and Abihu in Lev 10), and the silence of the prophet would contrast well with the loudness of the angelic voices, also pairing well with the "unclean lips" imagery to come.

5c	כִּ֣י אִ֤ישׁ טְמֵֽא־שְׂפָתַ֙יִם֙ אָנֹ֔כִי
	for I am a man of unclean lips,

כִּ֣י כִּי	for/because *ḵî*	---	conj
אִ֤ישׁ אִי	a man *ʾîš*	ABS	noun
טְמֵֽא־ טָמֵא	unclean *ṭə·mēʾ-*	MS CST	adj
שְׂפָתַ֙יִם֙ שָׂפָה	lips/speech *śə·fā·ta·yim*	ABS	noun
אָנֹ֔כִי אָנֹכִי	I *ʾā·nō·ḵî*	---	personal pron

Isaiah ends this phrase with אָנֹכִי ("I"), which casts attention on himself grammatically: "A man of unclean lips—*that's who I am!*"

5d	וּבְת֣וֹךְ עַם־טְמֵ֣א שְׂפָתַ֔יִם אָנֹכִ֖י יוֹשֵׁ֑ב

and in the middle of a people of unclean lips—
that's where I live,

וּבְת֣וֹךְ בְּתוֹךְ	and in the midst *û·və·**tôḵ***	--- W/ CONJ וְ	prep
עַם־ עַם	people *'am-*	CST	noun
טְמֵ֣א טָמֵא	unclean *ṭə·**mē'***	MS CST	adj
שְׂפָתַ֔יִם שָׂפָה	lips/speech *śə·fā·**ta**·yim*	ABS	noun
אָנֹכִ֖י אָנֹכִי	I *'ā·**nō**·ḵî*	---	personal pron
יוֹשֵׁ֑ב ישׁב	dwelling *yô·**šēv***	QAL PTCP MS	verb

The idea of "unclean lips" derives from the Levitical distinction between clean/unclean. Isaiah's speech—in contrast to the seraphim's—is dangerously unfit for ceremonial worship. As such, he reflects the Israelite people, who have similar qualities of ungodliness. If one anachronistically takes Jesus' words into account, that the words of our mouth overflow from the heart (Matt 12:34), then this may indicate that Isaiah's heart is not right with God.

5e	כִּ֗י אֶת־הַמֶּ֛לֶךְ יְהוָ֥ה צְבָא֖וֹת רָא֥וּ עֵינָֽי׃

for my eyes have seen the king, YHWH of hosts!"

כִּ֗י כִּי	for/because ***kî***	---	conj
אֶת־ אֵת	*(direct object marker)* *'et-*	---	particle
הַמֶּ֛לֶךְ מֶלֶךְ	the king *ham·**me**·leḵ*	ABS W/ DEF. ART.	noun

יְהוָה יהוה	the Lord *YHWH*	ABS	noun
צְבָאוֹת צָבָא	hosts/armies *ṣə·vā·**ʾôt***	ABS	noun
רָאוּ ראה	(they) have seen *rā·**ʾû***	QAL PF 3CP	verb
עֵינָי׃ עַיִן	my eyes *ʿê·**nāy***	CST W/ 1CS SX	noun

Isaiah's words are reminiscent of Manoah's in Judg 13:22 (cf. Gen 32:30; Judg 6:22). To behold God as a sinful man is to court death.

6:6–7

6a וַיָּ֣עָף אֵלַ֗י אֶחָד֙ מִן־הַשְּׂרָפִ֔ים

*way**yā**ʿāf ʾē**lay** ʾe**ḥād** min-haśśərā**fîm***

Then, one of the burning ones flew towards me,

6b וּבְיָד֖וֹ רִצְפָּ֑ה

*ûvəyā**dô** riṣ**pâ***

and in his hand was a live coal

6c בְּמֶ֨לְקַחַ֔יִם לָקַ֖ח מֵעַ֥ל הַמִּזְבֵּֽחַ׃

*bəmelqa**ḥayim** lā**qaḥ** mē**ʿal** hammiz**bē**aḥ.*

which he took from upon the altar with tongs.

7a וַיַּגַּ֣ע עַל־פִּ֔י

*wayyag**ga**ʿ ʿal-**pî***

Then he touched my mouth

7b וַיֹּ֕אמֶר הִנֵּ֛ה נָגַ֥ע זֶ֖ה עַל־שְׂפָתֶ֑יךָ

*way**yō**ʾmer hin**nē** nā**ga**ʿ **ze** ʿal-śəfā**tê**ḵā*

and he said, "Look! This has struck your lips,

7c וְסָ֣ר עֲוֹנֶ֔ךָ וְחַטָּאתְךָ֖ תְּכֻפָּֽר׃

*wə**sār** ʿăwō**ne**ḵā wəḥaṭṭāʾtə**ḵā** təḵup**pār**.*

and your iniquity has been turned aside
and your sin has been atoned for."

6a	וַיָּ֣עָף אֵלַ֗י אֶחָד֙ מִן־הַשְּׂרָפִ֔ים

Then, one of the burning ones flew towards me,

וַיָּ֣עָף עוף	and (they) flew *way·yā·ʿāf*	QAL WAYY 3MS	verb
אֵלַ֗י אֶל	to me *ʾē·lay*	--- W/ 1CS SX	prep
אֶחָד֙ אֶחָד	one *ʾe·ḥād*	ABS	cardinal number
מִן־ מִן	from *min-*	---	prep
הַשְּׂרָפִ֔ים שָׂרָף	the burning ones/ seraphim *haś·śə·rā·fîm*	ABS W/ DEF. ART.	noun

6b	וּבְיָד֖וֹ רִצְפָּ֑ה

and in his hand was a live coal

וּבְיָד֖וֹ יָד	and in his hand *û·və·yā·dô*	CST W/ CONJ וְ + PREP בְּ + 3MS SX	noun
רִצְפָּ֑ה רִצְפָּה	live coal *riṣ·pâ*	ABS	noun

"In his hand" may include the "tongs" that Isaiah mentions in the next phrase. Perhaps the intended thought is that the seraphim picks up the coal with the tongs, then transports the coal using its bare hand.

6c	בְּמֶ֨לְקַחַ֔יִם לָקַ֖ח מֵעַ֥ל הַמִּזְבֵּֽחַ׃

which he took from upon the altar with tongs.

בְּמֶ֨לְקַחַ֔יִם מֶלְקָחַיִם	with tongs *bə·mel·qa·ḥa·yim*	ABS W/ PREP בְּ	noun
לָקַ֖ח לקח	he took *lā·qaḥ*	QAL PF 3MS	verb

מֵעַל עַל	from upon *mē·**ʿal***	--- W/ PREP מִן	prep
הַמִּזְבֵּחַ׃ מִזְבֵּחַ	the altar *ham·miz·**bē**·aḥ*	ABS W/ DEF. ART.	noun

7a וַיַּגַּע עַל־פִּי

Then he touched my mouth

וַיַּגַּע נגע	and he touched *way·yag·**ga**ʿ*	HIPH WAYY 3MS	verb
עַל־ עַל	upon *ʿal-*	---	prep
פִּי פֶּה	my mouth ***pî***	CST W/ 1CS SX	noun

Preachers may want to draw attention to the preponderance of "mouth/lip/speech" imagery in this chapter. The motif reaches its climax in vv. 5–7, where Isaiah identifies with his people and then has his guilt atoned for by means of the coal touching his lips. The strong association between Isaiah and the people indicates that what has happened to the prophet also needs to happen to the people.

7b וַיֹּאמֶר הִנֵּה נָגַע זֶה עַל־שְׂפָתֶיךָ

and he said, "Look! This has struck your lips,

וַיֹּאמֶר אמר	and he said *way·**yō**ʾ·mer*	QAL WAYY 3MS	verb
הִנֵּה הִנֵּה	behold!/look! *hin·**nē***	---	particle
נָגַע נגע	it has touched/struck *nā·**ga**ʿ*	QAL PF 3MS	verb
זֶה זֶה	this ***ze***	---	demonstr pron
עַל־ עַל	upon *ʿal-*	---	prep

שְׂפָתֶ֑יךָ שָׂפָה	your lips *śə·fā·**tê**·ḵā*	CST W/ 2MS SX	noun

The verb **נגע** often has a more aggressive connotation than a light "touch." Recall especially Jacob's wrestling with the angel, who "struck" his hip to dislodge it (Gen 32:25). The significance of the coal touching the prophet's lips/mouth may relate to the nature of the prophetic role of representing the voice of God to the people.

7c **וְסָ֣ר עֲוֺנֶ֔ךָ וְחַטָּאתְךָ֖ תְּכֻפָּֽר׃**

and your iniquity has been turned aside
and your sin has been atoned for."

וְסָ֣ר סור	and (it) is turned aside *wə·**sār***	QAL PF 3MS W/ CONJ וְ	verb
עֲוֺנֶ֔ךָ עָוֺן	your iniquity *ʿă·wō·**ne**·ḵā*	CST W/ 2MS SX	noun
וְחַטָּאתְךָ֖ חַטָּאת	and your sin *wə·ḥaṭ·ṭā'·tə·**ḵā***	CST W/ CONJ וְ + 2MS SX	noun
תְּכֻפָּֽר׃ כפר	(it) has been atoned for *tə·ḵup·**pār***	PUAL IMPF 3FS	verb

The Hebrew phrase is arranged in a chiasm. The words used for "sin/iniquity" need not be too carefully distinguished, as they act synonymously here and elsewhere (Exod 34:9; Deut 19:15; 1 Sam 20:1; etc.). The verse highlights the beautiful effects of the gospel, with overt tones of forgiveness, propitiation, reconciliation, and atonement all evident in the text.

6:8–13

8a וָאֶשְׁמַע אֶת־קוֹל אֲדֹנָי אֹמֵר

*wāʾešma*ʿ *ʾet-qôl ʾădōnāy ʾōmēr*

Then I heard the voice of my Lord, saying,

8b אֶת־מִי אֶשְׁלַח

ʾet-mî ʾešlaḥ

"Who will I send?

8c וּמִי יֵלֶךְ־לָנוּ

ûmî yēlek̲-lānû

And who will go out for us?"

8d וָאֹמַר הִנְנִי שְׁלָחֵנִי׃

wāʾōmar hinnî šəlāḥēnî.

So I said, "Look at me! Send me!"

9a וַיֹּאמֶר לֵךְ

wayyōʾmer lēk̲

Then he said, "Go!

9b וְאָמַרְתָּ לָעָם הַזֶּה

wəʾāmartā lāʿām hazze

Now say to this people,

9c שִׁמְעוּ שָׁמוֹעַ וְאַל־תָּבִינוּ

šimʿû šāmôaʿ wəʾal-tāvînû

'Listen carefully, but do not discern,

9d וּרְאוּ רָאוֹ וְאַל־תֵּדָעוּ׃

ûrəʾû rāʾô wəʾal-tēdāʿû.

and look carefully, but do not truly understand.'

10a הַשְׁמֵן לֵב־הָעָם הַזֶּה

*haš**mēn** lēv-hā**ʿām** hazze*

Coagulate the heart of this people.

10b וְאָזְנָיו הַכְבֵּד וְעֵינָיו הָשַׁע

*wəʾoz**nāyw** hak**bēd** wəʿê**nāyw** hāšaʿ*

Make their ears deaf and make their eyes blind,

10c פֶּן־יִרְאֶה בְעֵינָיו וּבְאָזְנָיו יִשְׁמָע

*pen-yir**ʾe** vəʿê**nāyw** ûvəʾoz**nāyw** yiš**mā**ʿ*

lest his eyes see anything and his ears hear anything,

10d וּלְבָבוֹ יָבִין וָשָׁב וְרָפָא לוֹ׃

*ûləvā**vô** yā**vîn** wā**šāv** wərā**fā**ʾ **lô**.*

lest his heart discern and he returns and is healed."

11a וָאֹמַר עַד־מָתַי אֲדֹנָי

*wāʾō**mar** ʿad-mā**tay** ʾădō**nāy***

So I said, "How long, Lord?"

11b וַיֹּאמֶר עַד אֲשֶׁר אִם־שָׁאוּ

*way**yō**ʾmer **ʿad** ʾă**šer** ʾim-šā**ʾû***

And he said, "Until they are laid waste—

11c עָרִים מֵאֵין יוֹשֵׁב

*ʿā**rîm** mēʾ**ên** yô**šēv***

cities without inhabitant

11d וּבָתִּים מֵאֵין אָדָם

*ûvāt**tîm** mēʾ**ên** ʾā**dām***

and houses without a person in them

11e וְהָאֲדָמָה תִּשָּׁאֶה שְׁמָמָה׃

*wəhāʾădā**mâ** tiš**šāʾe** šəmā**mâ**.*

and the land is absolutely destroyed.

12a וְרִחַק יְהוָה אֶת־הָאָדָם

*wəri**ḥaq** YHWH ʾet-hāʾā**dām***

Then YHWH will send people far away,

12b וְרַבָּה הָעֲזוּבָה בְּקֶרֶב הָאָרֶץ׃

*wərab**bâ** hāʿăzû**vâ** bə**qe**rev hāʾā**reṣ**.*

and the abandoned places are many all around the land.

13a וְעוֹד בָּהּ עֲשִׂרִיָּה

*wəʿ**ôd bāh** ʿăśīriy**yâ***

And yet if there will remain a tenth in it,

13b וְשָׁבָה וְהָיְתָה לְבָעֵר

*wə**šā**vâ wəhāyə**tâ** ləvā**ʿēr***

so it will be burned up again.

13c כָּאֵלָה וְכָאַלּוֹן

*kāʾē**lâ** wək̠āʾal**lôn***

As the terebinth or as the oak

13d אֲשֶׁר בְּשַׁלֶּכֶת מַצֶּבֶת בָּם

*ʾă**šer** bəšal**le**k̠et maṣ**ṣe**vet **bām***

whose stump remains after being felled,

13e זֶרַע קֹדֶשׁ מַצַּבְתָּהּ׃

*ze**ra**ʿ **qō**deš maṣṣav**tāh**.*

the holy seed is its stump.

8a **וָאֶשְׁמַ֞ע אֶת־ק֤וֹל אֲדֹנָי֙ אֹמֵ֔ר**

Then I heard the voice of my Lord, saying,

וָאֶשְׁמַ֞ע שׁמע	and I heard *wā·ʾeš·**ma**ʿ*	QAL WAYY 1CS	verb
אֶת־ אֵת	*(direct object marker)* *ʾet-*	---	particle
ק֤וֹל קוֹל	sound/voice ***qôl***	CST	noun
אֲדֹנָי֙ אֲדֹנָי	my lord *ʾă·dō·**nāy***	ABS	noun
אֹמֵ֔ר אמר	saying *ʾō·**mēr***	QAL PTCP MS	verb

The "voice" of the Lord has been silent until now, with the seraphim filling the temple with the noise of their praise (6:3–4). First, the angels speak, then Isaiah, then the Lord. This may offer another good outline for the sermon.

8b **אֶת־מִ֥י אֶשְׁלַ֖ח**

"Who will I send?

אֶת־ אֵת	*(direct object marker)* *ʾet-*	---	particle
מִ֥י מִי	who?/whom? ***mî***	---	interr pron
אֶשְׁלַ֖ח שׁלח	I will send *ʾeš·**laḥ***	QAL IMPF 1CS	verb

8c **וּמִ֣י יֵֽלֶךְ־לָ֑נוּ**

And who will go out for us?"

וּמִ֣י מִי	and who?/whom? *û·**mî***	--- W/ CONJ וְ	interr pron
יֵֽלֶךְ־ הלך	(he) will walk/go ***yē**·lek-*	QAL IMPF 3MS	verb

לָ֫נוּ לְ	for us *__lā__·nû*	--- W/ 1CP SX	prep

The switch to the plural "us" in this clause has generated several plausible theories. Some see it as a plural of majesty/royalty. Others take it as God addressing the heavenly council or the angelic beings. Still other theories posit a reference to the fullness of God's being, or a hint at the Trinitarian relationship of the Godhead. Preachers would do well to steer clear of dogmatic decisions on the unsettled matter, but instead focus on the response of the prophet.

8d וָאֹמַ֕ר הִנְנִ֖י שְׁלָחֵֽנִי׃

So I said, "Look at me! Send me!"

וָאֹמַ֕ר אמר	and I said *wā·ʾō·__mar__*	QAL WAYY 1CS	verb
הִנְנִ֖י הִנֵּה	behold/look at me! *hin·__nî__*	--- W/ 1CS SX	particle
שְׁלָחֵֽנִי׃ שׁלח	send me *šə·lā·__ḥē__·nî*	QAL IMPV MS W/ 1CS SX	verb

The expressiveness of the Hebrew reminds us of the eager child in grade school, begging for the teacher to choose him to run an errand. "Ooh! Ooh! Pick me! Pick me!"

9a וַיֹּ֕אמֶר לֵ֖ךְ

Then he said, "Go!

וַיֹּ֕אמֶר אמר	and he said *way·__yōʾ__·mer*	QAL WAYY 3MS	verb
לֵ֖ךְ הלך	go! *__lēḵ__*	QAL IMPV MS	verb

God's command repeats the same verb (הלך, "go/walk") from the injunction in v. 8. God asks who will go, Isaiah volunteers, and God commands: "Then go!"

9b	וְאָמַרְתָּ לָעָם הַזֶּה

Now say to this people,

וְאָמַרְתָּ אמר	and you will say *wə·ʾā·mar·**tā***	QAL WEQATAL 2MS	verb
לָעָם עַם	to the people *lā·**ʿām***	ABS W/ PREP לְ + DEF. ART.	noun
הַזֶּה זֶה	this *haz·**ze***	--- W/ DEF. ART.	demonstr pron

"This people" (לָעָם הַזֶּה) may contain a hint of derision. God is none too pleased with "this people."

9c	שִׁמְעוּ שָׁמוֹעַ וְאַל־תָּבִינוּ

'Listen carefully, but do not discern,

שִׁמְעוּ שׁמע	hear/listen *šim·**ʿû***	QAL IMPV MP	verb
שָׁמוֹעַ שׁמע	to listen *šā·**mô**·aʿ*	QAL INF ABS	verb
וְאַל־ אַל	and do not *wə·ʾal-*	--- W/ CONJ וְ	particle
תָּבִינוּ בין	(you will) discern *tā·**vî**·nû*	QAL IMPF 2MP	verb

The use of the infinitive absolute here could be used to strengthen the force of the imperative or emphasize a continuation of the action of the imperative ("keep on listening"). We have chosen to translate it according to the former. The decision in part comes from the imperatives in v. 10.

9d	וּרְאוּ רָאוֹ וְאַל־תֵּדָעוּ׃

and look carefully, but do not truly understand.'

וּרְאוּ ראה	and see *û·rə·**ʾû***	QAL IMPV MP W/ CONJ וְ	verb

רָא֔וֹ ראה	to see *rā·ʾô*	QAL INF ABS	verb
וְאַל־ אַל	and do not *wə·ʾal-*	--- W/ CONJ וְ	particle
תֵּדָֽעוּ׃ ידע	(you will) perceive *tē·**dā**·ʿû.*	QAL IMPF 2MP	verb

See the comment on 9c for the impact of the infinitive absolute.

10a הַשְׁמֵן֙ לֵב־הָעָ֣ם הַזֶּ֔ה

Coagulate the heart of this people

הַשְׁמֵן֙ שׁמן	make fat *haš·**mēn***	HIPH IMPV MS	verb
לֵב־ לֵב	heart *lēv-*	CST	noun
הָעָ֣ם עַם	the people *hā·**ʿām***	ABS W/ DEF. ART.	noun
הַזֶּ֔ה זֶה	this *haz·**ze***	--- W/ DEF. ART.	demonstr pron

The verb הַשְׁמֵן literally means "make fat." The metaphor pictures a hardened or calloused heart that does not respond to God's word. Preachers will need to wrestle with the force of God's words to the prophet here. Are these commands sarcastic, simply a clever use of rhetoric? ("You might as well harden their hearts . . . they're not going to listen to you anyway!") Or does this represent God's sovereign choice to harden those whom he chooses? Preachers may want to allow Jesus' use of this passage to help them address these tricky theological questions (see below).

10b וְאָזְנָ֥יו הַכְבֵּ֖ד וְעֵינָ֣יו הָשַׁ֑ע

Make their ears deaf and make their eyes blind,

וְאָזְנָ֥יו אֹזֶן	and his ears *wə·ʾoz·**nāyw***	CST W/ CONJ וְ + 3MS SX	noun

הַכְבֵּד כבד	make heavy *hak·**bēd***	HIPH IMPV MS	verb
וְעֵינָיו עַיִן	and his eyes *wə·ʿê·**nāyw***	CST W/ CONJ וְ + 3MS SX	noun
הָשַׁע שׁעע	make blind *hā·**šaʿ***	HIPH IMPV MS	verb

The Hebrew here regarding "making heavy" (כבד) the ears is idiomatic. The figure calls for reduced sharpness in hearing (e.g., making deaf).

10c פֶּן־יִרְאֶה בְעֵינָיו וּבְאָזְנָיו יִשְׁמָע

lest his eyes see anything and his ears hear anything,

פֶּן־ פֶּן	lest *pen-*	---	conj
יִרְאֶה ראה	(he) will see *yir·**ʾe***	QAL IMPF 3MS	verb
בְעֵינָיו עַיִן	his eyes *və·ʿê·**nāyw***	CST W/ PREP בְּ + 3MS SX	noun
וּבְאָזְנָיו אֹזֶן	and with his ears *û·və·ʾoz·**nāyw***	CST W/ CONJ וְ + PREP בְּ + 3MS SX	noun
יִשְׁמָע שׁמע	(he) will hear *yiš·**māʿ***	QAL IMPF 3MS	verb

"Lest" (פֶּן) indicates that God's divine will was to harden hearts through Isaiah's ministry. Pastors and ministry workers will need to grapple with this difficult concept. Sometimes, preaching does not result in many conversions or visible revival; rather, the word may harden already stubborn hearts and invite judgment from God. Believers should not measure the success of their ministries by how others respond (otherwise, Isaiah himself would be a failure!). A minister's faithfulness to communicate the word accurately and boldly is a better indicator of success.

10d	וּלְבָבוֹ יָבִין וָשָׁב וְרָפָא לוֹ׃			
	lest his heart discern and he returns and is healed.”			
וּלְבָבוֹ לֵבָב	and with his heart *û·lə·vā·**vô***	CST W/ CONJ וּ + 3MS SX	noun	
יָבִין בין	he will discern *yā·**vîn***	QAL IMPF 3MS	verb	
וָשָׁב שׁוב	and he will return *wā·**šāv***	QAL WEQATAL 3MS	verb	
וְרָפָא רפא	and he will be healed *wə·**rā**·fā’*	QAL WEQATAL 3MS	verb	
לוֹ׃ לְ	to him ***lô***	--- W/ 3MS SX	prep	

The Hebrew of v. 10 is organized in a chiasm, with heart-ears-eyes, eyes-ears-heart. The structure balances cause and effect between the divine message and the people's reaction.

11a	וָאֹמַר עַד־מָתַי אֲדֹנָי			
	So I said, “How long, Lord?”			
וָאֹמַר אמר	and I said *wā·’ō·**mar***	QAL WAYY 1CS	verb	
עַד־ עַד	as far as/until *‘ad-*	---	prep	
מָתַי מָתַי	when? *mā·**tay***	---	adv	
אֲדֹנָי אֲדֹנָי	lord/master *’ă·dō·**nāy***	ABS	noun	

Isaiah asks a natural question. God's news of hard hearts and deaf ears does not encourage excitement from the prophet. Isaiah's wording recalls several psalms and other Scripture that laments the Lord's slowness to act, especially in dealing with wickedness (e.g., Num 14:11; Pss 79:5; 89:46; 94:3).

11b וַיֹּ֗אמֶר עַד֩ אֲשֶׁ֨ר אִם־שָׁא֜וּ

And he said, "Until they are laid waste—

וַיֹּ֗אמֶר אמר	and he said *way·yō'·mer*	QAL WAYY 3MS	verb
עַד֩ עַד	until *'ad*	---	prep
אֲשֶׁ֨ר אֲשֶׁר	who/which/that *'ă·šer*	---	relative pron
אִם־ אִם	if *'im-*	---	conj
שָׁא֜וּ שׁאה	they are laid waste/ devastated *šā·'û*	QAL PF 3CP	verb

11c עָרִ֗ים מֵאֵ֣ין יוֹשֵׁ֔ב

cities without inhabitant

עָרִ֗ים עִיר	cities *'ā·rîm*	ABS	noun
מֵאֵ֣ין אַיִן	without *mē·'ên*	--- W/ PREP מִן	particle
יוֹשֵׁ֔ב ישׁב	inhabitant *yô·šēv*	QAL PTCP MS	verb

The parallelism between this and the next line strongly indicates that both lines should be taken as subjects of the verb שָׁא֜וּ ("they are laid waste/ devastated"). In modern terminology, Isaiah depicts a postapocalyptic wasteland in Jerusalem.

11d וּבָתִּים֙ מֵאֵ֣ין אָדָ֔ם

and houses without a person in them

וּבָתִּים֙ בַּ֫יִת	and houses *û·vāt·tîm*	ABS W/ CONJ וְ	noun

מֵאֵין	without	---	particle
אַיִן	*mē·**ʾên***	W/ PREP מִן	
אָדָם	man/people	ABS	noun
אָדָם	*ʾā·**dām***		

11e וְהָאֲדָמָה תִּשָּׁאֶה שְׁמָמָה׃

and the land is absolutely destroyed.

וְהָאֲדָמָה	and the ground/land	ABS	noun
אֲדָמָה	*wə·hā·ʾă·dā·**mâ***	W/ CONJ וְ + DEF. ART.	
תִּשָּׁאֶה	(it) is laid waste	NIPH IMPF 3FS	verb
שׁאה	*tiš·šā·**ʾe***		
שְׁמָמָה׃	devastation/waste	ABS	noun
שְׁמָמָה	*šə·mā·**mâ***		

The last word, שְׁמָמָה, adds strong emphasis to an already bleak picture. Its final position in the sentence can be seen to summarize the rest of the verse—"a devastation."

12a וְרִחַק יְהוָה אֶת־הָאָדָם

Then YHWH will send people far away,

וְרִחַק	and (he) will send far away	PIEL WEQATAL 3MS	verb
רחק	*wə·ri·**ḥaq***		
יְהוָה	the Lord	ABS	noun
יהוה	*YHWH*		
אֶת־	*(direct object marker)*	---	particle
אֵת	*ʾet-*		
הָאָדָם	the man	ABS	noun
אָדָם	*hā·ʾā·**dām***	W/ DEF. ART.	

Isaiah's choice to use the definite article with the word הָאָדָם ("the man/person") may reference the earlier usage of the same word in v. 11. Where did "the person" go who should be occupying his own house? The Lord sent him into exile.

12b וְרַבָּ֥ה הָעֲזוּבָ֖ה בְּקֶ֥רֶב הָאָֽרֶץ׃

and the abandoned places are many all around the land.

וְרַבָּה רבב	and (she) will be many *wə·rab·**bâ***	QAL WEQATAL 3FS W/ CONJ וְ	verb
הָעֲזוּבָה עֲזוּבָה	the forsaken/abandoned places *hā·ʿă·zû·**vâ***	ABS W/ DEF. ART.	noun
בְּקֶרֶב קֶרֶב	in the midst/inward part *bə·**qe**·rev*	CST W/ PREP בְּ	noun
הָאָרֶץ׃ אֶרֶץ	the earth/land *hā·**ʾā**·reṣ*	ABS W/ DEF. ART.	noun

13a וְע֥וֹד בָּהּ֙ עֲשִׂ֣רִיָּ֔ה

And yet if there will remain a tenth in it,

וְעוֹד עוֹד	and still/yet/again/though *wə·**ʿôd***	--- W/ CONJ וְ	adv
בָּהּ בְּ	in her/it ***bāh***	--- W/ 3FS SX	prep
עֲשִׂרִיָּה עֲשִׂירִי	tenth *ʿă·śī·riy·**yâ***	---	ordinal number

The Hebrew here is complex and challenging. The text seems to communicate that if a remnant ("a tenth") survives the exile, even they will not escape God's judgment ("burned up again"; 13b). Yet simultaneously, the final line (13e) gives hope in the midst of such inescapable and seemingly comprehensive judgment.

13b וְשָׁ֖בָה וְהָיְתָ֣ה לְבָעֵ֑ר

so it will be burned up again.

וְשָׁבָה שׁוּב	and she/it will turn/return *wə·**šā**·vâ*	QAL WEQATAL 3FS	verb

וְהָיְתָה היה	and she/it will be *wə·hā·yə·**tâ***	QAL WEQATAL 3FS	verb
לְבָעֵר בער	to burn *lə·vā·**ʿēr***	PIEL INF CST W/ PREP לְ	verb

13c כָּאֵלָה וְכָאַלּוֹן

As the terebinth or as the oak

כָּאֵלָה אֵלָה	as the terebinth *kā·ʾē·**lâ***	ABS W/ PREP כְּ + DEF. ART.	noun
וְכָאַלּוֹן אַלּוֹן	and as the oak *wə·ḵā·ʾal·**lôn***	ABS W/ CONJ וְ + PREP כְּ + DEF. ART.	noun

The noun אֵלָה ("terebinth") literally refers to a large tree. Biblical authors sometimes use it with cultic significance, referring to a pagan place of worship (e.g., Hos 4:13). Here, we do not detect pagan associations.

13d אֲשֶׁר בְּשַׁלֶּכֶת מַצֶּבֶת בָּם

whose stump remains after being felled,

אֲשֶׁר אֲשֶׁר	who/which *ʾă·**šer***	---	relative pron
בְּשַׁלֶּכֶת שַׁלֶּכֶת	in felling *bə·šal·**le**·ḵet*	ABS W/ PREP בְּ	noun
מַצֶּבֶת מַצֵּבָה	pillar/stump *maṣ·**ṣe**·vet*	ABS	noun
בָּם בְּ	in them ***bām***	--- W/ 3MP SX	prep

Some emend the words here to refer to sacred pillars (מַצֵּבָה instead of מַצֶּבֶת), Asherah poles (אֲשֵׁרָה instead of אֲשֶׁר), and high places (בָּמָה instead of בָּם), comparing the felling of the tenth to the destruction of sacrilegious idols. This would then read the final phrase negatively, explicitly linking the destroyed pillar to the chosen people (see NET: "Even if only a tenth of the people remain in the land, it will again be destroyed, like one of the large sacred trees or an Asherah pole, when a sacred pillar on a high place is thrown down. That sacred pillar symbolizes the special chosen family." Some of these emendations are supported by 1QIsa[a]). However, the text is coherent without resorting to emendation, and thus it is better to read a positive glimmer of hope in the final phrases of this chapter.

13e	זֶ֥רַע קֹ֖דֶשׁ מַצַּבְתָּֽהּ׃		
	the holy seed is its stump.		
זֶ֥רַע זֶ֫רַע	seed *ze · ra'*	CST	noun
קֹ֖דֶשׁ קֹ֫דֶשׁ	holy *qō · deš*	ABS	noun
מַצַּבְתָּֽהּ׃ מַצֵּבָה	her/its pillar/stump *maṣ · ṣav · **tāh***	CST W/ 3FS SX	noun

Many have understood a messianic promise in this final phrase. See the similar phrase in Ezra 9:2 (זֶ֣רַע הַקֹּ֔דֶשׁ, "holy seed") for reference to the Israelite people (cf. Isa 4:3).

From Text to Sermon

- ***Big Idea.*** Behold God and proclaim his word.

- ***Avenues for Illustration and Application.*** One potential way to outline the passage is according to who/what Isaiah "beholds":

  A. Isaiah beholds God (6:1–4)
  B. Isaiah beholds himself (6:5–8)
  C. Isaiah beholds Israel (6:9–13)

  This structure leads to the Big Idea. Upon beholding the glorious holiness of God, Isaiah realizes just how sinfully unholy and unclean he is. Then, he identifies with his people Israel. In effect, he realizes, "I'm no better than those drunks! I'm no better than those who make their own standard of righteousness! I'm no better than the unfaithful, arrogant Israelites!"

  The ultimate standard of comparison is not the Israelites, but the perfectly holy God. Athletes could provide a potential illustration for this theological concept. Many fancy themselves fast swimmers, or accomplished weightlifters, or top-form runners. And perhaps they are, when compared with other amateurs. But watching professional athletes or Olympians perform magnifies the inadequacies of amateurs. Your time in the pool is nothing compared to that of Michael Phelps; your muscles are puny compared to Arnold Schwarzenegger's; your time is slow compared to Usain Bolt's. Likewise, when people who appear righteous are stacked up against a perfectly holy, glorious God, they immediately become aware of their sinfulness.

  Preachers will want to keep the outside context in mind when preaching Isa 6. As mentioned in the commentary, Isaiah's "Woe is me!" (v. 5) builds on the six "woes" of ch. 5 (5:8, 11, 18, 20–22; on a side note, the placement of ch. 6, though possibly not *chronologically* following ch. 5, certainly is *logically* and *theologically* in the correct position to contrast the woes of Israel with the woe of Isaiah). What a surprising turn of events! One would think that, of all the people not to get "woe-d" by God, it would be a prophet! This again serves to highlight the inadequacy of man's righteousness when compared to God's. Isaiah beholds God and it humbles him, making him infinitely more aware of his sin. Just as shining light through a gemstone will reveal previously unseen imperfections, so the light of God's glory exposes the sin of man. If you read your Bible and come away thinking about how good a person you are, you have failed to behold your God.

The contrast between the death of King Uzziah and the eternal reign of the Lord allows the preacher to challenge the church to carefully avoid putting too much trust in earthly kings and rulers. Uzziah was a long-reigning, mostly righteous king. Yet his reign and his righteousness do not even begin to compare to the reign and righteousness of God. Think about the number of people who feel devastated or even disillusioned when their political candidate loses an election. Think about how upset church members feel when a beloved pastor resigns or retires. Earthly rulers come and go, but our hope as Christians does not rest in an earthly president, an earthly ruler, or an earthly pastor. Our hope rests in the King of kings.

The burning coal from the altar gives the preacher an excellent opportunity to take the sermon to the gospel (6:6–7). The coal and its effects represent something of the Lord's atonement for sin, his cleansing power over iniquity, and perhaps by extension the theological concepts of propitiation and reconciliation. God removed Isaiah's guilt and atoned for his sins. This pictures the gospel's work on the sinful heart. Isaiah's recognition of his sinfulness becomes the starting place for unredeemed people today. First we must recognize that we are not good people. The starting place of salvation is a recognition of the need for a Savior because of one's sinfulness. Woe is you! It is only following this recognition that one then places their faith in the atoning work and resurrection of Jesus Christ (Rom 10:9–10).

Preachers should not miss the opportunity to infuse missional application in this sermon. Isaiah beheld God, recognized his sin, and was transformed by the atoning work of the altar; *then* came the essential mission to proclaim the word of God to the people. When the gospel transforms believers, they cannot help but spread the good news to others. Behold God, then proclaim his word.

One might even reflect on the nature of Isaiah's call. Did he know what God was calling him to do? Did he know the content of God's message before accepting the call? Did he know how long it would take, or how difficult it would be, or the reaction of the people when he said what God wanted him to say? God does not reveal the challenges of our mission or call to ministry ahead of time. He expects us to be willing to go, to be faithful to his message, and to trust in him. He does not ask ministers to know the future; rather, he expects us to respond in the present based on his faithfulness in the past.

Challenge the church based on Isaiah's call and the Israelites' predicted response. Would you still teach Sunday school if you knew no child would ever be saved in your ministry? Would you still go overseas as a missionary if you knew that your efforts would only harden people's hearts? Would you still preach if you knew no one would ever walk the aisle? Sometimes, it does not matter how great a preacher, minister, or leader you are; sometimes, people just simply refuse to listen to the truth. Effective ministry, then, is not evaluated by worldly definitions of success. God measures effective ministry by your faithfulness to his calling. This takes the responsibility of heart-change out of your hands and reorients success in ministry from a result-based model to a faith-based model.

New Testament Connections. Isaiah 6 offers several theological challenges which only increase when the preacher also considers the teaching of the New Testament. The most difficult of these comes in vv. 9–10, where God commands Isaiah to harden hearts, deafen ears, and blind eyes of the Israelites with his message. Our natural tendency is to want to water down this statement by making it say something less than what it says. We might desire for it to say, "The Israelites can't respond *because* they have blinded their own eyes." But that is not the cause and effect that God gives to Isaiah. God says, "Isaiah, *you make* the heart dull and eyes blind, *so that* they *can't* respond and see."

The New Testament Gospels complicate the matter. The Greek translation (Septuagint or LXX) puts the responsibility on the people rather than on God's message through Isaiah. Insofar as Matthew puts the emphasis on the people for not hearing or seeing or responding to God's word (Matt 13:14–15), he appears to be quoting the Septuagint, not the Hebrew (Mark and Luke do something similar to Matthew; see Mark 4:12; Luke 8:10). John, however, quotes the passage more in line with the Hebrew (John 12:39–40). He is clear: God's divine plan includes even the unbelief of the people.

Preachers will need to carefully walk the tightrope of this theological tension. John and Isaiah emphasize the *divine* perspective of the situation of unbelief: *God* has hardened the hearts of the people *so that* they don't respond. The Synoptic authors focus more on the *human* perspective: *the people* have responded with unbelief and therefore they incur judgment. Preachers will need to use wisdom and discernment to determine how much of this conversation enters a sermon on Isaiah (see Murawski 2021:131–46 for more help on preaching theologically loaded texts).

One more New Testament passage captures our attention as it intersects with Isa 6. John, after quoting Isa 6:9–10, follows up the quotation with the statement that "Isaiah said these things because he saw his glory and spoke of him" (John 12:41 ESV). Does John mean that Isaiah saw Jesus, perhaps in some preincarnate form? Was the voice that asked, "Who shall I send, and who will go for us?" the voice of the Messiah? Depending on how one takes the final phrase, "the holy seed is its stump" (Isa 6:13), the interpreter may see additional messianic references in the text. Preachers will want to consider the impact of John's statements and how Christ enters the picture in Isa 6.

ISAIAH 7:10–17

THE SIGN OF IMMANUEL

The Israelites were in a time of crisis. Isaiah 7 picks up the story about five years after ch. 6. King Pekah of northern Israel has joined forces with King Rezin of Syria. Together, they marched to Jerusalem to wage war against it, terrifying the Judean king Ahaz (7:1–2). Through Isaiah, the Lord reassures King Ahaz that these two nations will not succeed in overthrowing the Judean throne. To give him additional reassurance, the Lord then gives Ahaz and the entire house of David a sign: a boy named "Immanuel"—God-With-Us—is coming! God's presence with his people assures them that they need not fear the enemy. This chapter offers hope in the form of God's promises and the Messiah.

LARGER LITERARY CONTEXT ▸ 7:1–25

7:10–12

10a וַיֹּ֣וסֶף יְהוָ֔ה דַּבֵּ֥ר אֶל־אָחָ֖ז לֵאמֹֽר׃

*way**yô**sef YHWH da**bēr** ʾel-ʾā**ḥāz** lēʾ**mōr**.*

Then YHWH once again spoke to Ahaz, saying,

11a שְׁאַל־לְךָ֣ א֔וֹת מֵעִ֖ם יְהוָ֣ה אֱלֹהֶ֑יךָ

*šəʾal-lə**ḵā** **ʾôt** mē**ʿim** YHWH ʾĕlō**hê**ḵā*

"Ask for a sign for yourself from YHWH your God.

11b הַעְמֵ֣ק שְׁאָ֔לָה א֖וֹ הַגְבֵּ֥הַּ לְמָֽעְלָה׃

*haʿ**mēq** šə**ʾā**lâ **ʾô** hag**bē**ah lə**mā**ʿəlâ.*

Make it as deep as hell or as high as heaven!"

12a וַיֹּ֖אמֶר אָחָ֑ז

*way**yō**ʾmer ʾā**ḥāz***

So Ahaz responded,

12b לֹֽא־אֶשְׁאַ֥ל וְלֹֽא־אֲנַסֶּ֖ה אֶת־יְהוָֽה׃

*lōʾ-ʾešʾ**al** wə**lōʾ**-ʾăna**sse** ʾet-YHWH.*

"I won't ask or test YHWH!"

10a וַיֹּ֣וסֶף יְהוָ֔ה דַּבֵּ֥ר אֶל־אָחָ֖ז לֵאמֹֽר׃

Then YHWH once again spoke to Ahaz, saying,

וַיֹּ֣וסֶף יסף	again/and he added *way·**yô**·sef*	HIPH WAYY 3MS	verb
יְהוָ֔ה יהוה	the Lord *YHWH*	ABS	noun
דַּבֵּ֥ר דבר	to speak/speaking *da·**bēr***	PIEL INF CST	verb

אֶל־ אֶל	to *'el-*	---	prep
אָחָז אָחָז	Ahaz *'ā·ḥāz*	ABS	noun
לֵאמֹר׃ אמר	saying *lē'·mōr*	QAL INF CST W/ PREP לְ	verb

The use of וַיּוֹסֶף indicates that this is a continuation or addition to the conversation the Lord just had with Isaiah (7:7–9). Preachers will want to incorporate the historical context from the earlier part of the chapter (and perhaps even the parallel passages in 2 Kgs 16 // 2 Chr 28) as a backdrop to the present passage. It is important to keep in mind the division between the house of Judah and Ephraim/Samaria (southern vs. northern Israel) and the ever-present threat from the Assyrians during this stage in history.

11a שְׁאַל־לְךָ אוֹת מֵעִם יְהוָה אֱלֹהֶיךָ

"Ask for a sign for yourself from YHWH your God.

שְׁאַל־ שׁאל	ask *šə·'al-*	QAL IMPV MS	verb
לְךָ לְ	for yourself *lə·ḵā*	--- W/ 2MS SX	prep
אוֹת אוֹת	sign *'ôt*	ABS	noun
מֵעִם עִם	from with *mē·'im*	--- W/ PREP מִן	prep
יְהוָה יהוה	the Lord *YHWH*	ABS	noun
אֱלֹהֶיךָ אֱלֹהִים	your God *'ĕ·lō·hê·ḵā*	CST W/ 2MS SX	noun

"Sign" (אוֹת) does not necessarily indicate something miraculous (cf. Gen 1:14; 9:12–13), though it certainly can be (Exod 4:9; 7:3). In contrast to the second-person plural pronouns used later in this passage (Isa 7:13–14), God here speaks directly to king Ahaz (indicated by use of the singular pronouns). Preachers may want to draw attention to this feature of the text in order to set up the contrast between communication to Ahaz and communication to the house of David later in the passage.

11b	הַעְמֵק שְׁאָלָה אוֹ הַגְבֵּהַ לְמָעְלָה׃

Make it as deep as hell or as high as heaven!"

הַעְמֵק עמק	to make deep *ha'·**mēq***	HIPH INF ABS	verb
שְׁאָלָה שְׁאוֹל	sheol/underworld/grave *šə·'**ā**·lâ*	ABS W/ LOCATIVE ה	noun
אוֹ אוֹ	or *'ô*	---	conj
הַגְבֵּהַ גבה	to exalt/make high *hag·**bē**·ah*	HIPH INF ABS	verb
לְמָעְלָה׃ מַעַל	to above *lə·**mā**·'ə·lâ*	--- W/ PREP לְ + LOCATIVE ה	prep

The noun שְׁאָלָה ("sheol") can refer literally to the grave or to the place of the dead. Here, it works in combination with הַגְבֵּהַ לְמָעְלָה ("high as heaven") to form a merism, where the extreme contrast (cf. e.g., other merisms such as "top to bottom" or "from head to toe") amounts to a figurative way of saying, "Ask anything at all that you want!" God assigns no limits to what Ahaz can request.

12a	וַיֹּאמֶר אָחָז

So Ahaz responded,

וַיֹּאמֶר אמר	and he said *way·**yō**'·mer*	QAL WAYY 3MS	verb
אָחָז אָחָז	Ahaz *'ā·**ḥāz***	ABS	noun

12b	לֹא־אֶשְׁאַל וְלֹא־אֲנַסֶּה אֶת־יְהוָה׃

"I won't ask or test YHWH!"

לֹא־ לֹא	no/not *lō'-*	---	particle
אֶשְׁאַל שׁאל	I will ask *'eš·'**al***	QAL IMPF 1CS	verb

וְלֹא־ לֹא	and no/not *wə·lō*ʾ-	--- W/ CONJ וְ	particle
אֲנַסֶּה נסה	I will test/try *ʾă·nas·se*	PIEL IMPF 1CS	verb
אֶת־ אֵת	*(direct object marker)* *ʾet-*	---	particle
יְהוָה׃ יהוה	the LORD *YHWH*	ABS	noun

Ahaz's response seems pious; after all, one should not put the Lord to the test (Deut 6:16; cf. Matt 4:7; Luke 4:12). However, considering that God invited him to ask for a sign, and also considering all we know about Ahaz's character (or lack thereof; cf. 2 Kgs 16:2–4), we can probably surmise that Ahaz is not being genuinely righteous here. He is trying God's patience and ignoring God's mercies rather than expressing humble deference.

7:13–17

13a וַיֹּ֕אמֶר שִׁמְעוּ־נָ֖א בֵּ֣ית דָּוִ֑ד

*wayy**ō**ʾmer šimʿû-**nāʾ bêt** dā**wid***

So he said, "All of you, listen up, O house of David!

13b הַמְעַ֤ט מִכֶּם֙ הַלְא֣וֹת אֲנָשִׁ֔ים

*ham**ʿaṭ** mik**kem** hal**ʾôt** ʾănā**šîm***

Is it not enough for you to wear people down,

13c כִּ֥י תַלְא֖וּ גַּ֥ם אֶת־אֱלֹהָֽי׃

***kî** tal**ʾû** **gam** ʾet-ʾĕlō**hāy**.*

that you also wear God down?

14a לָ֠כֵן יִתֵּ֨ן אֲדֹנָ֥י ה֛וּא לָכֶ֖ם א֑וֹת

*lā**ḵēn** yit**tēn** ʾădō**nāy** **hûʾ** lā**ḵem** **ʾôt***

Therefore, the Lord himself will give you all a sign:

14b הִנֵּ֣ה הָעַלְמָ֗ה הָרָה֙ וְיֹלֶ֣דֶת בֵּ֔ן

*hin**nē** hāʿal**mâ** hā**râ** wəyō**le**det **bēn***

Look! A young woman will get pregnant
and she will give birth to a son,

14c וְקָרָ֥את שְׁמ֖וֹ עִמָּ֥נוּ אֵֽל׃

*wəqā**rāʾt** šə**mô** ʿim**mā**nû **ʾēl**.*

and she will call his name 'God-Is-With-Us.'

15a חֶמְאָ֥ה וּדְבַ֖שׁ יֹאכֵ֑ל

*ḥem**ʾâ** ûdə**vaš** yō**ʾḵēl***

He will eat curds and honey

15b לְדַעְתּ֛וֹ מָא֥וֹס בָּרָ֖ע וּבָח֥וֹר בַּטּֽוֹב׃

*ləda**ʿtô** mā**ʾôs** bā**rāʿ** ûvā**ḥôr** baṭ**ṭôv**.*

by the time he knows the difference between
refusing evil and choosing good.

16a כִּ֠י בְּטֶ֨רֶם יֵדַ֥ע הַנַּ֛עַר

*kî bəṭerem yē**da**ʿ han**na**ʿar*

For before the boy knows

16b מָאֹ֥ס בָּרָ֖ע וּבָחֹ֣ר בַּטּ֑וֹב

*mā**ʾōs** bā**rā**ʿ ûvā**ḥōr** baṭ**ṭôv***

the difference between refusing evil and choosing good,

16c תֵּעָזֵ֤ב הָאֲדָמָה֙

*tēʿā**zēv** hāʾădā**mâ***

the land will be deserted—

16d אֲשֶׁ֣ר אַתָּ֣ה קָ֔ץ מִפְּנֵ֖י שְׁנֵ֥י מְלָכֶֽיהָ׃

*ʾă**šer** ʾat**tâ** **qāṣ** mippə**nê** šə**nê** məlā**ḵê**hā.*

the land owned by the two kings you dread.

17a יָבִ֨יא יְהוָ֜ה עָלֶ֗יךָ וְעַל־עַמְּךָ֮ וְעַל־בֵּ֣ית אָבִיךָ֒

*yā**vî**ʾ YHWH ʿā**lê**ḵā wə**ʿal**-ʿammə**ḵā** wəʿal-**bêt** ʾā**vî**ḵā*

YHWH will bring upon you and upon your people
and upon your father's house

17b יָמִים֙ אֲשֶׁ֣ר לֹא־בָ֔אוּ

*yā**mîm** ʾă**šer** lōʾ-**vā**ʾû*

days which have never come

17c לְמִיּ֛וֹם סוּר־אֶפְרַ֥יִם מֵעַ֖ל יְהוּדָ֑ה

*ləmiy**yôm** sûr-ʾef**ra**yim mēʿ**al** yəhû**dâ***

since the day that Ephraim split from Judah—

17d אֵ֖ת מֶ֥לֶךְ אַשּֽׁוּר׃

***ʾēt** **me**leḵ ʾaš**šûr**.*

the king of Assyria!"

13a **וַיֹּ֕אמֶר שִׁמְעוּ־נָ֖א בֵּ֣ית דָּוִ֑ד**

So he said, "All of you, listen up, O house of David!

וַיֹּ֕אמֶר אמר	and he said *way·**yō**'·mer*	QAL WAYY 3MS	verb
שִׁמְעוּ־ שׁמע	hear/listen *šim·'û-*	QAL IMPV MP	verb
נָ֖א נָא	now/I pray ***nā'***	---	particle
בֵּ֣ית בַּ֫יִת	house ***bêt***	CST	noun
דָּוִ֑ד דָּוִד	David *dā·**wid***	ABS	noun

The subject of וַיֹּאמֶר ("and he said") could be God, but the use of "my God" later in the verse probably indicates that Isaiah is in view. Preachers must also pay careful attention to the change in object here. Previously, God had addressed Ahaz individually (note the singular pronouns in v. 11). Here and in much of the following, however, the referent switches to plural. It is the "house of David"—the Davidic dynasty as a whole, not just Ahaz—that God addresses. The first indication of this (besides the use of "house of David") is the plural imperative in this verse.

13b **הַמְעַ֤ט מִכֶּם֙ הַלְא֣וֹת אֲנָשִׁ֔ים**

Is it not enough for you to wear people down,

הַמְעַ֤ט מְעַט	if a few/little *ham·**'aṭ***	ABS W/ INTERR הֲ	noun
מִכֶּם֙ מִן	from you *mik·**kem***	--- W/ 2MP SX	prep
הַלְא֣וֹת לאה	to make weary *hal·**'ôt***	HIPH INF CST	verb
אֲנָשִׁ֔ים אִישׁ	men *'ă·nā·**šîm***	ABS	noun

The plural pronoun here once again indicates God addresses more than just Ahaz. Though Ahaz alone tests God's patience in this passage, the prophecy will point beyond the time and person of Ahaz and relate to the entire Davidic dynasty. Preachers might want to draw attention to the difference between singular/plural use of pronouns at this point in the sermon. Colloquializing the difference may help: southerners differentiate between "you" and "y'all"; certain parts of New Jersey and New York differentiate between "you" and "yous guys." The KJV does differentiate between the two, with "thee" (v. 11) for singular and "ye" (v. 13) for plural.

13c **כִּֽי תַלְא֖וּ גַּ֥ם אֶת־אֱלֹהָֽי׃**

that you also wear God down?

כִּ֣י כִּי	that *kî*	---	conj
תַלְא֖וּ לאה	you make weary *tal·ʾû*	HIPH IMPF 2MP	verb
גַּ֥ם גַּם	also *gam*	---	adv
אֶת־ אֵת	*(direct object marker)* *ʾet-*	---	particle
אֱלֹהָֽי׃ אֱלֹהִים	God *ʾĕ·lō·hāy*	CST W/ 1CS SX	noun

There is some irony in the use of תַלְאוּ ("make weary") in relation to God. How does one wear out the omnipotent God of the universe? The exaggerated claim puts emphasis on Ahaz's sinful stubbornness.

14a **לָ֠כֵן יִתֵּ֨ן אֲדֹנָ֥י ה֛וּא לָכֶ֖ם א֑וֹת**

Therefore, the Lord himself will give you all a sign:

לָ֠כֵן לָכֵן	thus/so/therefore *lā·kēn*	---	adv
יִתֵּ֨ן נתן	(he) will give *yit·tēn*	QAL IMPF 3MS	verb
אֲדֹנָ֥י אֲדֹנָי	Lord/Master *ʾă·dō·nāy*	ABS	noun

הָ֣וּא הוּא	he *hû'*	--- 	personal pron
לָכֶ֖ם לְ	to you *lā·kem*	--- W/ 2MP SX	prep
א֑וֹת אוֹת	sign *'ôt*	ABS	noun

The addition of the pronoun הוּא ("he") spotlights the Lord as subject. The sign does not just come from a human prophet; it comes directly from God himself.

14b הִנֵּ֣ה הָעַלְמָ֗ה הָרָה֙ וְיֹלֶ֣דֶת בֵּ֔ן

Look! A young woman will get pregnant
and she will give birth to a son,

הִנֵּ֣ה הִנֵּה	behold *hin·nē*	---	particle
הָעַלְמָ֗ה עַלְמָה	the young woman/virgin *hā·'al·mâ*	ABS W/ DEF. ART.	noun
הָרָה֙ הָרָה	pregnant *hā·râ*	FS PRED	adj
וְיֹלֶ֣דֶת ילד	and she will bear/ beget *wə·yō·le·det*	QAL PTCP FS W/ CONJ וְ	verb
בֵּ֔ן בֵּן	son *bēn*	ABS	noun

One cannot discount the possibility that הִנֵּה ("behold!/look!") indicates that Isaiah refers to a young woman in literal view at the present moment. The definite article on הָעַלְמָה ("the young woman") could lend additional support to such a view ("Behold–*that* woman right there!"). The word עַלְמָה has engendered great debate, especially when Matthew's Gospel is taken into account. Critics of Matthew's translation of עַלְמָה point out that the word בְּתוּלָה more precisely means "virgin." עַלְמָה, the word Isaiah uses, has a broader range than בְּתוּלָה and can simply mean, "young girl of marriageable age" or "young woman who has not yet had children" instead of the more narrow definition "virgin." "Virgin" could be the appropriate nuance in this context, but the word certainly has broader possibilities.

Walton (1997:415–19) concludes that childbearing is the pivotal issue with עַלְמָה. He writes, "The fact that a young woman has not borne a child may in fact suggest that she is a virgin, and perhaps even of marriageable age, but the lexical profile of the term does not require either of those to be true. To say this another way, a woman ceases to be an *ʿalma* when she becomes a mother—not when she becomes a wife or a sexual partner" (417).

Furthermore, it may be helpful to counter those who argue Isaiah *could not* have meant "virgin" by noting that even בְּתוּלָה has a wider range of meaning than the narrow "virgin." Joel 1:8 uses the term of a married woman; Esth 2:19 uses the term for women *after* they have had sex with the king. To summarize our conclusions: to translate עַלְמָה as "virgin" is not outside the range of the term, and to restrict עַלְמָה as anything other than "virgin" based on a narrow definition of בְּתוּלָה is to ignore the broader possibilities offered by בְּתוּלָה. See below for more on how Matthew's Gospel relates to this discussion. Finally, one can understand the predicate adjective הָרָה ("pregnant") in a future sense ("the young woman *will* get pregnant") or in a present sense ("the young woman *is* pregnant"). The construction is found in both senses elsewhere in Scripture (future: Judg 13:5; present: Gen 16:11). Context must determine the translator's choice.

14c	וְקָרָ֥את שְׁמ֖וֹ עִמָּ֥נוּ אֵֽל׃

and she will call his name 'God-Is-With-Us.'

וְקָרָ֥את קרא	and she will call *wə·qā·rā't*	QAL WEQATAL 3FS	verb
שְׁמ֖וֹ שֵׁם	his name *šə·mô*	CST W/ 3MS SX	noun
עִמָּ֥נוּ עִם	with us *ʿim·mā·nû*	--- W/ 1CP SX	prep
אֵֽל׃ אֵל	God *ʾēl*	ABS	noun

Traditionally, the phrase עִמָּנוּ אֵל has been translated either "God is with us" or "God with us," with the verb being implied. Either translational choice is fine and does not affect the meaning.

15a	חֶמְאָה וּדְבַשׁ יֹאכֵל		
	He will eat curds and honey		
חֶמְאָה חֶמְאָה	curd *ḥem·ʾâ*	ABS	noun
וּדְבַשׁ דְּבַשׁ	and honey *û·də·vaš*	ABS W/ CONJ וְ	noun
יֹאכֵל אכל	he will eat *yō·kēl*	QAL IMPF 3MS	verb

15b	לְדַעְתּוֹ מָאוֹס בָּרָע וּבָחוֹר בַּטּוֹב׃		
	by the time he knows the difference between refusing evil and choosing good.		
לְדַעְתּוֹ ידע	to know it *lə·daʿ·tô*	QAL INF CST W/ PREP לְ + 3MS SX	verb
מָאוֹס מאס	to reject/refuse *mā·ʾôs*	QAL INF ABS	verb
בָּרָע רַע	in the bad *bā·rāʿ*	ABS W/ PREP בְּ + DEF. ART.	noun
וּבָחוֹר בחר	and to choose *û·vā·ḥôr*	QAL INF ABS W/ CONJ וְ	verb
בַּטּוֹב׃ טוֹב	in the good *baṭ·ṭôv*	ABS W/ PREP בְּ + DEF. ART.	noun

The relationship between this clause and the previous has challenged interpreters. The preposition לְ in לְדַעְתּוֹ ("to know it") may indicate purpose or result here (e.g., KJV—"Butter and honey shall he eat, that he may know to refuse the evil, and choose the good"). This would understand the "curds and honey" as exilic staple food sources that poor Israelites must scrounge up in order to survive. Eating such food reminds them to make better choices in order to avoid God's judgment in the future. If the לְ is taken temporally (e.g., ESV, NASB), it may be a way of saying that by the time the child is weaned, the two kings threatening Judah will be destroyed (v. 16).

16a **כִּי בְּטֶרֶם יֵדַע הַנַּעַר**

For before the boy knows

כִּי כִּי	for *kî*	---	conj
בְּטֶרֶם טֶרֶם	before *bə·**ṭe**·rem*	--- W/ PREP בְּ	adv
יֵדַע ידע	(he) will know *yē·**da**ʿ*	QAL IMPF 3MS	verb
הַנַּעַר נַעַר	the boy/lad *han·**na**·ʿar*	ABS W/ DEF. ART.	noun

The verb **ידע** means not just cognitive awareness of good/bad, but behavioral decision, to "know" in the sense of "choose."

16b **מָאֹס בָּרָע וּבָחֹר בַּטּוֹב**

the difference between refusing evil and choosing good,

מָאֹס מאס	to reject/refuse *mā·**ʾōs***	QAL INF ABS	verb
בָּרָע רַע	in the bad *bā·**rā**ʿ*	ABS W/ PREP בְּ + DEF. ART.	noun
וּבָחֹר בחר	and to choose *û·vā·**ḥōr***	QAL INF ABS W/ CONJ וְ	verb
בַּטּוֹב טוֹב	in the good *baṭ·**ṭôv***	ABS W/ PREP בְּ + DEF. ART.	noun

16c **תֵּעָזֵב הָאֲדָמָה**

the land will be deserted—

תֵּעָזֵב עזב	(it) will be left/forsaken *tē·ʿā·**zēv***	NIPH IMPF 3FS	verb
הָאֲדָמָה אֲדָמָה	the land *hā·ʾă·dā·**mâ***	ABS W/ DEF. ART.	noun

The verb עזב is used twice in Isa 1 (1:4, 28), both times to refer to the people "forsaking" the Lord. The word most often characterizes the people's tendency to forsake their covenant obligations (e.g., Deut 31:16), which contrasts with the Lord's commitment to never forsake the covenant (e.g., Deut 31:6, 8). Here, in an ironic twist to the usual usages of this word, the territory occupied by the kings of Ephraim/Samaria (i.e., northern Israel) and Syria will be forsaken/deserted.

16d אֲשֶׁר אַתָּה קָץ מִפְּנֵי שְׁנֵי מְלָכֶיהָ׃

the land owned by the two kings you dread.

אֲשֶׁר אֲשֶׁר	which/that *ʾă·šer*	---	relative pron
אַתָּה אַתָּה	you *ʾat·tâ*	---	personal pron
קָץ קוץ	loathing/abhorring/ dread/fear *qāṣ*	QAL PTCP MS	verb
מִפְּנֵי מִפְּנֵי	from faces *mip·pə·nê*	---	prep
שְׁנֵי שְׁנַיִם	two *šə·nê*	CST	cardinal number
מְלָכֶיהָ׃ מֶלֶךְ	its kings *mə·lā·ḵê·hā*	CST W/ 3FS SX	noun

This phrase has some emphasis, coming at the end of the sentence, clarifying which "land" God is talking about. The verb קוץ here indicates that the king "dreads" or "fears" rather than "loathes" or "abhors." The (irrational) fear of King Ahaz is on display in this passage.

17a יָבִ֨יא יְהֹוָ֜ה עָלֶ֗יךָ וְעַֽל־עַמְּךָ֮ וְעַל־בֵּ֣ית אָבִיךָ֒

YHWH will bring upon you and upon your people
and upon your father's house

יָבִיא בוא	(he) will bring *yā·vîʾ*	HIPH IMPF 3MS	verb

יְהוָ֗ה יהוה	the LORD *YHWH*	ABS	noun
עָלֶ֙יךָ֙ עַל	upon you *ʿā·lɛ̂·ḵā*	--- W/ 2MS SX	prep
וְעַל־ עַל	and upon *wə·ʿal-*	--- W/ CONJ וְ	prep
עַמְּךָ֮ עַם	your people *ʿam·mə·ḵā*	CST W/ 2MS SX	noun
וְעַל־ עַל	and upon *wə·ʿal-*	--- W/ CONJ וְ	prep
בֵּ֣ית בַּ֫יִת	house *bêt*	CST	noun
אָבִ֒יךָ֒ אָב	your father *ʾā·vî·ḵā*	CST W/ 2MS SX	noun

The text once again reverts back to second-person singular pronouns (the singular pronoun אַתָּה, "you," also appeared in the previous clause, 16d), referring specifically to Ahaz. Since most English translations do not attempt to bring out the change in pronouns, and since proper interpretation in this passage hinges upon recognition of it, preachers will want to highlight this in their explanation of the text.

17b יָמִים֙ אֲשֶׁ֣ר לֹא־בָ֔אוּ

days which have never come

יָמִים֙ יוֹם	days *yā·mîm*	ABS	noun
אֲשֶׁ֣ר אֲשֶׁר	which *ʾă·šer*	---	relative pron
לֹא־ לֹא	not *lōʾ-*	---	particle
בָ֔אוּ בוא	(they) came *vā·ʾû*	QAL PF 3CP	verb

The phrase is idiomatic: "It's unlike *anything* you've ever seen!"

17c לְמִיּ֛וֹם סוּר־אֶפְרַ֖יִם מֵעַ֣ל יְהוּדָ֑ה

since the day that Ephraim split from Judah—

לְמִיּ֛וֹם יוֹם	to from day *lə·miy·**yôm***	ABS W/ PREP לְ + PREP מִן	noun
סוּר־ סוּר	to turn aside *sûr-*	QAL INF CST	verb
אֶפְרַ֖יִם אֶפְרַ֫יִם	Ephraim *ʾef·**ra**·yim*	ABS	noun
מֵעַ֣ל עַל	from upon *mē·**ʿal***	--- W/ PREP מִן	prep
יְהוּדָ֑ה יְהוּדָה	Judah *yə·hû·**dâ***	ABS	noun

Isaiah refers to the split in the time of Solomon's son, Rehoboam, when Jeroboam took over northern Israel and Davidic kings continued to rule over southern Israel (Judah) (see 1 Kgs 12).

17d אֵ֖ת מֶ֥לֶךְ אַשּֽׁוּר׃

the king of Assyria!"

אֵ֖ת אֵת	*(direct object marker)* *ʾēt*	---	particle
מֶ֥לֶךְ מֶ֫לֶךְ	king ***me**·leḵ*	CST	noun
אַשּֽׁוּר׃ אַשּׁוּר	Assyria *ʾaš·**šûr***	ABS	noun

This final phrase draws much emphasis, positioned as it is at the end of the clause. It is meant to evoke terror in Ahaz's heart. If Ahaz fears the kings of Israel and Syria (Pekah and Rezin, respectively), how much more should he fear the king of Assyria?

From Text to Sermon

Big Idea. Do not fear! God is with us!

Avenues for Illustration and Application. Isaiah 7 drops the reader down in the middle of the action. Congregants can quickly get lost in the melee of names. Especially if preaching the full chapter, preachers might help the church orient themselves in the text by providing a short list of names in the bulletin or on the screen (see below). Preachers will also want to take care to set the context, as this chapter picks up five years after the previous chapter. It might help reading a bit of 2 Kgs 16 // 2 Chr 28 to set the historical context.

Ahaz — King of Judah (South)
Pekah — King of Israel (North) (a.k.a. Ephraim/Samaria)
Rezin — King of Syria (a.k.a. Damascus)

The Lord's command for Ahaz to ask for a sign might be illustrated by popular depictions of genies granting three wishes. Imagine Aladdin finding the lamp and the genie comes out and offers him three wishes, and Aladdin says, "Nah!" and tosses the lamp back into the Cave of Wonders. Though we do not want to trivialize the depiction of God in the text, a short, humorous anecdote may help show the absurdity of such behavior from Ahaz.

The "curds and honey" comment in v. 15 will also need brief explanation. If this is another way of saying the child has been weaned and now eats solid food, as some commentators take it, then preachers can contemporize the meaning by saying "yogurt and bananas" or another baby-food substitute. If the preacher understands the text to mean the food of scavenging exiles, then perhaps "bread and water" or "beans and rice" might substitute as a way of illustrating.

Preachers must not fall into the temptation of spending so much time illustrating and explaining the text—especially when it comes to the prophetic/messianic portion in v. 14—that they forget to *apply* the text. The point of the passage is not to offer an exegetical treat for interpreters. The point is rather to offer prophetic hope in both the more immediate child born in Ahaz's day and also ultimately in the coming Messiah. The promise that "God is with us" (Immanuel) was designed to alleviate the fear of both King Ahaz and Israel. Drive home the point that God remains with his people even today and that his presence with believers should help us deal with our own struggle with fear. Examples of fears can be big (cancer diagnosis; fear of death; crippling anxiety) or small (fear of the dark; worry over lost business revenue). Our fears are inversely proportional to our confidence in the fact that God is with us.

New Testament Connections. Isaiah 7 gives any interpreter a daunting challenge, most especially when Matthew's Gospel comes into the discussion. Indeed, much of the sermon, even if rooted in the text of the Old Testament, will revolve around what Matthew does with the prophecy of the virgin. Many articles and excellent chapters have been written on the topic in much more detail than this volume affords. Here, our purpose will be to provide homiletical advice regarding how to guide a church through the many interpretive difficulties in the text. The exegetical problems are numerous: Does Matthew apply the prophecy in a different way than Isaiah intends? Does Isaiah's use of עַלְמָה mean "virgin" in this context? Does "the virgin" refer to someone in Isaiah's time, to the virgin Mary, or both? If Isaiah meant the sign only for King Ahaz, then why does Matthew apply it to Jesus? If Isaiah meant for the sign to refer to Jesus, then how did it have any relevance to King Ahaz? And so on. Here, I offer one possible method for organizing and answering the difficulties in a sermon.

When I preached this passage, after first raising the interpretive questions so that the church understood the problems, I dismissed the possibility that Matthew misapplied Isaiah. If Matthew inappropriately applied Isaiah, his argument would have lost all force for his Jewish readers. So I moved forward with the assumption that Matthew makes sense of Isaiah and "plays by the rules."

Second, I discussed the terms עַלְמָה and בְּתוּלָה as they relate to the text. The goal was to help the congregation understand that the former term *can* be applied more broadly than "virgin," but that the latter term is not necessarily so restrictive in its meaning. Thus, there is a possibility Isaiah could have been referring to either a virgin in the traditional sense or a young woman without child. Nothing is ultimately won or lost by this term due to its fluidity.

Third, I organized the rest of the discussion around two primary questions: (1) Is there evidence that this prophecy was originally meant for a future time? And (2) Is there evidence that this prophecy was fulfilled in Isaiah's time? With regard to the first question, I pointed to the plural usage of "you" throughout much of the prophecy, the references to the "house of David," and evidence from Isa 9:6–7 and 11:1–10 that may indicate that the Messiah will ultimately fulfill this prophecy. With regard to the second question, I reviewed three main interpretive possibilities on how to understand "virgin" if it refers to something in Isaiah's day: (1) "The virgin" refers to an unknown woman in Isaiah's time who had a baby and named the child "Immanuel"; (2) "The virgin" refers to Ahaz's wife giving birth to Hezekiah; (3) "The virgin" refers to Isaiah's own wife giving birth to Maher-shalal-hash-baz (8:1–4). Evidence from Isa 8:1–4 and also 7:15–17 led me to conclude that one could potentially understand the text as having reference to Isaiah's own day.

Bringing all of this together, my personal conclusions lent towards a double-fulfillment approach to the text. Whether the reader shares my personal conclusions is irrelevant. Preachers must study the text, determine their convictions on what they believe it says, and find a way to present the material in an engaging, humble, and biblical manner.

An outline of the passage (assuming one only preaches 7:10–17) might look like this:

- I. Introduction: Historical Context (2 Kgs 16; Isa 7:1–9)
- II. Isa 7:10–12 — Ask for a Sign
- III. Isa 7:13–14 — The Sign of Immanuel
  - A. Introduction to Interpretive Problems (cf. Matt 1:18–25)
  - B. Discussion of Hebrew Terms for "Virgin"
  - C. Evidence the Prophecy Was Meant for a Future Time
  - D. Evidence the Prophecy Was Meant for Isaiah's Time
  - E. Personal Conclusions
- IV. Isa 7:15–17 — The Coming Exile
- V. Conclusion: Do Not Fear! God Is With Us!

A CHILD IS BORN

On any given Sunday, the church enters the building with a mix of gloom and joy. Some are rejoicing—a recent promotion has lifted spirits, a child has brought home a good report card, a spiritual breakthrough has finally occurred in a spouse. Some are struggling—depression is creeping back in, the loss of a loved one brings anguish, financial pressures mount. If we were to ask Isaiah where he was when he wrote Isa 9, he might say a bit of both.

With the Assyrian threat looming over the nation, the people of Judah were in the shadow of death. Isaiah preaches judgment against the Northern Kingdom. Yet the Lord offers hope in the form of a messianic child. His light will soon shine through the darkness, offering salvation to all who fight despair.

LARGER LITERARY CONTEXT › 8:23–9:6 [9:1–7]

8:23 [9:1]

8:23a[9:1a] כִּי לֹא מוּעָף לַאֲשֶׁר מוּצָק לָהּ

__kî lō’__ mû‘__āf__ la’ă__šer__ mû__ṣāq lāh__

Now, there will be no gloom for her who is in a tight spot.

8:23b[9:1b] כָּעֵת הָרִאשׁוֹן הֵקַל

kā‘__ēt__ hāri’__šôn__ hē__qal__

In earlier times, he made light

8:23c[9:1c] אַרְצָה זְבֻלוּן וְאַרְצָה נַפְתָּלִי

’__ar__ṣâ zəvū__lūn__ wə’__ar__ṣâ naftā__lî__

of the land of Zebulun and the land of Naphtali,

8:23d[9:1d] וְהָאַחֲרוֹן הִכְבִּיד דֶּרֶךְ הַיָּם

wəhā’aḥă__rôn__ hiḵ__bîd__ __de__reḵ hay__yām__

but in later times, he will give weight to the way of the sea,

8:23e[9:1e] עֵבֶר הַיַּרְדֵּן גְּלִיל הַגּוֹיִם׃

‘__ē__ver hayyar__dēn__ gə__lîl__ haggô__yim__.

the region beyond the Jordan, the Galilee of the nations.

8:23a[9:1a] כִּי לֹא מוּעָף לַאֲשֶׁר מוּצָק לָהּ

Now, there will be no gloom for her who is in a tight spot.

כִּי כִּי	for/since/but *kî*	---	conj
לֹא לֹא	no/not *lō’*	---	particle
מוּעָף מוּעָף	gloom/anguish *mû·‘āf*	ABS	noun

לַאֲשֶׁר אֲשֶׁר	for/to that *la·ʾă·šer*	--- W/ PREP לְ	relative pron
מוּצָק מוּצָק	narrowness/constraint *mû·ṣāq*	ABS	noun
לָהּ לְ	for her *lāh*	--- W/ 3FS SX	prep

Students of Hebrew will notice that the MT and English versification differ at this point. The Hebrew Bible has this verse as 8:23, whereas the ninth chapter of Isaiah begins here in English. The verses coincide again at 10:1. Unless you preach to a group who regularly uses Hebrew, there is no need to mention this from the pulpit. The reason for such a difference is the opening כִּי, which could connect backwards or forwards. Isaiah 8:22 also uses מוּעָף ("gloom") and uses צוּקָה ("pressure/distress") instead of מוּצָק ("narrowness/constraint"). Isaiah 8:23 [9:1] enjoys some assonance between מוּעָף and מוּצָק, but this is difficult to bring about in translation (perhaps "there will be no *gloom* for her who feels *doom*"). The feminine suffixed לָהּ also requires an antecedent, so if this phrase does go with the following, it must act as a hinge also, keeping the preceding in context.

8:23b [9:1b] **כָּעֵת הָרִאשׁוֹן הֵקַל**

In earlier times, he made light of

כָּעֵת עֵת	as the time *kā·ʿēt*	ABS W/ PREP כְּ + DEF. ART.	noun
הָרִאשׁוֹן רִאשׁוֹן	the first/former *hā·riʾ·šôn*	MS ATTR W/ DEF. ART.	adj
הֵקַל קלל	he made light (of) *hē·qal*	HIPH PF 3MS	verb

Since the "later times" in 8:23d [9:1d] (וְהָאַחֲרוֹן) likely refers to a time future to Isaiah, "earlier times" (הָרִאשׁוֹן) here likely refers to Isaiah's own day, or at least Isaiah's present experience of the effects of the Lord's past actions.

8:23c[9:1c]	אַ֣רְצָה זְבֻל֙וּן וְאַ֣רְצָה נַפְתָּלִ֔י

the land of Zebulun and the land of Naphtali,

אַ֣רְצָה אֶ֫רֶץ	the land *ʾar·ṣâ*	CST W/ LOCATIVE ה	noun
זְבֻל֙וּן זְבוּלֻ֫ן	Zebulun *zə·vū·lūn*	ABS	noun
וְאַ֣רְצָה אֶ֫רֶץ	and the land *wə·ʾar·ṣâ*	CST W/ CONJ וְ + LOCATIVE ה	noun
נַפְתָּלִ֔י נַפְתָּלִי	Naphtali *naf·tā·lî*	ABS	noun

Zebulun and Naphtali were regions in northern Israel, near and above the Sea of Galilee. Because of their northern location, they were most vulnerable to attacks from the Assyrians. It may help to show these regions on a map to the congregation to explain Isaiah's comments here.

8:23d[9:1d]	וְהָאַחֲר֣וֹן הִכְבִּ֑יד דֶּ֣רֶךְ הַיָּ֗ם

but in later times, he will give weight to the way of the sea,

וְהָאַחֲר֣וֹן אַחֲרוֹן	but after *wə·hā·ʾa·ḥă·rôn*	MS SUBST W/ CONJ וְ + DEF. ART.	adj
הִכְבִּ֑יד כבד	he made heavy *hik̲·bîd*	HIPH PF 3MS	verb
דֶּ֣רֶךְ דֶּ֫רֶךְ	way/road *de·rek̲*	CST	noun
הַיָּ֗ם יָם	the sea *hay·yām*	ABS W/ DEF. ART.	noun

Note the contrast between God earlier "making light" (קלל) of the land of Zebulun/Naphtali and later "making heavy" (כבד) the way of the sea. Modern translations tend to obscure this intentional contrast, so the preacher may want to draw attention to this feature of the text. Though Isaiah uses a perfect verb here, he likely intends a "prophetic perfect," or a future orientation, written in past tense to emphasize that this prophecy is so certain he views it as already completed.

The Masoretic accenting, specifically the *atnakh* beneath הִכְבִּ֑יד ("he made heavy"), separates וְהָאַחֲר֣וֹן הִכְבִּ֑יד ("but in later times, he will give weight") from the second half of the clause, דֶּרֶךְ הַיָּם ("to the way of the sea"). In my opinion, breaking the verse at that point obscures the contrastive parallelism between lines b–c and d–e. Keeping the clause together—וְהָאַחֲרוֹן הִכְבִּיד דֶּרֶךְ הַיָּם ("but in later times, he will give weight to the way of the sea")—provides a nice contrast with כָּעֵת הָרִאשׁוֹן ("in earlier times") in 8:23b [9:1b].

8:23e [9:1e]	עֵ֣בֶר הַיַּרְדֵּ֔ן גְּלִ֖יל הַגּוֹיִֽם׃

the region beyond the Jordan, the Galilee of the nations.

עֵ֣בֶר עֵ֫בֶר	region beyond *ʿē·ver*	CST	noun
הַיַּרְדֵּ֔ן יַרְדֵּן	the Jordan *hay·yar·**dēn***	ABS W/ DEF. ART.	noun
גְּלִ֖יל גָּלִיל	Galilee *gə·**lîl***	CST	noun
הַגּוֹיִֽם׃ גּוֹי	the nations/peoples/ Gentiles *hag·gô·**yīm***	ABS W/ DEF. ART.	noun

This phrase further qualifies and defines דֶּרֶךְ הַיָּם ("the way of the sea"), still referring to the northernmost parts of Israel, but with an emphasis on the pagan character of the people.

9:1–4 [2–5]

9:1a [9:2a] הָעָם֙ הַהֹלְכִ֣ים בַּחֹ֔שֶׁךְ

*hā**ʿām** hahōlə**ḵîm** ba**ḥō**šeḵ*

Those who once walked in darkness

9:1b [9:2b] רָא֖וּ א֣וֹר גָּד֑וֹל

*rāʾ**û** ʾ**ôr** gā**dôl***

now see a great light;

9:1c [9:2c] יֹשְׁבֵי֙ בְּאֶ֣רֶץ צַלְמָ֔וֶת

*yōšə**vê** bəʾ**e**reṣ ṣal**mā**wet*

those who dwell in the land of shadows,

9:1d [9:2d] א֖וֹר נָגַ֥הּ עֲלֵיהֶֽם׃

*ʾ**ôr** nā**gah** ʿălê**hem**.*

light now shines on them!

9:2a [9:3a] הִרְבִּ֣יתָ הַגּ֔וֹי

*hir**bî**tā hag**gôy***

You caused the nations to explode in population;

9:2b [9:3b] ל֖וֹ הִגְדַּ֣לְתָּ הַשִּׂמְחָ֑ה

lô** hig**dal**tā haśśim**ḥâ

you have caused them to experience great joy!

9:2c [9:3c] שָׂמְח֤וּ לְפָנֶ֙יךָ֙

*śāmə**ḥû** ləfā**nê**ḵā*

They celebrate before you

9:2d [9:3d] כְּשִׂמְחַ֣ת בַּקָּצִ֔יר

*kəśim**ḥat** baqqā**ṣîr***

just like the joy at harvesttime,

9:2e[9:3e] כַּאֲשֶׁר יָגִילוּ בְּחַלְּקָם שָׁלָל׃

*ka'ă**šer** yā**gî**lû bəḥallə**qām** šā**lāl**.*

just like they rejoice when dividing the spoils.

9:3a[9:4a] כִּי ׀ אֶת־עֹל סֻבֳּלוֹ

kî** 'et-'**ōl** subbŏ**lô

For his burdensome yoke—

9:3b[9:4b] וְאֵת מַטֵּה שִׁכְמוֹ

*wə'**ēt** maṭ**ṭē** šiḵ**mô***

and his shoulder's staff—

9:3c[9:4c] שֵׁבֶט הַנֹּגֵשׂ בּוֹ

šē**veṭ hannō**gēś** **bô

his oppressor's rod—

9:3d[9:4d] הַחִתֹּתָ כְּיוֹם מִדְיָן׃

*haḥit**tō**tā kə**yôm** mid**yān**.*

you shattered, just as in the day of Midian!

9:4a[9:5a] כִּי כָל־סְאוֹן סֹאֵן בְּרַעַשׁ

***kî** ḵol-sə'**ôn** sō'**ēn** bə**ra**'aš*

For every treaded sole treading

9:4b[9:5b] וְשִׂמְלָה מְגוֹלָלָה בְדָמִים

*wəśim**lâ** məgôlā**lâ** vədā**mîm***

and cloak rolled in blood

9:4c[9:5c] וְהָיְתָה לִשְׂרֵפָה מַאֲכֹלֶת אֵשׁ׃

*wəhāyə**tâ** liśrē**fâ** ma'ăḵōlet '**ēš**.*

will be burned as fuel for the fire.

9:1a[9:2a]	הָעָם֙ הַהֹלְכִ֣ים בַּחֹ֔שֶׁךְ

Those who once walked in darkness

הָעָם֙ עַם	the people *hā·ʿ**ām***	ABS W/ DEF. ART.	noun
הַהֹלְכִ֣ים הלך	who walked *ha·hō·lə·**ḵîm***	QAL PTCP MP W/ DEF. ART.	verb
בַּחֹ֔שֶׁךְ חֹ֫שֶׁךְ	in the darkness *ba·**ḥō**·šeḵ*	ABS W/ PREP בְּ + DEF. ART.	noun

To "walk" is a common biblical idiom referring to the conduct of life. Walking in darkness extends the metaphor to absurd proportions. In the absence of modern electrical lighting, no Israelite would dare venture on the darkened roads without a torch.

9:1b[9:2b]	רָא֖וּ א֣וֹר גָּד֑וֹל

now see a great light;

רָא֖וּ ראה	(they) see *rā·ʾ**û***	QAL PF 3CP	verb
א֣וֹר אוֹר	light *ʾ**ôr***	ABS	noun
גָּד֑וֹל גָּדוֹל	great *gā·**dôl***	MS ATTR	adj

9:1c[9:2c]	יֹשְׁבֵי֙ בְּאֶ֣רֶץ צַלְמָ֔וֶת

those who dwell in the land of shadows,

יֹשְׁבֵי֙ ישׁב	those who dwell *yō·šə·**vê***	Q (CST) PTCP MP	verb
בְּאֶ֣רֶץ אֶ֫רֶץ	in the land/earth *bə·ʾ**e**·reṣ*	CST W/ PREP בְּ	noun
צַלְמָ֔וֶת צַלְמָ֫וֶת	deep shadow/darkness *ṣal·**mā**·wet*	ABS	noun

The word צַלְמָוֶת ("deep shadow/darkness") is perhaps best known for its use in Ps 23:4: "Even though I walk in the valley of *the shadow of death*" (ESV, emphasis mine). Though its etymology is debated, scriptural usage can help illuminate its meaning. It can be used literally to refer to darkness (Job 3:4–5) or figuratively to refer to terror (Job 24:17), grave danger (Ps 23:4), or the grave/Sheol (Job 10:20–22; 38:17). See Price 1997:807–10.

9:1d [9:2d]	אוֹר נָגַהּ עֲלֵיהֶם׃		
	light now shines on them!		
אוֹר אוֹר	light *'ôr*	ABS	noun
נָגַהּ נגה	(it) shines *nā·**gah***	QAL PF 3MS	verb
עֲלֵיהֶם׃ עַל	on them *'ă·lê·**hem***	--- W/ 3MP SX	prep

The impact of this statement can hardly be overestimated. Zebulun and Naphtali were not exactly known as bastions of godliness (putting it mildly). To say that they now enjoy great light would be akin to saying that the darkest parts of this country or this world are now known for their spirituality.

9:2a [9:3a]	הִרְבִּיתָ הַגּוֹי		
	You caused the nations to explode in population;		
הִרְבִּיתָ רבה	you made many *hir·**bî**·tā*	HIPH PF 2MS	verb
הַגּוֹי גּוֹי	the nation/people/ Gentiles *hag·**gôy***	ABS W/ DEF. ART.	noun

"The nations" (plural) was used in 8:23e [9:1e]; here, it is also articular, but singular. It likely refers to the entire nation of Israel, or at least northern Israel. Theologically, interpreters usually take this verse in one of two ways: (1) Some see this fulfilled in the church's spiritual population growth; (2) some understand its fulfillment in the end times, a literal revival for ethnic Israel.

9:2b[9:3b]	לוֹ הִגְדַּ֫לְתָּ הַשִּׂמְחָ֑ה

you have caused them to experience great joy!

לֽוֹ לְ	to him *lô*	--- W/ 3MS SX	prep
הִגְדַּ֫לְתָּ גדל	you made great *hig·**dal**·tā*	HIPH PF 2MS	verb
הַשִּׂמְחָ֑ה שִׂמְחָה	the joy/gladness *haś·śim·**ḥâ***	ABS W/ DEF. ART.	noun

9:2c[9:3c]	שָׂמְח֣וּ לְפָנֶ֔יךָ

They celebrate before you

שָׂמְח֣וּ שׂמח	they rejoice *śā·mə·**ḥû***	QAL PF 3CP	verb
לְפָנֶ֔יךָ לִפְנֵי	before/to your face *lə·fā·**nɛ̂**·ḵā*	--- W/ 2MS SX	prep

9:2d[9:3d]	כְּשִׂמְחַ֖ת בַּקָּצִ֑יר

just like the joy at harvesttime,

כְּשִׂמְחַ֖ת שִׂמְחָה	as the joy/gladness *kə·śim·**ḥat***	CST W/ PREP כְּ	noun
בַּקָּצִ֑יר קָצִיר	in the harvest *baq·qā·**ṣîr***	ABS W/ PREP בְּ + DEF. ART.	noun

9:2e[9:3e]	כַּאֲשֶׁ֥ר יָגִ֖ילוּ בְּחַלְּקָ֥ם שָׁלָֽל׃

just like they rejoice when dividing the spoils.

כַּאֲשֶׁ֥ר אֲשֶׁר	as that *ka·ʾă·**šer***	--- W/ PREP כְּ	relative
יָגִ֖ילוּ גיל	they will rejoice *yā·**gî**·lû*	QAL IMPF 3MP	verb

בְּחַלְּקָם חלק	when they divide them *bə·ḥal·lə·**qām***	PIEL INF CST W/ PREP בְּ + 3MP SX	verb
שָׁלָל׃ שָׁלָל	spoils *šā·**lāl***	ABS	noun

Two similes will qualify this phrase, both introduced by the preposition כְּ: (1) כְּשִׂמְחַת בַּקָּצִיר ("just like at harvesttime") and (2) כַּאֲשֶׁר יָגִילוּ בְּחַלְּקָם שָׁלָל ("just like when they divide the spoils"). Preachers can use both of these as launching points for illustrations. The harvest brought great joy to the Israelites, as another season of blessing had come to fruition. Dividing the spoils of war also brought great joy, as it symbolized the enemy's defeat and the blessings that came with it.

9:3a[9:4a] כִּ֣י ׀ אֶת־עֹ֣ל סֻבֳּל֗וֹ

For his burdensome yoke—

כִּ֣י ׀ כִּי	for ***kî***	---	conj
אֶת־ אֵת	*(direct object marker)* *ʾet-*	---	particle
עֹ֣ל עֹל	yoke ***ʿōl***	CST	noun
סֻבֳּל֗וֹ סֹבֶל	his burden *sub·bŏ·**lô***	CST W/ 3MS SX	noun

Verse 3a–c [4a–c] has three phrases, all objects of the verb in 3d. The first two phrases begin with the direct object marker, while the third is unmarked but functions similarly. Each phrase reflects a metaphor for slavery or oppression drawn from shepherding and agriculture. Once again, each phrase gives preachers the opportunity for built-in illustration. See below under "Avenues for Illustration and Application" for specific examples.

9:3b[9:4b] וְאֵת֙ מַטֵּ֣ה שִׁכְמ֔וֹ

and his shoulder's staff—

וְאֵת֙ אֵת	and *(direct object marker)* *wə·**ʾēt***	--- W/ CONJ וְ	particle

מַטֵּה	staff/rod	CST	noun
מַטֶּה	*maṭ·ṭē*		
שִׁכְמוֹ	his shoulder	CST	noun
שְׁכֶם	*šiḵ·mô*	W/ 3MS SX	

9:3c[9:4c] שֵׁבֶט הַנֹּגֵשׂ בּוֹ

his oppressor's rod—

שֵׁבֶט	rod/staff	CST	noun
שֵׁבֶט	*šē·veṭ*		
הַנֹּגֵשׂ	the oppressor	QAL PTCP MS	verb
נגשׂ	*han·nō·gēś*	W/ DEF. ART.	
בּוֹ	in him	---	prep
בְּ	*bô*	W/ 3MS SX	

This third phrase may syntactically differ in order to draw attention to itself. It is the least metaphorical of the three phrases and as such it recalls most directly the oppression of the Israelites.

9:3d[9:4d] הַחִתֹּתָ כְּיוֹם מִדְיָן׃

you shattered, just as in the day of Midian!

הַחִתֹּתָ	you shattered	HIPH PF 2MS	verb
חתת	*ha·ḥit·tō·tā*		
כְּיוֹם	as the day	CST	noun
יוֹם	*kə·yôm*	W/ PREP כְּ	
מִדְיָן׃	Midian	ABS	noun
מִדְיָן	*mid·yān*		

Here we note another כְּ phrase, recalling 2d–e [3d–e]. It gives a concrete illustration of what it looks like to break/shatter the yoke/staff/rod of oppression. Preachers might recall Judg 6–7 and the story of Gideon/Midian in order to biblically illustrate the text.

9:4a [9:5a]	כִּֽי כָל־סְא֤וֹן סֹאֵן֙ בְּרַ֔עַשׁ

For every treaded sole treading

כִּ֣י כִּי	for *kî*	---	conj
כָל־ כֹּל	all/each/every *k̲ol-*	CST	noun
סְא֤וֹן סְאוֹן	sandal/boot *sə·**ʾôn***	CST	noun
סֹאֵן֙ סאן	treading/marching *sō·**ʾēn***	QAL PTCP MS	verb
בְּרַ֔עַשׁ רַ֫עַשׁ	with shaking/quaking *bə·**ra**·ʿaš*	ABS W/ PREP בְּ	noun

The text literally reads, "for every boot booting with shaking." The imagery depicts soldiers marching out to battle.

9:4b [9:5b]	וְשִׂמְלָ֖ה מְגוֹלָלָ֣ה בְדָמִ֑ים

and cloak rolled in blood

וְשִׂמְלָ֖ה שִׂמְלָה	and cloak/mantle *wə·śim·**lâ***	ABS W/ CONJ וְ	noun
מְגוֹלָלָ֣ה גלל	rolled *mə·gô·lā·**lâ***	POAL PTCP FS	verb
בְדָמִ֑ים דָּם	in blood *və·dā·**mîm***	ABS W/ PREP בְּ	noun

This phrase continues the warrior metaphor, depicting the aftermath of battle with bloody garments. Even such stained garments were normally collected as spoils, as clothes could be expensive.

9:4c [9:5c]	וְהָיְתָ֥ה לִשְׂרֵפָ֖ה מַאֲכֹ֥לֶת אֵֽשׁ׃

will be burned as fuel for the fire.

וְהָיְתָ֥ה היה	and it will be *wə·hā·yə·**tâ***	QAL WEQATAL 3FS	verb

לִשְׂרֵפָ֖ה שְׂרֵפָה	to a burning *liś·rē·fâ*	ABS W/ PREP לְ	noun
מַאֲכֹ֥לֶת מַאֲכֹ֫לֶת	fuel *ma·ʾă·ḵō·let*	CST	noun
אֵֽשׁ׃ אֵשׁ	fire *ʾēš*	ABS	noun

To burn expensive boots and coats in the fire demonstrates how little need there will be to reuse the boots and coats for war in the future. The enemy will be defeated so thoroughly that Israel will experience a time of peace and prosperity unlike any other period of her existence.

9:5–6 [6–7]

9:5a [9:6a] כִּי־יֶ֣לֶד יֻלַּד־לָ֗נוּ

*kî-**ye**led yullad-**lā**nû*

For a child will be born to us,

9:5b [9:6b] בֵּ֚ן נִתַּן־לָ֔נוּ

***bēn** nittan-**lā**nû*

a son will be given to us;

9:5c [9:6c] וַתְּהִ֥י הַמִּשְׂרָ֖ה עַל־שִׁכְמ֑וֹ

*wattə**hî** hammiś**râ** ʿal-šiḵ**mô***

And dominion will be upon his shoulder,

9:5d [9:6d] וַיִּקְרָ֨א שְׁמ֜וֹ

*wayyiq**rā**ʾ šə**mô***

and people will call him,

9:5e [9:6e] פֶּ֠לֶא יוֹעֵ֗ץ

pe**leʾ yô**ʿēṣ

“Wonderful Counselor

9:5f [9:6e] אֵ֚ל גִּבּ֔וֹר

ʾēl** gib**bôr

Mighty God,

9:5g [9:6f] אֲבִיעַ֖ד

*ʾăvî**ʿad***

Forever Father

9:5h [9:6f] שַׂר־שָׁלֽוֹם׃

*śar-šā**lôm**.*

Prince of Peace.”

9:6a[9:7a] לְמַרְבֵּ֨ה הַמִּשְׂרָ֜ה וּלְשָׁל֣וֹם אֵֽין־קֵ֗ץ

ləmarbē hammiśrâ ûləšālôm ʾên-qēṣ

There will be no end to the abundance of rule and peace

9:6b[9:7b] עַל־כִּסֵּ֤א דָוִד֙ וְעַל־מַמְלַכְתּ֔וֹ

ʿal-kissēʾ dāwid wəʿal-mamlaktô

on the throne of David and over his kingdom,

9:6c[9:7c] לְהָכִ֥ין אֹתָהּ֙ וּֽלְסַעֲדָ֔הּ

ləhākîn ʾōtāh ûləsaʿădāh

to establish it and to support it

9:6d[9:7d] בְּמִשְׁפָּ֖ט וּבִצְדָקָ֑ה

bəmišpāṭ ûviṣdāqâ

with justice and with righteousness

9:6e[9:7e] מֵעַתָּה֙ וְעַד־עוֹלָ֔ם

mēʿattâ wəʿad-ʿôlām

both now and forever.

9:6f[9:7f] קִנְאַ֛ת יְהוָ֥ה צְבָא֖וֹת תַּֽעֲשֶׂה־זֹּֽאת׃

qinʾat YHWH ṣəvāʾôt taʿăśe-zōʾt.

The zeal of YHWH of hosts will accomplish this!

9:5a[9:6a]	כִּֽי־יֶ֣לֶד יֻלַּד־לָ֗נוּ		
	For a child will be born to us,		
כִּֽי־ / כִּי	for / *kî-*	---	conj
יֶ֣לֶד / יֶ֫לֶד	child/lad/boy / ***ye**·led*	ABS	noun

יֻלַּד־ יֻלַּד	will be born *yul·lad-*	PUAL PF 3MS	verb
לָ֫נוּ לְ	to us *lā·nû*	--- W/ 1CP SX	prep

Every word of this verse holds great theological significance and deserves careful study. The opening כִּי demonstrates *how* the Lord will accomplish the great revival promised in vv. 1–4 [2–5]. The fronting of the noun יֶלֶד ("child/lad/boy") puts emphasis on the word. The word enjoys alliteration with the verb ילד ("will be born"). The word לָנוּ ("to us") refers to Isaiah's audience. The promised child will be an Israelite.

9:5b [9:6b] בֵּ֚ן נִתַּן־לָ֔נוּ

a son will be given to us;

בֵּן בֵּן	son *bēn*	ABS	noun
נִתַּן־ נתן	(he) will be given *nit·tan-*	NIPH PF 3MS	verb
לָ֔נוּ לְ	to us *lā·nû*	--- W/ 1CP SX	prep

The clause enjoys perfect parallelism with the preceding (minus the opening conjunction כִּי). The child will be a male, implied by בֵּן ("son"). That נתן ("he will be given") is in the Niphal indicates a divine passive—the Lord will give the child as a gift to his people. The repetition of לָנוּ ("to us") emphasizes the Israelite nationality of the child and also shows the child will be the personal object of hope for God's people.

9:5c [9:6c] וַתְּהִ֥י הַמִּשְׂרָ֖ה עַל־שִׁכְמ֑וֹ

And dominion will be upon his shoulder,

וַתְּהִי היה	and it will be *wat·tə·hî*	QAL WAYY 3FS	verb
הַמִּשְׂרָה מִשְׂרָה	the rule/dominion *ham·miś·râ*	ABS W/ DEF. ART.	noun

עַל־	upon	---	prep
עַל	*'al-*		
שִׁכְמוֹ	his shoulder	CST W/ 3MS SX	noun
שְׁכֶם	*šik·mô*		

The noun שְׁכֶם ("shoulder") was also used in 9:3 [4]. The repetition here has ironic effect. The Israelites suffered under oppression, symbolized by the staff upon their shoulder. The Lord not only promises to break it, but the entire weight of the government shall one day be upon the "shoulder" of the coming child. The burden that the Israelites could not bear, the boy can. The image of an entire government (lit., "dominion") carried upon the shoulder of an infant is startling. Surely this child is omnipotent!

9:5d [9:6d] וַיִּקְרָא שְׁמוֹ

and people will call him,

וַיִּקְרָא	and he will call	QAL WAYY 3MS	verb
קרא	*way·yiq·rā'*		
שְׁמוֹ	his name	CST W/ 3MS SX	noun
שֵׁם	*šə·mô*		

In Hebrew thought, the "name" stands for the person. The following phrases do not merely represent titles for the child, but describe his essence. They describe who he *is*.

9:5e [9:6e] פֶּלֶא יוֹעֵץ

"Wonderful Counselor,

פֶּלֶא	wonderful	CST	noun
פֶּלֶא	*pe·le'*		
יוֹעֵץ	counselor	QAL PTCP MS	verb
יעץ	*yô·'ēṣ*		

Some versions, like the KJV, translate the first two words separately: "and his name shall be called Wonderful, Counselor . . ." But the following descriptions are each built on two Hebrew words, so the majority of translations correctly combine "wonderful" and "counselor." Additional support comes from the same roots used together in 25:1 and 28:29. The word פֶּלֶא ("wonderful") is often used in the Old Testament for God's miraculous acts of salvation and deliverance (e.g., Exod 3:20; Judg 6:13), not only for something that is above average and goes beyond normal human expectation (as we might use the word today). The participle יוֹעֵץ ("counselor") can sometimes refer to a king's advisor (e.g., 2 Sam 17:15; 1 Kgs 12:28). The child will lead the nation in wisdom. His counsel goes far beyond what one would normally expect to receive from a human.

9:5f[9:6f]	אֵ֣ל גִּבּ֔וֹר		
	Mighty God,		
אֵ֣ל אֵל	God *ʾēl*	ABS	noun
גִּבּ֔וֹר גִּבּוֹר	mighty/strong *gib·bôr*	MS ATTR	adj

The adjective גִּבּוֹר ("mighty/strong") frequently describes strong and brave warriors (e.g., Josh 10:7; Judg 11:1). Combining this adjective with the deific noun אֵל ("God") pictures a beautiful contrast: the "child" will be called "Warrior God"! These juxtaposed descriptions can only find fulfillment in the incarnation.

9:5g[9:6g]	אֲבִיעַ֖ד		
	Forever Father		
אֲבִיעַ֖ד אֲבִיעַד	forever/everlasting father *ʾă·vî·ʿad*	ABS	noun

The word אֲבִיעַד ("everlasting father") combines the word for "father" with a noun denoting long duration (עַד). The title at least indicates an incredibly long reign; the New Testament understands it to refer to the eternal reign of Jesus Christ (Luke 1:33). Preachers should be careful not to confuse Isaiah's purpose with this phrase. Isaiah does not reflect on the ontological relationship within the Trinity, confusing Father and Son. Isaiah uses "father" as a metaphorical protector and overseer of the people (cf. the sense of "father" in Isa 22:21).

9:5h [9:6h]	שַׂר־שָׁלֽוֹם׃		
	Prince of Peace."		
שַׂר־ / שַׂר	prince/ruler / *śar-*	CST	noun
שָׁלֽוֹם׃ / שָׁלוֹם	peace / *šā·**lôm***	ABS	noun

The title "prince of peace" would have had great impact on the people in Isaiah's time. The people were ravaged and continually threatened by war, from within the country and from outsiders (see Isa 7). The thought of a prince bringing everlasting, perfect *shalom* would have been warmly received.

9:6a [9:7a]	לְמַרְבֵּה הַמִּשְׂרָה וּלְשָׁלוֹם אֵין־קֵץ		
	There will be no end to the abundance of rule and peace		
לְמַרְבֵּה / מַרְבֶּה	to an abundance / *lə·mar·**bē***	CST W/ PREP לְ	noun
הַמִּשְׂרָה / מִשְׂרָה	the rule/dominion / *ham·miś·**râ***	ABS W/ DEF. ART.	noun
וּלְשָׁלוֹם / שָׁלוֹם	and peace / *û·lə·šā·**lôm***	ABS W/ CONJ וְ + PREP לְ	noun
אֵין־ / אַיִן	nothing/no / ***'ên-***	---	particle
קֵץ / קֵץ	end / ***qēṣ***	ABS	noun

Juxtaposing מִשְׂרָה ("rule/dominion") and שָׁלוֹם ("peace") has an ironic effect. What government continues forever in peace? Consider the greatest kingdoms the earth has ever seen—Babylon, Greece, Rome, America—*none* can claim this! Today, there is "no end" to war, to death, to violence, to bloodshed. But when the prophesied child reigns, there will be "no end" to peace.

9:6b[9:7b]	עַל־כִּסֵּ֤א דָוִד֙ וְעַל־מַמְלַכְתּ֔וֹ

on the throne of David and over his kingdom,

עַל־ עַל	upon/on *'al-*	---	prep
כִּסֵּא כִּסֵּא	throne/seat *kis·**sē'***	CST	noun
דָוִד דָּוִד	David *dā·**wid***	ABS	noun
וְעַל־ עַל	and upon/over *wə·'al-*	--- W/ CONJ וְ	prep
מַמְלַכְתּוֹ מַמְלָכָה	his kingdom *mam·lak·**tô***	CST W/ 3MS SX	noun

This phrase, though easy to translate, has engendered great theological debate. Does it refer only to the literal, physical kingdom of Israel, fulfilled in the Millennium to come? Or does it refer to a spiritual, present-day reign in heaven? The text itself offers no solution.

9:6c[9:7c]	לְהָכִ֤ין אֹתָהּ֙ וּֽלְסַעֲדָ֔הּ

to establish it and to support it

לְהָכִין כון	to fix/establish *lə·hā·**kîn***	HIPH INF CST W/ PREP לְ	verb
אֹתָהּ אֵת	*(direct object marker)* it *'ō·**tāh***	--- W/ 3FS SX	particle
וּלְסַעֲדָהּ סעד	and to support/uphold it *û·lə·sa·'ă·**dāh***	QAL INF CST W/ CONJ וְ + PREP לְ + 3FS SX	verb

The 3fs suffix must refer to the kingdom, the nearest feminine noun. The child establishes and upholds the kingdom through his reign.

9:6d[9:7d]	בְּמִשְׁפָּ֖ט וּבִצְדָקָ֑ה

with justice and with righteousness

בְּמִשְׁפָּט מִשְׁפָּט	in/with justice/judgment *bə·miš·**pāṭ***	ABS W/ PREP בְּ	noun
וּבִצְדָקָה צְדָקָה	and in/with righteousness *û·viṣ·dā·**qâ***	ABS W/ CONJ וְ + PREP בְּ	noun

Preachers can easily contrast the less-than-ideal condition of their country or government with the perfectly ideal conditions of the messianic kingdom. A few news stories of corrupt politics will highlight the contrasting beauty of a perfectly just, perfectly righteous kingdom to come.

9:6e[9:7e]	מֵעַתָּ֖ה וְעַד־עוֹלָ֑ם

both now and forever.

מֵעַתָּה עַתָּה	from now *mē·ʿat·**tâ***	--- W/ PREP מִן	adv
וְעַד־ עַד	and until *wə·ʿad-*	--- W/ CONJ וְ	prep
עוֹלָם עוֹלָם	forever *ʿô·**lām***	ABS	noun

Isaiah speaks from the perspective of the inauguration of this future ideal reign with his use of the present orientation מֵעַתָּה ("from now"). Preachers may want to take a page from the prophet's book and imagine such a kingdom in the sermon.

9:6f[9:7f]	קִנְאַ֛ת יְהוָ֥ה צְבָא֖וֹת תַּעֲשֶׂה־זֹּֽאת׃

The zeal of YHWH of hosts will accomplish this!

קִנְאַת קִנְאָה	zeal/passion *qin·**ʾat***	CST	noun
יְהוָה יהוה	the Lord *YHWH*	ABS	noun

צְבָאֽוֹת צָבָא	hosts/armies *ṣə · vā · ʾôt*	ABS	noun
תַּעֲשֶׂה־ עשׂה	(it) will do *ta · ʿă · śe-*	QAL IMPF 3FS	verb
זֹּֽאת׃ זאת	this *zōʾt*	---	demonstr pron

Assurance of the prophecy's fulfillment is rooted in the passionate covenant commitment of the Lord himself. There is no room for doubt that all this will be fully and finally fulfilled, because God keeps his covenant promises.

From Text to Sermon

Big Idea. Jesus brings everlasting political and spiritual hope.

Avenues for Illustration and Application. Churches will likely have strong familiarity with the two verses popularly read each year during Christmastime: 9:5–6 [6–7]. This may present challenges to preachers, as they will be tempted to preach primarily or only these verses in exclusion of the rest of the context. Though 9:5–6 [6–7] certainly packs a christologically loaded punch, a focus on the entire passage produces a better-rounded expository sermon. One might extract the following principles from the text and use the following structural outline:

(1) God brings glory out of anguish (8:23 [9:1])

(2) God brings joy out of darkness (9:1–2 [2–3])

(3) God brings peace out of oppression (9:3–4 [4–5])

(4) Jesus brings everlasting political and spiritual hope (9:5–6 [6–7])

The first principle (God brings glory out of anguish) may be illustrated by childbirth. There is hardly a better example of glory springing from pain than the suffering that gives way to holding a newborn baby. The labor pains might last a few hours, perhaps even more than a day, but what glory comes as a result! This physical reality illustrates the spiritual reality inherent in this passage. Suffering prepares believers for glory.

Preachers can contextualize the second principle (God brings joy out of darkness) by playing off of areas in the world known for spiritual or political darkness. Saying that people who once walked in darkness will now experience great light is as radical as saying that the projects in New York will be transformed into a retirement community, or the red light district in Amsterdam will one day become a religious sanctuary, or North Korea will one day be known for free religious expression.

The verses that stand behind the third principle (9:3–4 [4–5]; God brings peace out of oppression) provide several built-in illustrations for preachers to utilize. The trifold yoke-staff-rod in v. 3 [4] all picture Israelites in slavery under foreign oppressors. Reflection on texts like Exod 2 to biblically illustrate the principle may help. The warfare imagery of v. 4 [5] may also lend itself to helpful analogies and examples.

Preachers should not forget to help the church understand the characteristics given to the child/son in the final two verses of the sermon. Again, the familiarity of the passage presents challenges to listeners to hear it afresh, but simple illustrations help bring to light the meaning of even the most familiar verses. Perhaps giving the analogy of "shouldering the responsibility" for something may help congregations understand the common phrase, "the government shall be upon his shoulder." The image of a child shouldering the responsibility of an entire government is quite the picture, but often missed by those who gloss over the text because they have heard it a thousand times.

Contrast the "wonderful counselor" with a terrible piece of advice given to you. Compare the "mighty/warrior God" with the mighty warriors of history—Alexander the Great, Nebuchadnezzar of Babylon, et al.—to magnify the lasting nature of God's future victory. Consider what everlasting peace really looks like—Fox News and CNN side by side, *both* reporting nothing but peace and love. It will take nothing short of God himself to pull it off! Most people cannot even imagine what a conflict-free life looks like, working at a job where you never feud with your co-workers, living in a house where you never fight with your spouse, going to a church where no one ever gets nasty with each other. May we all look forward to this time!

New Testament Connections. Isaiah 9 offers a multitude of New Testament connections, too many to elaborate on in any detail here. Preachers will need to determine which to include in the sermon.

Matthew 4:12–17 offers inspired comments on Isa 8:23 [9:1]. After Jesus' baptism and wilderness temptation, he leaves Nazareth and goes to Galilee, in the territory of Zebulun and Naphtali, and there officially begins his ministry of preaching the gospel. Matthew says that Jesus' ministry in Zebulun and Naphtali fulfills the prophecy of Isa 8:23 [9:1] (Matt 4:14–16). Jesus brought glory where there was formerly anguish. He healed the shame and contempt of these tribes with the gospel.

Preachers might use texts like Rom 8:18, 2 Cor 4:17, or 1 Pet 4:13 to illustrate the principle of glory from anguish. Texts like John 8:12 and 12:46 beautifully illuminate the power of Jesus to bring light to the darkness. Depending on one's ecclesiology and eschatology, passages like Dan 9, Rom 9–11, and Rev 7 may point to the kind of revival among God's people that Isaiah prophesies about here. Revelation 11:15 points to a fulfillment of the kind of kingdom envisioned in the closing verses of the paragraph in Isaiah (and again, depending on one's ecclesiology or eschatology, preachers might see this fulfilled now in the church or yet to come in the future).

ISAIAH 11:1–10

THE MESSIAH'S KINGDOM

In a world where so many things are falling apart, Isa 11 gives hope for the future. Israel was experiencing a time of extreme terror and anxiety, with the nation of Assyria looming in her midst. But God promised to keep a remnant of Jacob's seed alive (10:20–23) and to chop down the giant "tree" of Assyria (10:33–34). On the heels of those promises, Isaiah prophesies of a special deliverer from king David's descent (11:10) who will bring perfect righteousness, justice, and peace—extending even to the animal kingdom! This passage gives believers something beautiful to look forward to, something trustworthy to place our hope in, and someone worthy in whom to rest our faith.

LARGER LITERARY CONTEXT ▸ 10:33–11:16

11:1–5

1a וְיָצָ֥א חֹ֖טֶר מִגֶּ֣זַע יִשָׁ֑י

*wəyā**ṣā’** **ḥō**ṭer mig**gē**za‘ yi**šāy***

But a shoot will spring forth from the stem of Jesse,

1b וְנֵ֖צֶר מִשָּׁרָשָׁ֥יו יִפְרֶֽה׃

*wə**nē**ṣer miššārā**šāyw** yif**re**.*

and a branch from his roots will produce fruit.

2a וְנָחָ֥ה עָלָ֖יו ר֣וּחַ יְהוָ֑ה

*wənā**ḥâ** ‘ā**lāyw** **rû**aḥ YHWH*

And YHWH's spirit will rest upon him:

2b ר֧וּחַ חָכְמָ֣ה וּבִינָ֗ה

rû**aḥ ḥok**mâ** ûvî**nâ

the spirit of wisdom and understanding,

2c ר֤וּחַ עֵצָה֙ וּגְבוּרָ֔ה

rû**aḥ ‘ē**ṣâ** ûgəvû**râ

the spirit of counsel and power,

2d ר֥וּחַ דַּ֖עַת וְיִרְאַ֥ת יְהוָֽה׃

***rû**aḥ **da**‘at wəyir’**at** YHWH.*

a spirit of knowledge and a fear of YHWH.

3a וַהֲרִיח֖וֹ בְּיִרְאַ֣ת יְהוָ֑ה

*wahărî**ḥô** bəyir’**at** YHWH*

Also, the fear of YHWH is like a delightful smell to him,

3b וְלֹֽא־לְמַרְאֵ֤ה עֵינָיו֙ יִשְׁפּ֔וֹט

*wə**lō’**-ləmar’**ē** ‘ê**nāyw** yiš**pôṭ***

and he will not judge merely by external sight,

3c וְלֹֽא־לְמִשְׁמַ֥ע אָזְנָ֖יו יוֹכִֽיחַ׃

wəlōʾ-ləmišmaʿ ʾoznāyw yôḵîaḥ.

nor will he reprove based on rumors he hears.

4a וְשָׁפַ֤ט בְּצֶ֙דֶק֙ דַּלִּ֔ים

wəšāfaṭ bəṣedeq dallîm

But with perfect equity he will judge society's lowest,

4b וְהוֹכִ֥יחַ בְּמִישׁ֖וֹר לְעַנְוֵי־אָ֑רֶץ

wəhôḵîaḥ bəmîšôr ləʿanwê-ʾāreṣ

and he will reprove with uprightness the meek of the earth.

4c וְהִֽכָּה־אֶ֙רֶץ֙ בְּשֵׁ֣בֶט פִּ֔יו

wəhikkâ-ʾereṣ bəšēveṭ pîw

And he will smite the earth with the rod of his mouth,

4d וּבְר֥וּחַ שְׂפָתָ֖יו יָמִ֥ית רָשָֽׁע׃

ûvərûaḥ śəfātāyw yāmît rāšāʿ.

and with a puff of his breath he will kill the wicked.

5a וְהָ֥יָה צֶ֖דֶק אֵז֣וֹר מָתְנָ֑יו

wəhāyâ ṣedeq ʾēzôr motnāyw

And righteousness will be the belt of his pants,

5b וְהָאֱמוּנָ֖ה אֵז֥וֹר חֲלָצָֽיו׃

wəhāʾĕmûnâ ʾēzôr ḥălāṣāyw.

and steadfastness will be the belt of his loins.

1a	וְיָצָ֥א חֹ֖טֶר מִגֵּ֣זַע יִשָׁ֑י		
	But a shoot will spring forth from the stem of Jesse,		
וְיָצָ֥א יצא	and (it) will go out *wə·yā·ṣā'*	QAL WEQATAL 3MS	verb
חֹ֖טֶר חֹ֫טֶר	branch/shoot/rod *ḥō·ṭer*	ABS	noun
מִגֵּ֣זַע גֶּ֫זַע	from a stem *mig·gē·za'*	CST W/ PREP מִן	noun
יִשָׁ֑י יִשַׁי	Jesse *yi·šāy*	ABS	noun

The verse begins with a *weqatal* rather than a *wayyiqtol*. This, along with the agricultural tree imagery, should connect this oracle in the minds of the readers with the previous one. In 10:33–34, Isaiah prophesied that God would "lop off the boughs" and "cut down the thickets" of Assyria, there depicted as a tall tree and a forest. Isaiah 11:1 continues this prophecy by giving hope to Israel through a Davidic king to come. Preachers should carefully demonstrate the connection between Isa 10 and 11, not allowing the artificial chapter break to hinder the message of the prophet.

1b	וְנֵ֖צֶר מִשָּׁרָשָׁ֥יו יִפְרֶֽה׃		
	and a branch from his roots will produce fruit.		
וְנֵ֖צֶר נֵ֫צֶר	and a sprout/shoot/ branch *wə·nē·ṣer*	ABS W/ CONJ וְ	noun
מִשָּׁרָשָׁ֥יו שֹׁ֫רֶשׁ	from his/its roots *miš·šā·rā·šāyw*	CST W/ PREP מִן + 3MS SX	noun
יִפְרֶֽה׃ פרה	(it) will bear fruit *yif·re*	QAL IMPF 3MS	verb

Many commentators have noted that the fact that the shoot stems from the roots of *Jesse* slights Judah's current king (Ahaz) and represents some discontinuity with his dynasty (e.g., Oswalt 1986:278–79). "Branch/shoot" in 11:1 (נֵ֫צֶר) is not the same word as that translated "branch" in 4:2 (צֶמַח), though the contexts predict similar hope through a Davidic king to come. The different choice of words may be prophetic in that the one who fulfilled this prophecy—Jesus the Messiah—came from the ignoble town of Nazareth. Though the etymology is debated, there is some evidence that the word "Nazareth" may be related to נֵ֫צֶר, with a meaning akin to "Branchburg" (I owe this word to my professor and now colleague Bill Krewson, who drew it to my attention in an undergraduate Bible class on 2/21/05; see Hagner 1993:40–42 for an excellent discussion summarizing the scholarly opinions on the "Nazareth" wordplay). Jesus of Branchburg is the branch that comes from Jesse's roots. Preachers may want to cross-reference other similar prophetic passages such as Jer 23:5; 33:15; Ezek 34:23–24; Hos 3:5.

2a	וְנָחָה עָלָיו רוּחַ יְהוָה
	And YHWH's spirit will rest upon him:

Hebrew	Gloss	Parsing	POS
וְנָחָה נוח	and (it) will rest *wə·nā·ḥâ*	QAL WEQATAL 3FS	verb
עָלָיו עַל	upon him *ʿā·lāyw*	--- W/ 3MS SX	prep
רוּחַ רוּחַ	spirit/Spirit *rû·aḥ*	CST	noun
יְהוָה יהוה	the LORD *YHWH*	ABS	noun

We left "spirit" translated without the capitalization, though we recognize it may (likely) refer to the third member of the Trinity. The decision to translate as such should not dissuade the interpreter or preacher from such an understanding of the text; rather, it leaves the ambiguity of the original Hebrew intact and allows individuals to make their own decisions regarding what exactly Isaiah refers to here. The verb "rest" (נוח) is used with "spirit" in Num 11:25–26 as a clear reference to the Holy Spirit. However, the "spirit" of Elijah "rested" upon Elisha in 2 Kgs 2:15, a reference not to the deity but to the prophet's power. The present text in Isaiah emphasizes the blessedness of the coming Messiah, empowered by God himself.

2b רֽוּחַ חָכְמָה וּבִינָה

the spirit of wisdom and understanding,

רֽוּחַ רוּחַ	spirit/Spirit ***rû***·*aḥ*	CST	noun
חָכְמָה חָכְמָה	wisdom *ḥok*·***mâ***	ABS	noun
וּבִינָה בִּינָה	and understanding *û*·*vî*·***nâ***	ABS W/ CONJ וְ	noun

Preachers should not feel the need to differentiate too particularly between some of these pairings, as some might even be hendiadys (e.g., "wise understanding"). Instead, focus on the overall meaning behind each phrase: the Messiah will enjoy a depth of wisdom and understanding like no other ruler in human history.

2c רֽוּחַ עֵצָה וּגְבוּרָה

the spirit of counsel and power,

רֽוּחַ רוּחַ	spirit/Spirit ***rû***·*aḥ*	CST	noun
עֵצָה עֵצָה	counsel/advice *ʿē*·***ṣâ***	ABS	noun
וּגְבוּרָה גְּבוּרָה	and strength/might *û*·*gə*·*vû*·***râ***	ABS W/ CONJ וְ	noun

The pairing here may seem odd at first until one recognizes the usefulness of proper counsel in application to one's strength. The Messiah will use his power correctly, always in proper measure and directed appropriately. He is not only omnipotent to accomplish whatever he desires to do; he also applies that ability correctly.

2d רֽוּחַ דַּעַת וְיִרְאַת יְהוָה׃

a spirit of knowledge and a fear of YHWH.

רֽוּחַ רוּחַ	spirit/Spirit ***rû***·*aḥ*	CST	noun

דָּ֫עַת דַּ֫עַת	knowledge *da·ʿat*	ABS	noun
וְיִרְאַ֖ת יִרְאָה	and a fear *wə·yir·ʾat*	CST W/ CONJ וְ	noun
יְהוָֽה׃ יהוה	the LORD *YHWH*	ABS	noun

This phrase recalls the key statement in Prov 1:7a: "The fear of the LORD is the beginning of knowledge" (ESV). To fear the Lord is to obey him out of reverent worship. One demonstrates a fear of God through obedience to his word (cf. Ps 111:10; Eccl 12:13).

3a וַהֲרִיח֖וֹ בְּיִרְאַ֣ת יְהוָ֑ה

Also, the fear of YHWH is like a delightful smell to him,

וַהֲרִיח֖וֹ ריח	and his smell/ enjoyment/delight *wa·hă·rî·ḥô*	HIPH INF CST W/ CONJ וַ + 3MS SX	verb
בְּיִרְאַ֣ת יִרְאָה	in fear *bə·yir·ʾat*	CST W/ PREP בְּ	noun
יְהוָ֑ה יהוה	the LORD *YHWH*	ABS	noun

The word וַהֲרִיחוֹ literally refers to enjoying a wonderful smell, like a perfume, or when you come home to a house that smells like brownies. The imagery derives from Levitical sacrifices, where the noun form of the word is often translated as a "soothing/pleasing aroma" (e.g., Lev 1:9; 2:2; 3:5; etc.). The Messiah so delights in obeying/fearing the Lord that it is akin to a pleasing sacrifice, or the scent of a well-cooked meal.

3b וְלֹֽא־לְמַרְאֵ֤ה עֵינָיו֙ יִשְׁפּ֔וֹט

and he will not judge merely by external sight,

וְלֹֽא־ לֹא	and not *wə·lōʾ-*	--- W/ CONJ וְ	particle

לְמַרְאֵה מַרְאֶה	towards sight/ appearance *lə·mar·ʾē*	CST W/ PREP לְ	noun
עֵינָיו עַיִן	his eyes *ʿê·**nāyw***	CST W/ 3MS SX	noun
יִשְׁפּוֹט שׁפט	he will judge *yiš·**pôṭ***	QAL IMPF 3MS	verb

Though the Hebrew elides the idea, the context demands the understanding that it is not *merely* by sight or hearing that he will judge and reprove. He will surely make use of these faculties, but unlike human judges, his evaluation will go far beyond the five senses.

3c וְלֹֽא־לְמִשְׁמַ֥ע אָזְנָ֖יו יוֹכִֽיחַ׃

nor will he reprove based on rumors he hears.

וְלֹֽא־ לֹא	and not *wə·**lō**ʾ-*	--- W/ CONJ וְ	particle
לְמִשְׁמַ֥ע מִשְׁמָע	towards rumor/hearsay *lə·miš·**ma**ʿ*	CST W/ PREP לְ	noun
אָזְנָ֖יו אֹזֶן	his ears *ʾoz·**nāyw***	CST W/ 3MS SX	noun
יוֹכִֽיחַ׃ יכח	he will reprove/decide *yô·**ḵî**·aḥ*	HIPH IMPF 3MS	verb

Lines 3b and 3c are perfectly balanced in Hebrew:

- a — and not towards sight
  - b — his eyes
    - c — he will judge
- a′ — and not towards rumor
  - b′ — his ears
    - c′ — he will reprove

The symmetry heightens the emphasis that reveals how the Messiah will judge and evaluate, and how common/earthly rulers typically judge and evaluate. “Judge” (שׁפט) and “reprove” (יכח) are both courtroom terms.

4a	וְשָׁפַט בְּצֶדֶק דַּלִּים

But with perfect equity he will judge society's lowest,

Hebrew	Gloss	Parsing	POS
וְשָׁפַט שׁפט	and he will judge *wə·šā·**faṭ***	QAL WEQATAL 3MS	verb
בְּצֶדֶק צֶדֶק	with righteousness *bə·**ṣe**·deq*	ABS W/ PREP בְּ	noun
דַּלִּים דַּל	lowly/weak/poor *dal·**lîm***	MP SUBST	adj

Notice how Isaiah repeats the two verbs from 3b and 3c here (שׁפט and יכח), this time with application to the lowest social classes of society. Preachers must be careful when contextualizing this so as not to offend those who might find themselves in such positions (e.g., referencing people who work in a fast-food chain or big-box store, or people who rely on welfare or subsidized income, can be demoralizing for listeners in such positions). Perhaps an illustration from how Jesus treated the lower social classes will suffice (cf. Luke 8:43–48).

4b	וְהוֹכִיחַ בְּמִישׁוֹר לְעַנְוֵי־אָרֶץ

and he will reprove with uprightness the meek of the earth.

Hebrew	Gloss	Parsing	POS
וְהוֹכִיחַ יכח	and he will decide/ reprove *wə·hô·**ḵî**·aḥ*	HIPH WEQATAL 3MS	verb
בְּמִישׁוֹר מִישׁוֹר	with/in uprightness/ level ground *bə·mî·**šôr***	ABS W/ PREP בְּ	noun
לְעַנְוֵי־ עָנָו	to poor/afflicted/humble *lə·ʿan·wê-*	CST W/ PREP לְ	noun
אָרֶץ אֶרֶץ	land/earth *ʾ**ā**·reṣ*	ABS	noun

The word translated here "meek" (עָנָו) can also mean "afflicted" or even "humble." Whoever it refers to, they occupy a lower position in the eyes of the world.

4c	וְהִכָּה־אֶ֙רֶץ֙ בְּשֵׁ֣בֶט פִּ֔יו

And he will smite the earth with the rod of his mouth,

וְהִכָּה־ נכה	and he will smite *wə·**hik**·kâ-*	HIPH WEQATAL 3MS	verb
אֶ֙רֶץ֙ אֶרֶץ	land/earth *ʾ**e**·reṣ*	ABS	noun
בְּשֵׁ֣בֶט שֵׁבֶט	with rod/staff/club *bə·**šē**·veṭ*	CST W/ PREP בְּ	noun
פִּ֔יו פֶּה	his mouth ***pîw***	CST W/ 3MS SX	noun

Notice the immediate repetition of the word "earth/land" in this and the preceding clause. Though v. 9 refers to God's holy mountain in the land of Israel, the references in vv. 10a, 11, and 12 appear to extend the scope of God's activity to the whole earth. Other possible references to this text also seem to interpretively expand it to the entire world (2 Thess 2:8; Rev 19:15).

4d	וּבְר֥וּחַ שְׂפָתָ֖יו יָמִ֥ית רָשָֽׁע׃

and with a puff of his breath he will kill the wicked.

וּבְר֥וּחַ רוּחַ	and with the breath/ spirit *û·və·**rû**·aḥ*	CST W/ CONJ וְ + PREP בְּ	noun
שְׂפָתָ֖יו שָׂפָה	his lips *śə·fā·**tāyw***	CST W/ 3MS SX	noun
יָמִ֥ית מות	he will kill *yā·**mît***	HIPH IMPF 3MS	verb
רָשָֽׁע׃ רָשָׁע	wicked *rā·**šāʿ***	MS SUBST	adj

"Spirit" may be used here ironically, as the fourfold usage in v. 4 appeared to be a very positive application of the Lord's spirit. Here we see the terrifying application of Messiah's spirit of "counsel and power."

5a	וְהָיָה צֶּדֶק אֵזוֹר מָתְנָיו

And righteousness will be the belt of his pants,

וְהָיָה היה	and it will be *wə·hā·yâ*	QAL WEQATAL 3MS	verb
צֶּדֶק צֶדֶק	righteousness *ṣe·deq*	ABS	noun
אֵזוֹר אֵזוֹר	waistcloth *ʾē·zôr*	CST	noun
מָתְנָיו מָתְנַיִם	his hips/loins *mot·nāyw*	CST W/ 3MS SX	noun

Most translations gloss the term “belt” (אֵזוֹר), but the word may actually refer to clothing worn *under* the robe (what we would normally call underwear). Either way, the item is essential to the clothing of an Israelite. Preachers can anachronistically refer to a belt around one’s pants, but must keep in mind that Israelites rarely wore pants but typically dressed with a robe or tunic tied around the waist.

5b	וְהָאֱמוּנָה אֵזוֹר חֲלָצָיו׃

and steadfastness will be the belt of his loins.

וְהָאֱמוּנָה אֱמוּנָה	and steadfastness/ faithfulness *wə·hā·ʾĕ·mû·nâ*	ABS W/ CONJ וְ + DEF. ART.	noun
אֵזוֹר אֵזוֹר	waistcloth *ʾē·zôr*	CST	noun
חֲלָצָיו׃ חָלָץ	his loins *ḥă·lā·ṣāyw*	CST W/ 3MS SX	noun

The words צֶדֶק (“righteousness”) and אֱמוּנָה (“steadfastness”) are used together in Pss 96:13; 119:75, 138; Prov 12:17; and Isa 59:4. The references from Psalms show a clear link between God’s judgment/discipline and his righteousness and steadfastness.

11:6–9

6a וְגָר זְאֵב עִם־כֶּבֶשׂ

*wə**gār** zə'**ēv** 'im-**keveś***

And these shall sojourn together: the wolf with the lamb,

6b וְנָמֵר עִם־גְּדִי יִרְבָּץ

*wənā**mēr** 'im-gə**dî** yir**bāṣ***

and the leopard with the baby goat: they will sleep in the same bed!

6c וְעֵגֶל וּכְפִיר וּמְרִיא יַחְדָּו

*wə'**ēgel** ûḵə**fîr** ûmə**rî'** yaḥ**dāw***

Also a calf and a lion and even a fattened calf—all together!

6d וְנַעַר קָטֹן נֹהֵג בָּם׃

*wə**na**'ar qā**ṭōn** nō**hēg** **bām**.*

And a small child shall lead them all.

7a וּפָרָה וָדֹב תִּרְעֶינָה

*ûfā**râ** wā**dōv** tir'**ênâ***

And a cow and a bear—they will graze!

7b יַחְדָּו יִרְבְּצוּ יַלְדֵיהֶן

*yaḥ**dāw** yirbə**ṣû** yal**dêhen***

Together all their young will sleep in the same bed,

7c וְאַרְיֵה כַּבָּקָר יֹאכַל־תֶּבֶן׃

*wə'ar**yē** kabbā**qār** **yō**'ḵal-**teven**.*

and the lion will eat straw, just like the ox.

8a וְשִׁעֲשַׁע יוֹנֵק עַל־חֻר פָּתֶן

*wəši'**ăša**' yô**nēq** 'al-**ḥur** **pā**ten*

And a toddler will play right over the hole of a cobra,

8b וְעַל֙ מְא֣וּרַ֣ת צִפְעוֹנִ֔י

*wəʿ**al** məʾû**rat** ṣif**ônî***

and over the den of a viper

8c גָּמ֖וּל יָד֥וֹ הָדָֽה׃

*gā**mûl** yā**dô** hā**dâ**.*

the weaned child will stick his hand.

9a לֹא־יָרֵ֥עוּ וְלֹא־יַשְׁחִ֖יתוּ

*l**ō**ʾ-yā**rē**ʿû wəl**ō**ʾ-yaš**ḥî**tû*

They will neither harm nor ruin

9b בְּכָל־הַ֣ר קָדְשִׁ֑י

*bəḵol-**har** qod**šî***

anything in all my holy mountain,

9c כִּֽי־מָלְאָ֣ה הָאָ֗רֶץ דֵּעָה֙ אֶת־יְהוָ֔ה

*k**î**-mālə**ʾâ** hā**ʾā**reṣ dē**ʿâ** ʾet-YHWH*

for the earth will be filled with the knowledge of YHWH

9d כַּמַּ֖יִם לַיָּ֥ם מְכַסִּֽים׃

*ka**ma**yim lay**yām** məḵas**sîm**.*

just like the waters cover the oceans.

6a	וְגָ֤ר זְאֵב֙ עִם־כֶּ֔בֶשׂ		
And these shall sojourn together: the wolf with the lamb,			
וְגָר גור	and (he will) sojourn *wə · **gār***	QAL WEQATAL 3MS	verb
זְאֵב֙ זְאֵב	wolf *zə · **ʾēv***	ABS	noun

עִם־	with	---	prep
עִם	*ʿim-*		
כֶּ֫בֶשׂ	lamb	ABS	noun
כֶּ֫בֶשׂ	***ke***·*veś*		

"Sojourn" (גור) implies more than a quick meeting; it indicates a longer journey together. Preachers will need to determine whether this passage speaks metaphorically or literally. They should proceed with proper humility and respect for the other position, on whichever side they fall. The peaceful coexistence within the animal kingdom (and between humans and animals) depicts a future ideal resembling a return to Eden.

6b **וְנָמֵ֖ר עִם־גְּדִ֣י יִרְבָּ֑ץ**

and the leopard with the baby goat: they will sleep in the same bed!

וְנָמֵ֖ר	and leopard	ABS W/ CONJ וְ	noun
נָמֵר	*wə·nā·**mēr***		
עִם־	with	---	prep
עִם	*ʿim-*		
גְּדִ֣י	young goat	ABS	noun
גְּדִי	*gə·**dî***		
יִרְבָּ֑ץ	(he) will lie down	QAL IMPF 3MS	verb
רבץ	*yir·**bāṣ***		

The verb positioned at the end of the sentence has a surprising effect on the reader. What will the leopard and young goat do? Wait for it . . . they will *lie down together!*

6c **וְעֵ֨גֶל וּכְפִ֤יר וּמְרִיא֙ יַחְדָּ֔ו**

Also a calf and a lion and even a fattened calf—all together!

וְעֵ֨גֶל	and a calf	ABS W/ CONJ וְ	noun
עֵ֫גֶל	*wə·**ʿē**·gel*		
וּכְפִ֤יר	and lion	ABS W/ CONJ וְ	noun
כְּפִיר	*û·ḵə·**fîr***		

וּמְרִיא מְרִיא	and fattened calf *û · mə · rî'*	ABS W/ CONJ וְ	noun
יַחְדָּו יַחְדָּו	together *yaḥ · dāw*	---	adv

"Fattened calf" (מְרִיא) usually refers to an animal ready for slaughter or sacrifice—in other words, one prime for the picking for a hungry lion. Sandwiching the lion between "calf" and "fattened calf" magnifies the peace that will characterize the Messiah's rule.

6d **וְנַ֥עַר קָטֹ֖ן נֹהֵ֥ג בָּֽם׃**

And a small child shall lead them all.

וְנַעַר נַעַר	and boy/lad/youth *wə · na · 'ar*	ABS W/ CONJ וְ	noun
קָטֹן קָטֹן	little/small *qā · ṭōn*	MS ATTR	adj
נֹהֵג נהג	driving/leading *nō · hēg*	QAL PTCP MS	verb
בָּם׃ בְּ	with them *bām*	--- W/ 3MP SX	prep

Isaiah could have made his point clear by only using נַעַר ("boy/lad/youth"), which by itself denotes a young/small boy. By adding the adjective קָטֹן ("little/small"), he again manages to heighten the coexistence of unlikely creatures.

7a **וּפָרָ֤ה וָדֹב֙ תִּרְעֶ֔ינָה**

And a cow and a bear—they will graze!

וּפָרָה פָּרָה	and a cow *û · fā · râ*	ABS W/ CONJ וְ	noun
וָדֹב דֹּב	and a bear *wā · dōv*	ABS W/ CONJ וְ	noun
תִּרְעֶינָה רעה	they will pasture/graze *tir · 'ɛ̄ · nâ*	QAL IMPF 3FP	verb

By placing the verb after the dual subject, Isaiah throws an element of surprise into the phrase. The imagery of a bear grazing next to a cow should evoke some humor.

7b	יַחְדָּו יִרְבְּצוּ יַלְדֵיהֶן		
	Together all their young will sleep in the same bed,		
יַחְדָּו יַחְדָּו	together *yaḥ·**dāw***	---	adv
יִרְבְּצוּ רבץ	(they) will lie down *yir·bə·**ṣû***	QAL IMPF 3MP	verb
יַלְדֵיהֶן יֶלֶד	their children/sons/boys *yal·dê·**hen***	CST W/ 3FP SX	noun

The adverb "together" (יַחְדָּו) is grammatically unnecessary. Its inclusion here gives emphasis on the joint nature of their activity. They will not lie in separate beds, but rather sleep in the same exact place, without conflict. Parents of toddlers know how difficult this task can be even with humans!

7c	וְאַרְיֵה כַּבָּקָר יֹאכַל־תֶּבֶן׃		
	and the lion will eat straw, just like the ox.		
וְאַרְיֵה אַרְיֵה	and lion *wə·ʾar·**yē***	ABS W/ CONJ וְ	noun
כַּבָּקָר בָּקָר	as the ox *kab·bā·**qār***	ABS W/ PREP כְּ + DEF. ART.	noun
יֹאכַל־ אכל	(he) shall eat ***yōʾ**·ḵal-*	QAL IMPF 3MS	verb
תֶּבֶן׃ תֶּבֶן	straw ***te**·ven*	ABS	noun

Like the image of the bear grazing with the cow, so goes the image of the lion eating straw like an ox. The *shalom* of Messiah's kingdom will be so extensive that the most ferocious of beasts will act like the most docile livestock.

8a	וְשִׁעֲשַׁע יוֹנֵק עַל־חֻר פָּתֶן

And a toddler will play right over the hole of a cobra,

וְשִׁעֲשַׁע שׁעע	and (he) will delight in/ take sport in *wə·ši·ʿă·**šaʿ***	PILPEL WEQATAL 3MS	verb
יוֹנֵק ינק	infant/child *yô·**nēq***	QAL PTCP MS	verb
עַל־ עַל	over/upon *ʿal-*	---	prep
חֻר חֻר	hole ***ḥur***	CST	noun
פָּתֶן פֶּתֶן	venomous snake ***pā**·ten*	ABS	noun

"Infant child" (ינק) properly refers to a child still nursing. It was common for Israelite mothers to nurse their children into their toddler years. "Cobra" (פֶּתֶן) is a generic word referring to any kind of venomous snake.

8b	וְעַל מְאוּרַת צִפְעוֹנִי

and over the den of a viper

וְעַל עַל	and over/upon *wə·**ʿal***	--- W/ CONJ וְ	prep
מְאוּרַת מְאוּרָה	hole *mə·ʾû·**rat***	CST	noun
צִפְעוֹנִי צִפְעוֹנִי	viper *ṣif·ʿô·**nî***	ABS	noun

8c	גָּמוּל יָדוֹ הָדָה׃

the weaned child will stick his hand.

גָּמוּל גמל	he who is weaned *gā·**mûl***	QAL PASS PTCP MS	verb
יָדוֹ יָד	his hand *yā·**dô***	CST W/ 3MS SX	noun

הָדָה׃ הדה	(he) stretched out *hā·dâ*	QAL PF 3MS	verb

"The weaned child" (גמל) is a participle referring to a child who is slightly older than a יוֹנֵק ("infant child"), but not by much. The two halves of v. 8 are meant to parallel one another in chiastic form.

9a לֹא־יָרֵעוּ וְלֹא־יַשְׁחִיתוּ

They will neither harm nor ruin

לֹא־ לֹא	not *lō'-*	---	particle
יָרֵעוּ רעע	they will harm *yā·rē·'û*	HIPH IMPF 3MP	verb
וְלֹא־ לֹא	and not *wə·lō'-*	--- W/ CONJ וְ	particle
יַשְׁחִיתוּ שׁחת	they will ruin/spoil *yaš·ḥî·tû*	HIPH IMPF 3MP	verb

Hurt and ruin characterize the fallenness of creation. Isaiah pictures a reversal of the curse of Gen 3.

9b בְּכָל־הַר קָדְשִׁי

anything in all my holy mountain,

בְּכָל־ כֹּל	in all *bə·kol-*	CST W/ PREP בְּ	noun
הַר הַר	mountain/hill *har*	CST	noun
קָדְשִׁי קֹדֶשׁ	my holy *qod·šî*	CST W/ 1CS SX	noun

The holy mountain of the Lord is likely a reference to Jerusalem, which by metonymy represents all Israel, or better, the entire universe. "All" (כֹּל) casts a comprehensive shadow here. Just as "all" creation suffers now under the effects of the curse, so also "all" creation will enjoy complete restoration one day under the Messiah's renewed kingdom.

9c	כִּֽי־מָלְאָ֣ה הָאָ֗רֶץ דֵּעָה֙ אֶת־יְהוָ֔ה

for the earth will be filled with the knowledge of YHWH

כִּֽי־ כִּי	for *kî-*	---	conj
מָלְאָ֣ה מלא	(she) filled *mā·lə·ʾâ*	QAL PF 3FS	verb
הָאָ֗רֶץ אֶ֫רֶץ	the earth *hā·ʾā·reṣ*	ABS W/ DEF. ART.	noun
דֵּעָה֙ דֵּעָה	knowledge *dē·ʿâ*	ABS	noun
אֶת־ אֵת	*(direct object marker)* *ʾet-*	---	particle
יְהוָ֔ה יהוה	the LORD *YHWH*	ABS	noun

Preachers will want to connect the "spirit of knowledge" in v. 2 with the "knowledge of YHWH" here. The same s/Spirit that gave the Messiah perfect knowledge will give the world perfect knowledge. Note also the function of כִּי—the *reason* that the animals will peacefully coexist is because the fullness of the knowledge of God covers the land. The more one knows God, the more that experiential, relational knowledge drives out evil and strife.

9d	כַּמַּ֖יִם לַיָּ֥ם מְכַסִּֽים׃

just like the waters cover the oceans.

כַּמַּ֖יִם מַ֫יִם	as the waters *ka·ma·yim*	ABS W/ PREP כְּ + DEF. ART.	noun
לַיָּ֥ם יָם	to the sea *lay·yām*	ABS W/ PREP לְ + DEF. ART.	noun
מְכַסִּֽים׃ כסה	(they) are covering *mə·ḵas·sîm*	PI PTCP MP	verb

11:10

10a וְהָיָה בַּיּוֹם הַהוּא

wəhāyâ bayyôm hahû'

And it will come to pass on that day

10b שֹׁרֶשׁ יִשַׁי אֲשֶׁר עֹמֵד לְנֵס עַמִּים

šoreš yišay 'ăšer 'ōmēd lənēs 'ammîm

the root of Jesse—who stands as a sign for the peoples—

10c אֵלָיו גּוֹיִם יִדְרֹשׁוּ

'ēlāyw gôyim yidrōšû

the nations will seek him,

10d וְהָיְתָה מְנֻחָתוֹ כָּבוֹד׃

wəhāyətâ mənūḥātô kāvôd.

and his place of rest will be glorious.

10a וְהָיָה בַּיּוֹם הַהוּא

And it will come to pass on that day

וְהָיָה היה	and it will be *wə·hā·yâ*	QAL WEQATAL 3MS	verb
בַּיּוֹם יוֹם	on (the) day *bay·yôm*	ABS W/ PREP בְּ + DEF. ART.	noun
הַהוּא הוּא	that *ha·hû'*	--- W/ DEF. ART.	demonstr pron

The challenge here concerns the time of "that day." The phrase appears often in Isaiah and other prophets (2:11, 17, 20; 3:7, 18; 4:1–2; 5:30; 7:18, 20–21, 23, etc.). The immediate context must always control interpretation of this phrase. See below under "New Testament Connections" for a brief discussion on how preachers can handle the timing of this passage.

10b	שֹׁ֣רֶשׁ יִשַׁ֗י אֲשֶׁ֤ר עֹמֵד֙ לְנֵ֣ס עַמִּ֔ים		
	the root of Jesse—who stands as a sign for the peoples—		
שֹׁ֣רֶשׁ שֹׁ֫רֶשׁ	root *šo·reš*	CST	noun
יִשַׁ֗י יִשַׁי	Jesse *yi·šay*	ABS	noun
אֲשֶׁ֤ר אֲשֶׁר	who *ʾă·šer*	---	relative pron
עֹמֵד֙ עמד	is standing *ʿō·mēd*	QAL PTCP MS	verb
לְנֵ֣ס נֵס	to a sign/standard *lə·nēs*	CST W/ PREP לְ	noun
עַמִּ֔ים עַם	people/peoples *ʿam·mîm*	ABS	noun

The root of Jesse will act like a banner or flag in the midst of war, raised high above everyone's heads so they can see. He will be a signal of peace and victory, a standard around which all will rally. Preachers can draw attention to the "peoples," which broadens the scope of the Messiah's influence to not only God's ethnic people Israel, but to other nations as well (cf. 10c).

10c	אֵלָ֖יו גּוֹיִ֣ם יִדְרֹ֑שׁוּ		
	the nations will seek him,		
אֵלָ֖יו אֶל	to him *ʾē·lāyw*	--- W/ 3MS SX	prep
גּוֹיִ֣ם גּוֹי	nations *gô·yim*	ABS	noun
יִדְרֹ֑שׁוּ דרשׁ	(they) will seek *yid·rō·šû*	QAL IMPF 3MP	verb

“Seek” (דרשׁ) indicates that the nations will look to the Messiah for guidance, wisdom, and direction. Preachers will not want to miss the most radical change of all in this text. It is remarkable enough that the lion will lie down with the lamb and the child will play with the serpent; it is beyond remarkable that once-pagan Gentiles will stream to a Davidic king, seeking purpose and hope and peace.

10d	וְהָיְתָה מְנֻחָתוֹ כָּבוֹד׃
	and his place of rest will be glorious.

וְהָיְתָה היה	and (it) will be *wə·hā·yə·**tâ***	QAL WEQATAL 3FS	verb
מְנֻחָתוֹ מְנוּחָה	his rest/resting place *mə·nū·ḥā·**tô***	CST W/ 3MS SX	noun
כָּבוֹד׃ כָּבוֹד	honor/glory *kā·**vôd***	ABS	noun

“His resting place” (מְנֻחָתוֹ) probably refers to the land of Israel, or to Jerusalem specifically. This final line indicates that the land itself will be transformed by the reign of the Messiah. The curse’s effects will reverse course and earth will revert to an Edenic state.

From Text to Sermon

- ***Big Idea.*** Remain righteous while longing for the Messiah's reign.

- ***Avenues for Illustration and Application.*** In application of these main ideas, first, preachers can help the church recognize that such a messianic kingdom gives believers hope for a better tomorrow. Isaiah 11 does not hang its hat on present-day hope. The condition of our world frustrates us, but knowing that Jesus has something much better in store gives us hope. Second, the Messiah's righteousness and faithfulness motivates our own godliness. Jesus sets the ideal—belted with righteousness, faithfulness, seeking the good of the meek and poor. That is what true religion looks like (Jas 1:27). It stretches us to measure ourselves against these future-kingdom ideals. Third, the Messiah's kingdom challenges us to live prepared for his return. As we long for the kind of kingdom pictured in Isa 11, we also keep in mind that at any moment, Christ's return can usher in this eternal future (1 Cor 15:52; 1 Thess 4:16–17). All believers should be urged to live considering this eschatological reality.

  Isaiah 11 presents several opportunities to illustrate the text using the language, imagery, and metaphors in the text. The opening metaphor of the shoot stemming from Jesse's root suggests agricultural imagery, especially in connection with the hacked forest of 10:33–34. Preachers can use projected pictures or time-lapse videos to capture the attention of the listeners. A few illustrations that can help explain the concept of the "scent" of the fear of the Lord (11:3a; see commentary) might be a husband coming in from work to the smell of a home-cooked meal, or walking into a bakery and enjoying the aroma of freshly baked goodies. In the same way these scents please us, fearing God pleases the Messiah.

  The messianic kingdom and messianic moral character should stand in stark contrast with today's rulers. Preachers should always use caution when "calling out" modern presidents, governors, and rulers (as they should treat them biblically, with respect and honor, no matter what their politics; Rom 13:1–7; 1 Pet 2:13–17), but carefully giving examples of failed policies, broken justice, and imperfect harmony will stir up a greater longing for the perfect ruler, perfect justice, and perfect harmony of this passage. We do not know what Isa 11 leadership is like. We have never experienced it. No one will be favored because of their social or economic status, the color of their skin, their family connections (or lack thereof). Christ's judgment will be perfect in all ways.

Likewise, we do not know what perfect harmony among the animal kingdom and between humans and animals looks like. Preachers can draw upon listeners' knowledge of National Geographic specials and Shark Week and other such programming that highlights the ferocity and dangers of wild predators, then give people freedom to imagine (along with the text) what this will feel like. You can snuggle up with a lion. You can high-five a grizzly bear. Children can play peak-a-boo with a viper. It will be the Garden of Eden all over again.

Perhaps extend these images to make relevant illustrations and applications. The Messiah's kingdom will be like Republicans and Democrats seeing eye to eye on all issues. It will be like Michigan and Michigan State wearing the same colors. It will be like Calvinists and Arminians talking about salvation without arguing. We can hardly imagine such harmony!

New Testament Connections. Isaiah 11 focuses on the coming Davidic king's reign (the Messiah's kingdom). The most challenging part of this for many preachers may be to determine their own theological-eschatological understanding of the prophet's message. Does Isaiah refer to a future, literal Millennial kingdom? Does he speak in metaphors and symbols of a spiritual reality experienced by the body of Christ now? Other texts in the New Testament will likely need to be examined in order to make any headway toward an answer (preachers might begin by examining texts such as 1 Cor 15:22–25 and Rev 20).

However, a preacher need not have everything "figured out" before preaching this text. The meaning of such prophecy is clear, even if the timing and exact mode of fulfillment remains elusive. In 11:1–3a, Isaiah writes that the Messiah's reign will be characterized by perfect wisdom; 11:3b–5 demonstrates that the Messiah's reign will be characterized by perfect godliness; 11:6–9 reveals the Messiah's reign will be characterized by perfect harmony. And 11:10 pictures the Messiah's reign characterized by widespread salvation and restoration.

Other New Testament passages may help demonstrate to the church that Jesus is indeed the fulfillment of this messianic prophecy from Isaiah. Luke 4:14–21 shows Jesus preaching in the power of the Spirit (4:14, 18; cf. 4:1), even quoting from Isa 61:1 to show that he fulfills the hopes of the prophet. Acts 13:22–23 indicates that Jesus is the fulfillment of Israelite hope, the descendant of David. Revelation 5:5 and 22:16 explicitly call Jesus "the root of David." Romans 15:12 quotes our text from Isaiah and applies it directly to Jesus. The New Testament message is unanimous: Jesus is the root of Jesse, fulfilling the hopes of the prophecy in Isa 11.

THE FALL OF THE KING OF BABYLON

Chapters 13–23 of Isaiah are typically known as "The Woes against the Nations." Each chapter focuses on one or more nations surrounding Israel. God condemns these nations for their sins and then declares the appropriate judgment coming against them. Though these oracles concerned foreign nations, they were written for the ears of the Israelites as a warning to God's people not to fall into similar sin. Here in Isa 14, God sets his sights on Babylon. The pride of the Babylonian king led to his downfall. In graphic fashion, Isaiah illustrates the consequences of arrogance and gives a shocking example of the common proverb: God humbles the exalted and exalts the humble.

LARGER LITERARY CONTEXT › 13:1–14:23

12a אֵיךְ נָפַלְתָּ מִשָּׁמַיִם

*ʾ**ēḵ** nā**fal**tā miššā**ma**yim*

How you fell from heaven,

12b הֵילֵל בֶּן־שָׁחַר

*hê**lēl** ben-**šā**ḥar*

O Shining One, Son of Dawn!

12c נִגְדַּעְתָּ לָאָרֶץ

*nig**da**ʿtā lāʾ**ā**reṣ*

You have been hewn down to the earth,

12d חוֹלֵשׁ עַל־גּוֹיִם׃

*ḥô**lēš** ʿal-gô**yim**.*

you who have submitted the nations!

13a וְאַתָּה אָמַרְתָּ בִלְבָבְךָ

*wəʾat**tâ** ʾā**mar**tā bilvāvə**ḵā***

But you—you said in your heart,

13b הַשָּׁמַיִם אֶעֱלֶה

*hašš**āma**yim ʾeʿĕ**le***

“To the heavens I will go up,

13c מִמַּעַל לְכוֹכְבֵי־אֵל

*mim**ma**ʿal lə**ḵô**ḵəvê-ʾ**ēl***

above even the stars of God

13d אָרִים כִּסְאִי

*ʾā**rîm** kisʾ**î***

I will raise my throne,

13e וְאֵשֵׁב בְּהַר־מוֹעֵד

*wəʾē**šēv** bəhar-mô**ʿēd***

and I will sit on the mountain of meeting

13f בְּיַרְכְּתֵי צָפוֹן׃

*bəyarkə**tê** ṣā**fôn**.*

in the uttermost parts of the north!

14a אֶעֱלֶה עַל־בָּמֳתֵי עָב

*ʾeʿĕ**le** ʿal-**bā**mŏtê **ʿāv***

I will go up above the high places of the clouds!

14b אֶדַּמֶּה לְעֶלְיוֹן׃

*ʾeddam**me** ləʿel**yôn**.*

I will make myself like the Most High God!"

15a אַךְ אֶל־שְׁאוֹל תּוּרָד

ʾaḵ** ʾel-šə**ʾôl** tû**rād

On the contrary, you will be led down to the grave,

15b אֶל־יַרְכְּתֵי־בוֹר׃

*ʾel-yarkətê-**vôr**.*

to the uttermost parts of the pit!

12a	אֵיךְ נָפַלְתָּ מִשָּׁמַיִם		
	How you fell from heaven,		
אֵיךְ אֵיךְ	how *ʾêḵ*	---	particle
נָפַלְתָּ נפל	you fell *nā·**fal**·tā*	QAL PF 2MS	verb

מִשָּׁמַ֫יִם שָׁמַ֫יִם	from heaven *miš·šā·**ma**·yim*	ABS W/ PREP מִן	noun

The singular suffix on נָפַלְתָּ ("you fell") may appear at first to point to a specific, individual king. After all, 14:4 already indicated that this taunt is "against the king of Babylon." However, even if an individual king is primarily in view, the plurals "wicked" and "rulers" in 14:5 likely indicate that the Babylonian king represents all those who act in a similarly haughty manner. The preposition and noun מִשָּׁמַ֫יִם ("from heaven") should not be pressed too literally, as the heightened poetic language could symbolize a metaphorical "fall" from a powerful political position.

12b הֵילֵ֣ל בֶּן־שָׁ֑חַר

O Shining One, Son of Dawn!

הֵילֵ֣ל הֵילֵל	shining one *hê·**lēl***	ABS	noun
בֶּן־ בֵּן	son *ben-*	CST	noun
שָׁ֑חַר שַׁ֫חַר	dawn ***šā**·ḥar*	ABS	noun

This phrase has drawn controversy disproportional to its brevity. Much centers around the translation and transliteration of הֵילֵל. Some take this as a reference to "Lucifer," understanding it to be a moniker for Satan. The name "Lucifer" derives from the KJV and is not a "translation" at all, but a transliteration of the Latin Vulgate, which here reads in part, "*quomodo cecidisti de caelo lucifer qui mane oriebaris*." The Vulgate's "lucifer" refers to Venus, known as the "morning star," a bright luminary that rises a few hours before the sun, then fades just as quickly as it came. Isaiah's הֵילֵל can be translated "morning star" or "shining one" or the like. With the appositional בֶּן־שָׁחַר ("son of dawn") it may indeed refer to Venus, but it remains to be proven that it refers to Satan. Even if so, the title "Lucifer" should be discarded as a proper name for the devil, as it is a transliteration of a Latin phrase rather than a direct translation (or even transliteration) of the Hebrew into English. Space does not permit a full discussion here, so preachers will need to educate themselves on the debate over the poem's meaning (perhaps by consulting the brief but excellent discussion

in Smith 2007:313–15) and consider the possibility that Isaiah may be riffing on Ugaritic mythos.

12c נִגְדַּעְתָּ לָאָרֶץ

You have been hewn down to the earth,

נִגְדַּעְתָּ גדע	you were cut down *nig·**da**ʿ·tā*	NIPH PF 2MS	verb
לָאָרֶץ אֶרֶץ	to the earth *lā·**ʾā**·reṣ*	ABS W/ PREP לְ + DEF. ART.	noun

The verb גדע ("hewn down") often describes the cutting down of sacred trees/pillars (e.g., Deut 7:5; 12:3; 2 Chr 14:3; Ezek 6:6). The imagery pictures the Babylonian king felled like a tree.

12d חוֹלֵשׁ עַל־גּוֹיִם׃

you who have submitted the nations!

חוֹלֵשׁ חלשׁ	he who prostrates *ḥô·**lēš***	QAL PTCP MS	verb
עַל־ עַל	on/above *ʿal-*	---	prep
גּוֹיִם׃ גּוֹי	nations/peoples *gô·**yim***	ABS	noun

13a וְאַתָּה אָמַרְתָּ בִלְבָבְךָ

But you—you said in your heart,

וְאַתָּה אַתָּה	and/but you *wə·ʾat·**tâ***	--- W/ CONJ וְ	personal pron
אָמַרְתָּ אמר	you said *ʾā·**mar**·tā*	QAL PF 2MS	verb
בִלְבָבְךָ לֵבָב	in your heart *bil·vā·və·**ḵā***	CST W/ PREP בְּ + 2MS SX	noun

The pronoun אַתָּה ("you") here is emphatic and singular, putting the focus squarely on the Babylonian king.

13b	הַשָּׁמַיִם אֶעֱלֶה		
	"To the heavens I will go up,		
הַשָּׁמַיִם שָׁמַיִם	the heavens *haš·šā·**ma**·yim*	ABS W/ DEF. ART.	noun
אֶעֱלֶה עלה	I will go up *'e·'ĕ·**le***	QAL IMPF 1CS	verb

Preachers will want to note the preponderance of first-person pronouns ("I") in vv. 13–14, as they appear no less than five times. This highlights the self-centered arrogance of the king. A king elevating himself "to the heavens" is common poetic imagery depicting a lofty position and need not be taken literally (Jer 51:53; Dan 8:10; cf. Job 20:6; Ps 139:8; Ezek 28:2).

13c	מִמַּעַל לְכוֹכְבֵי־אֵל		
	above even the stars of God		
מִמַּעַל מַעַל	above *mim·**ma**·'al*	--- W/ PREP מִן	prep
לְכוֹכְבֵי־ כּוֹכָב	to the stars of *lə·**ḵô**·ḵə·vê-*	CST W/ PREP לְ	noun
אֵל אֵל	God *'ēl*	ABS	noun

Once again, similar imagery in this line appears elsewhere in the Hebrew Bible (Obad 4). As such, interpreters should guard against understanding this too literally.

13d	אָרִים כִּסְאִי		
	I will raise my throne,		
אָרִים רום	I will raise/lift *'ā·**rîm***	HIPH IMPF 1CS	verb

כִּסְאִ֑י כִּסֵּא	my throne *kis·ʾî*	CST W/ 1CS SX	noun

13e	וְאֵשֵׁ֥ב בְּהַר־מוֹעֵ֖ד

and I will sit on the mountain of meeting

וְאֵשֵׁ֥ב ישׁב	and I will sit/dwell *wə·ʾē·šēv*	QAL IMPF 1CS W/ CONJ וְ	verb
בְּהַר־ הַר	on mountain *bə·har-*	CST W/ PREP בְּ	noun
מוֹעֵ֖ד מוֹעֵד	meeting/assembly *mô·ʿēd*	ABS	noun

The "mountain of meeting" may play off the supposed meeting place of the gods on Mount Zaphon (a.k.a. Mt. Cassius), the sacred mountain and site of the royal palace of the Canaanite deity Baal. From here, Baal would utter divine decrees and even engage in cosmic battles on occasion (see Avalos 1992:1040–41; cf. Oswalt 1986:322). At this point in the poem, the Babylonian king set his sights on ruling over the gods.

13f	בְּיַרְכְּתֵ֥י צָפֽוֹן׃

in the uttermost parts of the north!

בְּיַרְכְּתֵ֥י יַרְכָה	in uttermost parts *bə·yar·kə·tê*	CST W/ PREP בְּ	noun
צָפֽוֹן׃ צָפוֹן	north *ṣā·fôn*	ABS	noun

The word יַרְכָה refers to the most distant or most inwards parts of something. This prepositional phrase adds further emphasis to the (absurd) claim of the Babylonian king to dwell and reign on the mountain of the gods.

14a	אֶעֱלֶה עַל־בָּמֳתֵי עָב

I will go up above the high places of the clouds!

אֶעֱלֶה עלה	I will go up *ʾe·ʿĕ·**le***	QAL IMPF 1CS	verb
עַל־ עַל	on/above *ʿal-*	---	prep
בָּמֳתֵי בָּמָה	high places ***bā**·mŏ·tê*	CST	noun
עָב עָב	cloud *ʿ**āv***	ABS	noun

This is the second use of אֶעֱלֶה ("I will go up") in so many verses (cf. 14:13b). Here, it replaces "heavens" with "the high places of the clouds." This does not only mean the highest of clouds, but the choice of בָּמָה ("high place"), which is most commonly used as a cultic term for a place of (often illicit) worship (cf. 15:2; 16:12; 36:7), indicates that the Babylonian king desires to be worshiped as chief among the gods.

14b	אֶדַּמֶּה לְעֶלְיוֹן׃

I will make myself like the Most High God!"

אֶדַּמֶּה דמה	I will make myself like *ʾed·dam·**me***	HITH IMPF 1CS	verb
לְעֶלְיוֹן׃ עֶלְיוֹן	Elyon/Most High *lə·ʿel·**yôn***	ABS W/ PREP לְ	noun

Here, the king's desire becomes explicit. What he alluded to poetically becomes literally clear: he wants to be worshiped as God (cf. Ezek 28:2). The word עֶלְיוֹן denotes the uppermost of something, like the highest story of Ezekiel's temple (Ezek 41:7), or the highest basket on the chief baker's head (Gen 40:17). When used as a title for God, it highlights the universal sovereignty of the Lord over all other creation and so-called deities. The Babylonian king desires this lofty position for himself.

15a	אַךְ אֶל־שְׁאוֹל תּוּרָד

On the contrary, you will be led down to the grave,

אַךְ	surely/nevertheless	---	adv
אַךְ	*'ak̲*		
אֶל־	to	---	prep
אֶל	*'el-*		
שְׁאוֹל	Sheol/grave	ABS	noun
שְׁאוֹל	*šə·'ôl*		
תּוּרָד	you will be led/brought down	HOPH IMPF 2MS	verb
ירד	*tû·rād*		

The emphatic adverbial particle אַךְ forms a strong contrast between the king's desires and God's reality. He desires to go up to the heavens and become a chief god; instead, he will be led down to Sheol. Note that אֶל־שְׁאוֹל ("to Sheol") is fronted, creating more emphatic contrast with where the king wants to go versus where he will actually go. Additionally, the Hophal imperfect תּוּרָד implies another more powerful being acting upon the will of the Babylonian king, further denigrating his delusions of grandeur. Isaiah attacks the king's arrogance with every single word of this clause!

15b	אֶל־יַרְכְּתֵי־בוֹר׃

to the uttermost parts of the pit!

אֶל־	to	---	prep
אֶל	*'el-*		
יַרְכְּתֵי־	rear/flank	CST	noun
יַרְכָּה	*yar·kə·tê-*		
בוֹר׃	pit	ABS	noun
בּוֹר	*vôr*		

Isaiah ironically spins the king's use of יַרְכָּה ("uttermost parts") from vv. 13–14 in order to further heighten the contrast between where the king thinks he will ascend and where the king actually will descend. Preachers would do well to point out these clever rhetorical plays.

14:16–20c

16a רֹאֶ֫יךָ אֵלֶ֫יךָ יַשְׁגִּ֫יחוּ

*rō'**ê**ḵā 'ēl**ê**ḵā yaš**gî**ḥû*

Those who see you—at you they will stare,

16b אֵלֶ֫יךָ יִתְבּוֹנָ֫נוּ

*'ēl**ê**ḵā yitbô**nā**nû*

you they will mentally dissect:

16c הֲזֶה הָאִישׁ מַרְגִּיז הָאָ֫רֶץ

*hă**ze** hā'**îš** mar**gîz** hā'**ā**reṣ*

"Is this the man who shook the earth,

16d מַרְעִישׁ מַמְלָכוֹת׃

*mar'**îš** mamlā**ḵôt**.*

the one who shook kingdoms,

17a שָׂם תֵּבֵל כַּמִּדְבָּר

śām** tē**vēl** kammid**bār

the one who made the world like the wilderness

17b וְעָרָיו הָרָס

*wə'ā**rā**yw hā**rās***

and tore down its cities,

17c אֲסִירָיו לֹא־פָתַח בָּיְתָה׃

*'ăsî**rā**yw lō'-**fā**taḥ **bā**yətâ.*

not permitting his prisoners to go home?"

18a כָּל־מַלְכֵי גוֹיִם

*kol-mal**ḵê** gô**yim***

All the kings of the nations—

18b כֻּלָּם שָׁכְבוּ בְכָבוֹד

*kul**lām** šāḵə**vû** vəḵā**vôd***

all of them lie in glory,

18c אִישׁ בְּבֵיתוֹ׃

*ʾ**îš** bəvê**tô**.*

each man in his tomb.

19a וְאַתָּה הָשְׁלַכְתָּ מִקִּבְרְךָ

*wəʾat**tâ** hoš**laḵ**tā miqqivrə**ḵā***

Yet you—you have been tossed from your grave,

19b כְּנֵצֶר נִתְעָב

*kə**nē**ṣer nit**ʿāv***

as an abominable branch,

19c לְבוּשׁ הֲרֻגִים מְטֹעֲנֵי חָרֶב

*lə**vûš** hărū**gîm** məṭ**ō**ʿănê **ḥā**rev*

wearing the dead bodies of the slain,
those pierced with the sword,

19d יוֹרְדֵי אֶל־אַבְנֵי־בוֹר

*yôr**dê** ʾel-ʾavnê-**vôr***

those who go down to the stones of the pit

19e כְּפֶגֶר מוּבָס׃

*kə**fe**ger mû**vās**.*

like a trampled corpse.

20a לֹא־תֵחַד אִתָּם בִּקְבוּרָה

*lōʾ-tē**ḥad** ʾit**tām** biqvû**râ***

You won't join them in the grave,

20b כִּי־אַרְצְךָ שִׁחַתָּ

*kî-ʾarṣə**ḵā** šiḥatā*

for you have spoiled your land,

20c

עַמְּךָ הָרָגְתָּ

ʿamməḵā hārāgtā

you killed your own people!

16a רֹאֶיךָ אֵלֶיךָ יַשְׁגִּיחוּ

Those who see you—at you they will stare,

רֹאֶיךָ ראה	those who see you *rō·ʾɛ̂·ḵā*	QAL PTCP MP W/ 2MS SX	verb
אֵלֶיךָ אֶל	to/at you *ʾē·**lɛ̂**·ḵā*	--- W/ 2MS SX	prep
יַשְׁגִּיחוּ שׁגח	they will gaze *yaš·**gî**·ḥû*	HIPH IMPF 3MP	verb

By attempting to ascend the mountain of the gods, the Babylonian king wanted to be beheld by the masses. Instead, the masses will indeed behold him, but he will be an object of disgust and ridicule instead of worship.

16b אֵלֶיךָ יִתְבּוֹנָנוּ

you they will mentally dissect:

אֵלֶיךָ אֶל	to/at you *ʾē·**lɛ̂**·ḵā*	--- W/ 2MS SX	prep
יִתְבּוֹנָנוּ בין	they will consider/ give attention to *yit·bô·**nā**·nû*	HITHPOLEL IMPF 3MP	verb

This short phrase is parallel with the last, both beginning with אֵלֶיךָ ("to you"). This creates ironic wordplay with those who "stare" at the king as he descends. *At him* they will stare derisively. The verb בין indicates a careful consideration of, giving deep thought to something. Preachers should encourage the church to likewise give deep consideration to the reason for this king's rise and fall.

16c	הֲזֶה הָאִישׁ מַרְגִּיז הָאָרֶץ

"Is this the man who shook the earth,

הֲזֶה זֶה	this *hă·ze*	--- W/ INTERR הֲ	demonstr pron
הָאִישׁ אִישׁ	the man *hā·ʾîš*	ABS W/ DEF. ART.	noun
מַרְגִּיז רגז	one who caused to quake *mar·gîz*	HIPH PTCP MS	verb
הָאָרֶץ אֶרֶץ	the earth *hā·ʾā·reṣ*	ABS W/ DEF. ART.	noun

Many translations insert verbs like "saying" or "thinking" before this phrase, noting that these are the thoughts of the deceased who watch the Babylonian king descend into the netherworld. Notice the use of הָאִישׁ ("the man"), a subtle shot at the king who desired to become a god.

16d	מַרְעִישׁ מַמְלָכוֹת׃

the one who shook kingdoms,

מַרְעִישׁ רעשׁ	one who caused to shake *mar·ʿîš*	HIPH PTCP MS	verb
מַמְלָכוֹת׃ מַמְלָכָה	kingdoms *mam·lā·ḵôt*	ABS	noun

Both this and the phrase before use similar metaphors. In a contemporary illustration, we can imagine the king like Godzilla, shaking the world with each thunderous step in his power. Yet now, what has he become? The dead can hardly recognize him who was once so great in power.

17a	שָׂם תֵּבֵל כַּמִּדְבָּר

the one who made the world like the wilderness

שָׂם שׂים	one who put/set *śām*	QAL PTCP MS	verb

תֵּבֵל תֵּבֵל	world *tē·**vēl***	ABS	noun
כַּמִּדְבָּר מִדְבָּר	as the wilderness *kam·mid·**bār***	ABS W/ PREP כְּ + DEF. ART.	noun

This metaphor depicts the Babylonian's power to destroy a land so thoroughly that nothing was left, neither city nor soul. What was once a bustling metropolis was made a wild wasteland after he came to town.

17b **וְעָרָיו הָרָס**

and tore down its cities,

וְעָרָיו עִיר	and its cities/towns *wə·ʿā·**rāyw***	CST W/ CONJ וְ + 3MS SX	noun
הָרָס הרס	(he) threw down *hā·**rās***	QAL PF 3MS	verb

17c **אֲסִירָיו לֹא־פָתַח בָּיְתָה׃**

not permitting his prisoners to go home?"

אֲסִירָיו אָסִיר	his prisoners *ʾă·sî·**rāyw***	CST W/ 3MS SX	noun
לֹא־ לֹא	no/not *lōʾ-*	---	particle
פָתַח פתח	he opened ***fā**·taḥ*	QAL PF 3MS	verb
בָּיְתָה׃ בַּיִת	to house ***bā**·yə·tâ*	ABS W/ LOCATIVE ה	noun

This phrase speaks to the unmerciful attitude of the Babylonian king, who relished power over even his prisoners by refusing their release.

18a	כָּל־מַלְכֵ֥י גוֹיִ֖ם

All the kings of the nations—

כָּל־ כֹּל	all *kol-*	CST	noun
מַלְכֵ֥י מֶ֫לֶךְ	kings *mal·ke̱ê*	CST	noun
גוֹיִ֖ם גּוֹי	nations/peoples *gô·**yim***	ABS	noun

18b	כֻּלָּ֛ם שָׁכְב֥וּ בְכָב֖וֹד

all of them lie in glory,

כֻּלָּ֛ם כֹּל	all of them *kul·**lām***	CST W/ 3MP SX	noun
שָׁכְב֥וּ שׁכב	(they) lie *šā·ḵə·**vû***	QAL PF 3CP	verb
בְכָב֖וֹד כָּבוֹד	in glory *və·ḵā·**vôd***	ABS W/ PREP בְּ	noun

The repetition of כֹּל ("all") puts great emphasis on the comprehensive nature of the audience: *every single one of the other kings* watched the Babylonian king's descent. Preachers may want to draw out this emphasis since most English translations fail to pick up on it.

18c	אִ֥ישׁ בְּבֵיתֽוֹ׃

each man in his tomb.

אִ֥ישׁ אִישׁ	man *ʾîš*	ABS	noun
בְּבֵיתֽוֹ׃ בַּ֫יִת	in his house *bə·vê·**tô***	CST W/ PREP בְּ + 3MS SX	noun

Though בַּ֫יִת ("house") likely represents the permanent "home" of a deceased king (his grave), there may also be a subtle play on words with the usage of the same term in the previous verse. The Babylonian king refused to allow prisoners to return to their "homes," but now has gone on to a place where other kings in their permanent "homes" view his descent from glory.

19a	וְאַתָּ֛ה הָשְׁלַ֥כְתָּ מִֽקִּבְרְךָ֖

Yet you—you have been tossed from your grave,

וְאַתָּ֛ה אַתָּה	and/but you *wə·'at·**tâ***	--- W/ CONJ וְ	personal pron
הָשְׁלַ֥כְתָּ שׁלך	you have been cast *hoš·**lak**·tā*	HOPH PF 2MS	verb
מִֽקִּבְרְךָ֖ קֶ֫בֶר	from your grave *miq·qiv·rə·**kā***	CST W/ PREP מִן + 2MS SX	noun

The fronted independent pronoun וְאַתָּה ("Yet you") heightens the contrast with the "all of them" in the previous verse. The focus is now squarely on the Babylonian king. In contrast to other kings lying in their homes in glory, his has been cast (a word with violent intonations) *from* his grave. The use of the preposition מִן ("from") instead of the expected לְ ("to/toward") indicates that the king has experienced an ignoble burial, or no burial at all; quite the curse in the ancient world (cf. Deut 21:23).

19b	כְּנֵ֣צֶר נִתְעָ֔ב

as an abominable branch,

כְּנֵ֣צֶר נֵ֫צֶר	as a sprout/shoot/branch *kə·**nē**·ṣer*	ABS W/ PREP כְּ	noun
נִתְעָ֔ב תעב	being abhorred *nit·'**āv***	NIPH PTCP MS	verb

The use of נֵ֫צֶר ("branch") here likely recalls the highly messianic usage in 11:1. See below under "New Testament Connections" for further discussion.

19c	לְבוּשׁ הֲרֻגִים מְטֹעֲנֵי חָרֶב

wearing the dead bodies of the slain,
those pierced with the sword,

לְבוּשׁ לְבוּשׁ	garment/clothes *lə·**vûš***	CST	noun
הֲרֻגִים הרג	those who were killed *hă·rū·**gîm***	QAL PASS PTCP MP	verb
מְטֹעֲנֵי טען	those who were pierced *mə·**ṭō**·ʿă·nê*	PUAL (CST) PTCP MP	verb
חָרֶב חֶ֫רֶב	sword ***ḥā**·rev*	ABS	noun

The description here gives hint to what may have caused the Babylonian king's disgraceful death. Isaiah envisions a battle scenario where the king has been unceremoniously dumped into a mass grave of other slain warriors, left unburied. "The wages of sin is death" (Rom 6:23), and an ignoble death at that.

19d	יוֹרְדֵי אֶל־אַבְנֵי־בוֹר

those who go down to the stones of the pit

יוֹרְדֵי ירד	those who come down *yôr·**dê***	QAL (CST) PTCP MP	verb
אֶל־ אֶל	to *ʾel-*	---	prep
אַבְנֵי־ אֶ֫בֶן	stones *ʾav·nê-*	CST	noun
בוֹר בּוֹר	pit ***vôr***	ABS	noun

This phrase is another creative way of describing the grave, in the darkest of terms. Isaiah really strives to paint a darker picture with each stroke of the brush.

19e	כְּפֶ֖גֶר מוּבָֽס׃

like a trampled corpse.

כְּפֶ֖גֶר פֶּ֫גֶר	as corpse/carcass *kə·**fe**·ger*	ABS W/ PREP כְּ	noun
מוּבָֽס׃ בוס	is trodden down *mû·**vās***	HOPH PTCP MS	verb

Again, with each phrase, the description of the king's doom is amplified.

20a	לֹֽא־תֵחַ֤ד אִתָּם֙ בִּקְבוּרָ֔ה

You won't join them in the grave,

לֹֽא־ לֹא	no/not ***lō'**-*	---	particle
תֵחַ֤ד יחד	you will be united *tē·**ḥad***	QAL IMPF 2MS	verb
אִתָּם֙ אֵת	with them *'it·**tām***	--- W/ 3MP SX	prep
בִּקְבוּרָ֔ה קְבֻרָה	in grave *biq·vû·**râ***	ABS W/ PREP בְּ	noun

Here Isaiah explicitly spells out the fate of the king's unburied corpse—he will not receive a normal, honorary burial, but his body will be left to rot in the open. Or, with the images in 19c of the king wearing the bodies of the slain, perhaps we are meant to understand him lying in the battlefield, covered with corpses from other fallen soldiers in his army.

20b	כִּֽי־אַרְצְךָ֥ שִׁחַ֖תָּ

for you have spoiled your land,

כִּֽי־ כִּי	for/because ***kî**-*	---	conj
אַרְצְךָ֥ אֶ֫רֶץ	your land *'ar·ṣə·**kā***	CST W/ 2MS SX	noun
שִׁחַ֖תָּ שׁחת	you spoiled/ruined *ši·**ḥa**·tā*	PIEL PF 2MS	verb

20c	עַמְּךָ הָרַגְתָּ

you killed your own people!

עַמְּךָ עַם	your people *ʿam·mə·**ḵā***	CST W/ 2MS SX	noun
הָרַגְתָּ הרג	you killed *hā·**rāg**·tā*	QAL PF 2MS	verb

This phrase lacks a conjunction, giving the phrase an abrupt, surprising feel. By fronting עַמְּךָ ("your people"), Isaiah draws attention to the heinousness of the king's crimes.

From Text to Sermon

Big Idea. God humbles the exalted and exalts the humble.

Avenues for Illustration and Application. Isaiah 14 is the second chapter in the section of the book commonly called "The Woes to the Nations" (Isa 13–23). Preachers will want to contextualize the oracles for modern congregations by explaining that each oracle is written *about* foreign nations surrounding Israel, but they were written *for* the ears of the Israelites. Isaiah probably did not hike five hundred miles to hand deliver these scrolls to Merodach-baladan. The message *might* have reached the pagans, but it *certainly* reached the ears of the Judeans. Just like if a preacher condemns the human rights atrocities of the North Koreans, he likely does not expect Kim Jong Un to be listening in and taking notes. The message uses the sins of foreign dictators to illustrate the potential sins and possible judgments of the contemporary audience.

This oracle concerns a king of Babylon. Isaiah does not name the particular king, so the preacher should not spend inordinate time trying to pinpoint exactly who he speaks of (in fact, the plurals in v. 5 may indicate that one particular king was never the point, but the king here represents the whole of the Babylonians, who in turn represent the whole of God's enemies).

If only preaching vv. 12–20a, preachers may want to at least read vv. 9–11 for context. The scene is set: this king has died and descends to Sheol. Death is the great equalizer for all people, no matter how much power or influence they enjoyed while living.

The most difficult part of the sermon may be vv. 12–15, depending on which view one takes of the identity of the Babylonian king, and how much of the opposing views one decides to incorporate into the sermon. If one argues this text has nothing to do with Satan, keep in mind that early Church Fathers (including Origen, Cyprian, Tertullian, Gregory the Great, to name a few) believed otherwise. If one argues this text does speak of Satan, keep in mind the entire Reformation held a different opinion. Either way, preach humbly, with respect for the other opinion. This is not an issue that decides church membership or entrance into heaven.

Even more important to keep in mind is that even *if* this is about Satan, the text is not really about Satan! Isaiah makes a critical commentary on the proud arrogance of *humans*, especially human leaders. This is an indictment of the pride of the Babylonian king, and in turn, the pride of the Israelites. This is where the true application centers. Death mocks everyone who claims to be something in this life. Unless one lives for eternal rewards and eternal values, one has nothing to show for their efforts here. Preachers can apply this message by helping people to consider the wages of sin and by encouraging them to live for an eternal reward and to humble themselves before God and man.

Preachers might also want to consider texts from Ecclesiastes on the meaninglessness of life without God to illustrate and strengthen the point of this message.

New Testament Connections. Luke 14:11 perfectly summarizes Isaiah's point: "For everyone who exalts himself will be humbled, and he who humbles himself will be exalted" (ESV). Perhaps using Jesus as the ultimate contrast with the Babylonian king would be a helpful road towards the gospel. Death equalizes everyone. The king of Babylon claimed to be God. Death mocks all who claim to be God . . . *except Jesus!* Jesus conquered death and thus proved his deity to the world.

This avenue towards the cross is not invented; rather, it draws from the subtle yet purposeful messianic reference in v. 19. Isaiah 14:19 calls the Babylonian king an "abominable branch." The use of נֵצֶר recalls the same term in Isa 11:1: "There shall come forth a shoot from the stump of Jesse, and a branch (נֵצֶר) from his roots shall bear fruit" (ESV). Isaiah may purposefully reuse the term as a contrast between the messianic Davidic king to come and the abominable Babylonian king. If this is the case, it gives explicit permission for the interpreter to draw a contrastive line between the Babylonian king and Christ. The Israelites could not hope to overcome such pride on their own, but one day, a new King would indeed live a perfect, humble life, and be exalted above every name (Phil 2:9–11).

A PLEASANT VINEYARD

Back in Isa 5, the Lord sings a song about a vineyard. Though the farmer plants and cultivates the vineyard to perfection, the grapes rot and become worthless and, in the end, the farmer destroys the crop. The vineyard there represents Israel and her rebellion and judgment. Here in Isa 27, we hear another song about a vineyard, but it appears to be set to a different tune. Just like the first song, this one has a vineyard and a farmer. Just like the first song, the vineyard represents the Israelites, and the farmer represents God. But here in ch. 27, the vine blossoms appropriately and its shoots fill the entire world with delicious fruit. Isaiah 27 pictures a time when God's people have responded appropriately to his grace and judgment, a beautiful time when nations stream together to worship the Lord, a time when covenant promises find their fulfillment. It is a purposeful contrast with the previous Song of the Vineyard, one ripe for preaching and presenting glorious gospel hope.

LARGER LITERARY CONTEXT › 27:1–13

27:1

1a בַּיּ֣וֹם הַה֡וּא יִפְקֹ֣ד יְהוָ֡ה

*bay**yôm** ha**hû'** yif**qōd** YHWH*

In that day, YHWH will destroy

1b בְּחַרְבּ֗וֹ הַקָּשָׁה וְהַגְּדוֹלָ֣ה וְהַחֲזָקָ֔ה

*bəḥar**vô** haqqā**šâ** wəhaggədô**lâ** wəhaḥăzā**qâ***

with his hard and great and strong sword

1c עַ֚ל לִוְיָתָן֙ נָחָ֣שׁ בָּרִ֔חַ

*'**al** liwyā**tān** nā**ḥāš** bā**rī**aḥ*

against Leviathan, the fugitive serpent,

1d וְעַל֙ לִוְיָתָ֔ן נָחָ֖שׁ עֲקַלָּת֑וֹן

*wə'**al** liwyā**tān** nā**ḥāš** 'ăqallā**tôn***

yes, even Leviathan, the crooked serpent;

1e וְהָרַ֥ג אֶת־הַתַּנִּ֖ין אֲשֶׁ֥ר בַּיָּֽם׃

*wəhā**rag** 'et-hattan**nîn** 'ă**šer** bay**yām**.*

namely, he will kill the dragon who swims in the sea.

1a	בַּיּ֣וֹם הַה֡וּא יִפְקֹ֣ד יְהוָ֡ה
	In that day, YHWH will destroy

בַּיּ֣וֹם יוֹם	in/on the day *bay·**yôm***	ABS W/ PREP בְּ + DEF. ART.	noun
הַה֡וּא הוּא	that *ha·**hû'***	--- W/ DEF. ART.	demonstr pron

יִפְקֹד פקד	(he) will attend to/ visit/punish *yif·**qōd***	QAL IMPF 3MS	verb
יְהוָה יהוה	the LORD *YHWH*	ABS	noun

As always in prophetic literature, the preacher will need to determine through context when "in that day" refers to. Most interpreters see this text fulfilled in Christ, either wholly and spiritually at his resurrection, or in a future time period (the Millennium) still to come.

1b בְּחַרְבּוֹ הַקָּשָׁה וְהַגְּדוֹלָה וְהַחֲזָקָה

with his hard and great and strong sword

בְּחַרְבּוֹ חֶרֶב	with his sword *bə·ḥar·**vô***	CST W/ PREP בְּ + 3MS SX	noun
הַקָּשָׁה קָשֶׁה	the hard/heavy *haq·qā·**šâ***	FS ATTR W/ DEF. ART.	adj
וְהַגְּדוֹלָה גָּדוֹל	and the great *wə·hag·gə·dô·**lâ***	FS ATTR W/ CONJ וְ + DEF. ART.	adj
וְהַחֲזָקָה חָזָק	and the strong/mighty *wə·ha·ḥă·zā·**qâ***	FS ATTR W/ CONJ וְ + DEF. ART.	adj

The three adjectives lend great emphasis to the power of this sword. Any one of them would have described the power of the Lord's sword just fine; putting all three together is literal overkill.

1c עַל לִוְיָתָן נָחָשׁ בָּרִחַ

against Leviathan, the fugitive serpent,

עַל עַל	over/against *ʿ**al***	---	prep
לִוְיָתָן לִוְיָתָן	Leviathan *liw·yā·**tān***	ABS	noun
נָחָשׁ נָחָשׁ	serpent *nā·**ḥāš***	ABS	noun

בָּרִ֫חַ בָּרִיחַ	fugitive *bā·rī·aḥ*	MS ATTR	adj

The identity of "Leviathan" will need careful explanation. The serpent appears at various times in Scripture and, notably, in apocryphal texts (2 Esdr 6:47–52; 2 Bar 29:3–4). Sometimes in the Bible, Leviathan represents a pagan mythological creature symbolizing evil or chaos (e.g., Ps 74:13–14; cf. Isa 51:9; Ps 89:10, there called "Rahab"). Other times in the Bible, Leviathan represents a created sea creature (e.g., Gen 1:20–21, 23; Ps 104:26; possibly Job 41). Other ancient Near Eastern cultures had similar myths with great sea creatures, such as the Babylonian Tiamat, the Hittite Illuyankas, and the Ugaritic Lotan, each ultimately defeated by their respective gods (Oswalt 1986:490; Smith 2007:456; Wegner 2021:214–15). Preachers may want to see the excellent summaries of Leviathan theology and literature in Ortlund 2021 and Fyall 2002.

1d וְעַ֗ל לִֽוְיָתָ֔ן נָחָ֖שׁ עֲקַלָּת֑וֹן

yes, even Leviathan, the crooked serpent;

Hebrew	Gloss	Parsing	POS
וְעַ֗ל עַל	and/even upon/against *wə·ʿal*	--- W/ CONJ וְ	prep
לִֽוְיָתָ֔ן לִוְיָתָן	Leviathan *liw·yā·tān*	ABS	noun
נָחָ֖שׁ נָחָשׁ	serpent *nā·ḥāš*	CST	noun
עֲקַלָּת֑וֹן עֲקַלָּתוֹן	crooked/twisted *ʿă·qal·lā·tôn*	MS ATTR	adj

The ו (here and in the following phrase) can be translated conjunctively ("and") or appositionally ("even"). The former would yield at least two creatures (Leviathan the fugitive serpent and Leviathan the crooked serpent), whereas the latter would yield just one (Leviathan the fugitive serpent, namely, Leviathan the crooked serpent). For example, the KJV has "Leviathan the piercing serpent, *even* Leviathan that crooked serpent; *and* he shall slay the dragon that is in the sea." This translation yields at least two creatures. NIV, however, has one: "Leviathan the gliding serpent, Leviathan the coiling serpent; he will slay the monster of the sea." We have chosen the latter as the best option, with all three lines referring to the same creature in poetic synonymous parallelism. The word translated "serpent" (נָחָשׁ) is used of the serpent in Gen 3 (vv. 1–2, 4, 13–14), Aaron's staff that turned into a serpent (Exod 4:3; 7:15), and the venomous serpents in the wilderness that bit the Israelites to deadly effect (Num 21:6–7, 9; cf. Deut 8:15). Its typical use references venomous serpents of various kinds.

1e **וְהָרַג אֶת־הַתַּנִּין אֲשֶׁר בַּיָּם׃**

namely, he will kill the dragon who swims in the sea.

וְהָרַג הרג	and/namely he will kill *wə·hā·**rag***	QAL WEQATAL 3MS	verb
אֶת־ אֵת	*(direct object marker)* *ʾet-*	---	particle
הַתַּנִּין תַּנִּין	the dragon/sea monster *hat·tan·**nîn***	ABS W/ DEF. ART.	noun
אֲשֶׁר אֲשֶׁר	who *ʾă·**šer***	---	relative pron
בַּיָּם׃ יָם	in the sea *bay·**yām***	ABS W/ PREP בְּ + DEF. ART.	noun

"The Dragon" (הַתַּנִּין) is notably used in Gen 1:21 to refer to the great sea creatures God created on the fifth day (though translations sometimes use different English words for each of these occurrences). It is also used of Aaron's staff turning into a serpent in Exodus (7:9–10, 12; note that נָחָשׁ ["serpent"] in v. 1c is also used of the staff [Exod 4:3; 7:15], a strong indication that the words are not always precisely differentiated in biblical literature). Both Nebuchadnezzar (Jer 51:34) and Pharaoh (Ezek 29:3; 32:2) are unfavorably compared to a תַּנִּין.

27:2–6

2a בַּיּ֖וֹם הַה֑וּא

*bay**yôm** ha**hû**’*

In that day—

2b כֶּ֥רֶם חֶ֖מֶד עַנּוּ־לָֽהּ׃

*kerem ḥemed ‘annû-**lāh**.*

a delightful vineyard! Sing about it!

3a אֲנִ֤י יְהוָה֙ נֹֽצְרָ֔הּ

*’ă**nî** YHWH nōṣə**râ***

I, YHWH, am tending it.

3b לִרְגָעִ֖ים אַשְׁקֶ֑נָּה

*lirgā‘**îm** ’aš**qen**nâ*

Every single second I give it something to drink,

3c פֶּ֚ן יִפְקֹ֣ד עָלֶ֔יהָ

***pen** yif**qōd** ‘ā**lê**hā*

lest anyone tries to destroy it,

3d לַ֥יְלָה וָי֖וֹם אֶצֳּרֶֽנָּה׃

***lay**lâ wā**yôm** ’eṣṣŏ**ren**nâ.*

Night and day I will tend it.

4a חֵמָ֖ה אֵ֣ין לִ֑י

*ḥē**mâ** **’ên** **lî***

I have no rage.

4b מִֽי־יִתְּנֵ֜נִי שָׁמִ֥יר שַׁ֙יִת֙ בַּמִּלְחָמָ֔ה

mî**-yittənē**nî** šā**mîr** **ša**yit bammilḥā**mâ

Who would put thorns and thornbushes
in front of me in the battle?

4c אֶפְשְׂעָ֣ה בָ֑הּ

*ʾefśəʿ**â** **vāh***

I would trample over it,

4d אֲצִיתֶ֖נָּה יָּֽחַד׃

*ʾăṣî**ten**nâ **yā**ḥad.*

I would burn it all up!

5a א֚וֹ יַחֲזֵ֣ק בְּמָעוּזִּ֔י

*ʾô yaḥă**zēq** bəmāʿûz**zî***

Or let him enjoy the protection of my fortress,

5b יַעֲשֶׂ֥ה שָׁל֖וֹם לִ֑י

*yaʿă**śe** šā**lôm** **lî***

let him make peace with me,

5c שָׁל֖וֹם יַֽעֲשֶׂה־לִּֽי׃

*šā**lôm** yaʿă**śe**-**lî**.*

peace let him make with me.

6a הַבָּאִים֙ יַשְׁרֵ֣שׁ יַעֲקֹ֔ב

*habbā**ʾîm** yaš**rēš** yaʿă**qōv***

In coming times, Jacob shall take root,

6b יָצִ֥יץ וּפָרַ֖ח יִשְׂרָאֵ֑ל

*yā**ṣîṣ** ûfā**raḥ** yiśrā**ʾēl***

Israel will blossom and bud,

6c וּמָלְא֥וּ פְנֵי־תֵבֵ֖ל תְּנוּבָֽה׃

*ûmālə**ʾû** fə**nê**-tē**vēl** tənû**vâ**.*

and he will fill the entire world with fresh fruit.

2a	בַּיּ֣וֹם הַה֔וּא

In that day—

בַּיּ֣וֹם יוֹם	in (the) day *bay·**yôm***	ABS W/ PREP בְּ + DEF. ART.	noun
הַה֔וּא הוּא	that *ha·**hû’***	--- W/ DEF. ART.	demonstr pron

Once again, the phrase "in that day" appears (cf. 24:21; 25:9; 26:1; 27:1). Rather than ignoring it or passing over it too quickly, preachers can capitalize on this repetition by using it as a reminder of Isaiah's context and focus. Isaiah 24–27 form a literary unit oftentimes referred to as "Isaiah's Little Apocalypse." Most interpreters understand it to point forward to eschatological events, many of which may still be future of Isaiah's readers and even Christians today.

2b	כֶּ֥רֶם חֶ֖מֶד עַנּוּ־לָֽהּ׃

a delightful vineyard! Sing about it!

כֶּ֥רֶם כֶּרֶם	vineyard ***ke**·rem*	CST	noun
חֶ֖מֶד חֶ֫מֶד	beauty/desire/delight ***ḥe**·med*	ABS	noun
עַנּוּ־ ענה	sing *‘an·nû-*	PIEL IMPV MP	verb
לָֽהּ׃ לְ	of it ***lāh***	--- W/ 3FS SX	prep

The Hebrew puts some emphasis on "vineyard" (כֶּרֶם). This would immediately recall the original "Song of the Vineyard" in Isa 5 and invite comparison. Preachers can remind congregants of this original song in order to set up the contrast in the text to follow.

3a	אֲנִי יְהוָה נֹצְרָהּ

I, YHWH, am tending it.

אֲנִי אֲנִי	I *ʾă·nî*	---	personal pron
יְהוָה יהוה	the Lord *YHWH*	ABS	noun
נֹצְרָהּ נצר	watching/guarding it *nō·ṣə·râ*	QAL PTCP MS W/ 3FS SX	verb

The pronoun casts extra attention on the subject, YHWH. This song may be about the vineyard, but really, it focuses on YHWH.

3b	לִרְגָעִים אַשְׁקֶנָּה

Every single second I give it something to drink,

לִרְגָעִים רֶגַע	to a moment/instant *lir·gā·ʿîm*	ABS W/ PREP לְ	noun
אַשְׁקֶנָּה שׁקה	I will give it drink *ʾaš·qen·nâ*	HIPH IMPF 1CS W/ 3FS SX	verb

The noun and preposition לִרְגָעִים (translated idiomatically "every single second") indicates the unceasing nature of the Lord's watering activity. The object is not to drown the plant with nonstop streams of water; rather, we should understand the metaphor hyperbolically. God never neglects his duties towards the vine, not even for a second.

3c	פֶּן יִפְקֹד עָלֶיהָ

lest anyone tries to destroy it,

פֶּן פֶּן	lest *pen*	---	conj
יִפְקֹד פקד	he will attend to/ visit/punish *yif·qōd*	QAL IMPF 3MS	verb
עָלֶיהָ עַל	over/against it *ʿā·lê·hā*	--- W/ 3FS SX	prep

We have translated יִפְקֹד as "destroy" here and in v. 1a in order to draw out the identical usage of the verb. What the Lord does to Leviathan he also prevents others from doing to the vine.

3d	לַיְלָה וָיוֹם אֶצֳּרֶנָּה׃		
	Night and day I will tend it.		
לַיְלָה לַיְלָה	night *lay·lâ*	ABS	noun
וָיוֹם יוֹם	and day *wā·yôm*	ABS W/ CONJ וְ	noun
אֶצֳּרֶנָּה׃ נצר	I will watch/guard it *ʾeṣ·ṣŏ·ren·nâ*	QAL IMPF 1CS W/ 3FS SX	verb

The verb נצר ("keep") forms an inclusio in the beginning and end of this verse. If the emphasis here lands on God's protection, it may be better translated, "guard." However, the continual nature of the Lord's watering activities caused us to translate it "tend" in this context. Preachers can use the illustration of cultivating a garden by both tending to its needs and erecting a fence to keep out predators. Both are essential for the garden's health. Both are highlighted in this verse.

4a	חֵמָה אֵין לִי		
	I have no rage.		
חֵמָה חֵמָה	wrath/heat *ḥē·mâ*	ABS	noun
אֵין אַיִן	nothing *ʾên*	---	particle
לִי לְ	to me *lî*	--- W/ 1CS SX	prep

This standalone expression at first seems to be disconnected from the rest of the thought, but when considered with the song in Isa 5, it sets up a contrast to the way this vineyard responds to the farmer's vigilance and the farmer's subsequent pleased reaction.

4b מִֽי־יִתְּנֵנִי שָׁמִיר שַׁיִת בַּמִּלְחָמָה

Who would put thorns and thornbushes in front of me in the battle?

מִֽי־ מִי	who? *mî-*	---	interr pron
יִתְּנֵנִי נתן	(he) will give/set me *yit·tə·**nē**·nî*	QAL IMPF 3MS W/ 1CS SX	verb
שָׁמִיר שָׁמִיר	thorn *šā·**mîr***	ABS	noun
שַׁיִת שַׁיִת	thornbush ***ša**·yit*	ABS	noun
בַּמִּלְחָמָה מִלְחָמָה	in the battle/war *bam·mil·ḥā·**mâ***	ABS W/ PREP בְּ + DEF. ART.	noun

This phrase could be taken as an interrogative (presently translated) or an exclamatory statement (ESV: "Would that I had thorns and briers to battle!"). The point remains the same either way. If the Leviathan was no match for the Lord, how much less thorns and thistles?

4c אֶפְשְׂעָה בָהּ

I would trample over it,

אֶפְשְׂעָה פשׂע	I would step/march *ʾef·śə·**ʿâ***	QAL COHORT 1CS	verb
בָהּ בְּ	against it ***vāh***	--- W/ 3FS SX	prep

4d אֲצִיתֶנָּה יָּחַד׃

I would burn it all up!

אֲצִיתֶנָּה יצת	I will burn it *ʾă·ṣî·**ten**·nâ*	HIPH IMPF 1CS W/ 3FS SX	verb
יָחַד׃ יַחַד	altogether/completely ***yā**·ḥad*	---	adv

The expressions in 4c and 4d both vividly depict the farmer annihilating any potential obstacles, but the inclusion of the adverb יָחַד ("completely") truly puts the image over the top. Every last thorn will burn if anyone tries to get in the way of the farmer and his vine!

5a	אֹו יַחֲזֵק בְּמָעוּזִּי		
	Or let him enjoy the protection of my fortress,		
אֹו אוֹ	or *ʾô*	---	conj
יַחֲזֵק חזק	let him seize/strengthen *ya·ḥă·**zēq***	HIPH JUSS 3MS	verb
בְּמָעוּזִּי מָעוֹז	in my protection/ stronghold *bə·mā·ʿûz·**zî***	CST W/ PREP בְּ + 1CS SX	noun

Though this phrase offers translational difficulties, the **אֹו** ("or") indicates an opposing situation to the one previously described. Either the enemy can (futilely) try to thwart the farmer, or he can submit to the farmer's power and join him. Preachers can use these two choices to illustrate the two choices of every person—either we are for God or against him (Matt 12:30).

5b	יַעֲשֶׂה שָׁלֹום לִֽי		
	let him make peace with me,		
יַעֲשֶׂה עשׂה	let him do/make *ya·ʿă·**śe***	QAL JUSS 3MS	verb
שָׁלֹום שָׁלוֹם	peace *šā·**lôm***	ABS	noun
לִֽי לְ	to me ***lî***	--- W/ 1CS SX	prep

5c

שָׁלוֹם יַעֲשֶׂה־לִּֽי׃

peace let him make with me.

שָׁלוֹם שָׁלוֹם	peace *šā·**lôm***	ABS	noun
יַעֲשֶׂה־ עשׂה	let him do/make *ya·ʿă·**śe**-*	QAL JUSS 3MS	verb
לִּֽי׃ לְ	to me ***lî***	--- W/ 1CS SX	prep

This phrase nearly duplicates 5b, though with the noun and verb reversed. If both phrases are original, they work together to emphasize the need to make peace with the farmer.

6a

הַבָּאִים יַשְׁרֵשׁ יַעֲקֹב

In coming times, Jacob shall take root,

הַבָּאִים בוא	coming *hab·bā·**ʾîm***	QAL PTCP MP W/ DEF. ART.	verb
יַשְׁרֵשׁ שׁרשׁ	(he) shall take root *yaš·**rēš***	HIPH JUSS 3MS	verb
יַעֲקֹב יַעֲקֹב	Jacob *ya·ʿă·**qōv***	ABS	noun

The verb שׁרשׁ ("take root") will remind careful readers of the root of Jesse (the noun form שֹׁרֶשׁ is used in 11:1, 10). The use of הַבָּאִים ("in coming times") instead of the typical "in that day" (בַּיּוֹם הַהוּא) may simply be a stylistic variation with little to no difference in meaning.

6b

יָצִיץ וּפָרַח יִשְׂרָאֵל

Israel will blossom and bud,

יָצִיץ צוץ	(he) will blossom *yā·**ṣîṣ***	QAL IMPF 3MS	verb
וּפָרַח פרח	and (he) will bud *û·fā·**raḥ***	QAL WEQATAL 3MS	verb

יִשְׂרָאֵֽל יִשְׂרָאֵל	Israel *yiś·rā·ʾēl*	ABS	noun

Though it may be obvious to the astute reader, for the first time in this song, Isaiah explicitly states the vine's identity: Israel.

6c וּמָלְא֥וּ פְנֵי־תֵבֵ֖ל תְּנוּבָֽה׃

and he will fill the entire world with fresh fruit.

וּמָלְא֥וּ מלא	and he will fill *û·mā·lə·ʾû*	QAL WEQATAL 3CP	verb
פְנֵי־ פָּנֶה	face *fə·nê-*	CST	noun
תֵבֵ֖ל תֵּבֵל	world *tē·vēl*	ABS	noun
תְּנוּבָֽה׃ תְּנוּבָה	fruit *tə·nû·vâ*	ABS	noun

This phrase reflects on the creational mandate to "be fruitful and multiply and fill the earth" in Gen 1:28. This is the language of fulfillment.

27:7–11

7a הַכְּמַכַּת מַכֵּהוּ הִכָּהוּ

*hakkəmak**kat** mak**kē**hû hik**kā**hû*

Has God struck the Israelites as God struck their enemies?

7b אִם־כְּהֶרֶג הֲרֻגָיו הֹרָג׃

*ʾim-kə**he**reg hăru**gāyw** hō**rāg**.*

Have the Israelites been killed as their enemies were killed?

8a בְּסַאסְּאָה בְּשַׁלְחָהּ תְּרִיבֶנָּה

*bəssaʾssə**ʾâ** bəšal**ḥāh** tərî**ven**nâ*

You will fight with her by exiling her away.

8b הָגָה בְּרוּחוֹ הַקָּשָׁה בְּיוֹם קָדִים׃

*hā**gâ** bərû**ḥô** haqqā**šâ** bə**yôm** qā**dîm**.*

He separated them with his strong breath in the day of the east wind.

9a לָכֵן בְּזֹאת יְכֻפַּר עֲוֹן־יַעֲקֹב

*lā**ḵēn** bə**zōʾt** yəḵup**par** ʿă**wōn**-yaʿă**qōv***

Therefore, by this the iniquity of Jacob will be atoned for,

9b וְזֶה כָּל־פְּרִי הָסִר חַטָּאתוֹ

*wə**ze** kol-pə**rî** hā**sîr** ḥaṭṭā**ʾtô***

and this will be the full fruit of the removal of his sin:

9c בְּשׂוּמוֹ ׀ כָּל־אַבְנֵי מִזְבֵּחַ כְּאַבְנֵי־גִר מְנֻפָּצוֹת

*bəśû**mô** kol-ʾav**nê** miz**bē**aḥ kəʾavnê-**gir** mənuppā**ṣôt***

when he makes all the altar stones just like pulverized chalk.

9d לֹא־יָקֻמוּ אֲשֵׁרִים וְחַמָּנִים׃

*__lōʾ__-yā**qū**mû ʾăšē**rîm** wəḥammā**nîm**.*

Asherim and incense altars will not stand.

10a כִּי עִיר בְּצוּרָה בָּדָד

kî ʿîr bəṣûrâ bādād

For the impregnable city is isolated,

10b נָוֶה מְשֻׁלָּח וְנֶעֱזָב כַּמִּדְבָּר

nāwe məšullāḥ wəneʿĕzāv kammidbār

a dismissed residence, abandoned like the wilderness.

10c שָׁם יִרְעֶה עֵגֶל

šām yirʿe ʿēgel

There the calf will graze

10d וְשָׁם יִרְבָּץ וְכִלָּה סְעִפֶיהָ׃

wəšām yirbāṣ wəkillâ səʿifêhā.

and there he will lie down and put an end to its branches.

11a בִּיבֹשׁ קְצִירָהּ תִּשָּׁבַרְנָה

bîvōš qəṣîrāh tiššāvarnâ

When its branches dry up, they will be broken off.

11b נָשִׁים בָּאוֹת מְאִירוֹת אוֹתָהּ

nāšîm bāʾôt məʾîrôt ʾôtāh

Women come and use them for fire,

11c כִּי לֹא עַם־בִּינוֹת הוּא

kî lōʾ ʿam-bînôt hûʾ

for they are not the smartest people.

11d עַל־כֵּן לֹא־יְרַחֲמֶנּוּ עֹשֵׂהוּ

ʿal-kēn lōʾ-yəraḥămennû ʿōśēhû

Therefore, he will not have any compassion on them,

11e וְיֹצְרוֹ לֹא יְחֻנֶּנּוּ׃

wəyōṣərô lōʾ yəḥunnennû.

and his creator will not show him any favor.

7a	הַכְּמַכַּת מַכֵּהוּ הִכָּהוּ

Has God struck the Israelites as God struck their enemies?

הַכְּמַכַּת מַכָּה	if as a blow/wound *hak·kə·mak·**kat***	CST W/ INTERR הֲ + PREP כְּ	noun
מַכֵּהוּ נכה	smiting/striking him *mak·**kē**·hû*	HIPH PTCP MS W/ 3MS SX	verb
הִכָּהוּ נכה	(he) smote/struck him *hik·**kā**·hû*	HIPH PF 3MS W/ 3MS SX	verb

This phrase is as confusing as it is alliterative. Interpreters must answer: who do the pronominal suffixes refer to, and who is doing the action? Both suffixes are 3ms (but Hebrew commonly uses a singular pronoun to refer collectively), and they do not necessarily have the same referent. The sense is likely, "Has God struck the Israelites as God struck their enemies?" (I have replaced the pronouns in the translation with the nouns they refer to.) God has not struck the Israelites with a blow as severe as he has struck Israel's enemies. Preachers may want to provide their own interpretive translation (much as we have done here) in order to give clarity to this enigmatic verse.

7b	אִם־כְּהֶרֶג הֲרֻגָיו הֹרָג׃

Have the Israelites been killed as their enemies were killed?

אִם־ אִם	if *ʾim-*	---	conj
כְּהֶרֶג הֶרֶג	like a slaughter *kə·**he**·reg*	CST W/ PREP כְּ	noun
הֲרֻגָיו הרג	(he) has been killed by him *hă·ru·**gāyw***	QAL PASS PTCP MP W/ 3MS SX W/ 3MS SX	verb
הֹרָג׃ הרג	(he) was killed *hō·**rāg***	PUAL PF 3MS	verb

Once again, this verse is highly alliterative (using the same root three times) and difficult to translate. We suggest that preachers provide a more interpretive translation for church members to understand the meaning behind this verse.

8a	בְּסַאסְּאָה בְּשַׁלְּחָהּ תְּרִיבֶנָּה		
	You will fight with her by exiling her away.		
בְּסַאסְּאָה סאסא	by banishing *bəs·sa's·sə·'â*	PILPEL INF CST W/ PREP בְּ + 3FS SX	verb
בְּשַׁלְּחָהּ שׁלח	to send her away *bə·šal·ḥāh*	PIEL INF CST W/ PREP בְּ + 3FS SX	verb
תְּרִיבֶנָּה ריב	you will strive/contend with her *tə·rî·ven·nâ*	QAL IMPF 2MS W/ 3FS SX	verb

The interpretive difficulties continue with this phrase. Though ריב ("contend") at times dredges up legal terminology, the phrase better relates to the judgment of exile. God punished Israel through exile, which felt to her like God contending/fighting against her. Preachers can point to the feeling a child gets when the father sends her to her room for disobedience. The child feels like the parent opposes her, but the discipline ultimately has a sanctifying purpose.

8b	הָגָה בְּרוּחוֹ הַקָּשָׁה בְּיוֹם קָדִים׃		
	He separated them with his strong breath in the day of the east wind.		
הָגָה הגה	he removed/separated *hā·gâ*	QAL PF 3MS	verb
בְּרוּחוֹ רוּחַ	with his breath *bə·rû·ḥô*	CST W/ PREP בְּ + 3MS SX	noun
הַקָּשָׁה קָשֶׁה	the hard/difficult/severe *haq·qā·šâ*	FS ATTR W/ DEF. ART.	adj
בְּיוֹם יוֹם	in day *bə·yôm*	CST W/ PREP בְּ	noun

קָדִים׃ קָדִים	east/east wind *qā·**dîm***	ABS	noun

As in many other passages (e.g., Gen 41:6, 23, 27; Exod 10:13; etc.), "east wind" (קָדִים) represents the judgment of God blowing in upon Israel. The verb הָגָה ("he separated") here relates to the judgment of exile by the Assyrians and/or the Babylonians, who dwelled to the literal east of Israel.

9a **לָכֵן בְּזֹאת יְכֻפַּר עֲוֺן־יַעֲקֹב**

Therefore, by this the iniquity of Jacob will be atoned for,

לָכֵן לָכֵן	therefore *lā·**ḵēn***	---	adv
בְּזֹאת זֹאת	in/by this *bə·**zō't***	--- W/ PREP בְּ	demonstr pron
יְכֻפַּר כפר	(it) will be atoned for *yə·ḵup·**par***	PUAL IMPF 3MS	verb
עֲוֺן־ עָוֺן	iniquity/guilt/ punishment *'ă·**wōn**-*	CST	noun
יַעֲקֹב יַעֲקֹב	Jacob *ya·'ă·**qōv***	ABS	noun

Preachers should not quickly pass over the phrase "by this" (בְּזֹאת). "This" refers to the preceding judgment of exile (vv. 7–8). The judgment of exile (vv. 7–8) functioned as atonement by removing the guilt from the Israelites. The punishment had a purifying effect.

9b **וְזֶה כָּל־פְּרִי הָסִר חַטָּאתוֹ**

and this will be the full fruit of the removal of his sin:

וְזֶה זֶה	and this *wə·**ze***	--- W/ CONJ וְ	demonstr pron
כָּל־ כֹּל	all *kol-*	CST	noun
פְּרִי פְּרִי	fruit *pə·**rî***	ABS	noun

הָסֵר סור	to take away/remove *hā·sîr*	HIPH INF CST	verb
חַטָּאתוֹ חַטָּאת	his sin *ḥaṭ·ṭā'·tô*	CST W/ 3MS SX	noun

Once again, preachers should carefully note the second זֶה ("this") in the verse, which this time refers *forward* to the next two lines (9c–d). The "full fruit" (or the result, the proof of) Israel's removal of sins will be evidenced in her destruction of her idols (9c–d). To capture the full process of these verses: God judged the Israelites through the punishment of exile (vv. 7–8), which ultimately purified and atoned for Israel's guilt (9a). Israel's contrition and full repentance will be evidenced by her destroying all her adulterous idols (9b–d). To put it another way, why does the vine of Isa 27 respond positively to God's care, whereas the vine of Isa 5 produces rotten fruit and incurs judgment? *The judgment of the vine in Isa 5 has a sanctifying effect on Israel, producing better "fruit" the next time around.* In addition to carefully following this spiritual/historical process in the text, preachers may also want to draw attention to the ironic use of "fruit" (פְּרִי), which ties in nicely with the vine metaphor that began this chapter.

9c בְּשׂוּמוֹ ׀ כָּל־אַבְנֵי מִזְבֵּחַ כְּאַבְנֵי־גִר מְנֻפָּצוֹת

when he makes all the altar stones just like pulverized chalk.

בְּשׂוּמוֹ ׀ שׂים	in putting/setting him *bə·śû·mô*	QAL INF CST W/ PREP בְּ + 3MS SX	verb
כָּל־ כֹּל	all *kol-*	CST	noun
אַבְנֵי אֶבֶן	stones *'av·nê*	CST	noun
מִזְבֵּחַ מִזְבֵּחַ	altar *miz·bē·aḥ*	ABS	noun
כְּאַבְנֵי־ אֶבֶן	as stones *kə·'av·nê-*	CST W/ PREP כְּ	noun
גִר גִּר	lime/chalk *gir*	ABS	noun
מְנֻפָּצוֹת נפץ	pulverized/smashed *mə·nup·pā·ṣôt*	PUAL PTCP FP	verb

Isaiah calls for nothing less than the complete (כֹּל, "all") destruction (נפץ) of altars and idols to demonstrate the fruit of repentance. The verb נפץ can mean "spread out," such as the disbursement of the people over the face of the earth after the flood (Gen 9:19). It can also have a more violent overtone (as here), such as Gideon and his men "smashing" the jars (Judg 7:19) or the Messiah dashing to pieces his enemies like one smashes a clay pot (Ps 2:9). Additionally, Isaiah uses the verb here in the Pual stem, intensifying the meaning of an already brutal word. For those curious, Ps 137:9 has perhaps the most graphically violent usage of the term in Scripture.

9d לֹֽא־יָקֻ֥מוּ אֲשֵׁרִ֖ים וְחַמָּנִֽים׃

Asherim and incense altars will not stand.

לֹֽא־ לֹא	no/not *lōʾ-*	---	particle
יָקֻ֥מוּ קוּם	(they) will stand *yā·qū·mû*	QAL IMPF 3MP	verb
אֲשֵׁרִ֖ים אֲשֵׁרָה	Asherim *ă·šē·rîm*	ABS	noun
וְחַמָּנִֽים׃ חַמָּן	and incense altars *wə·ḥam·mā·nîm*	ABS W/ CONJ וְ	noun

10a כִּ֣י עִ֤יר בְּצוּרָה֙ בָּדָ֔ד

For the impregnable city is isolated,

כִּ֣י כִּי	for *kî*	---	conj
עִ֤יר עִיר	city *ʿîr*	ABS	noun
בְּצוּרָה֙ בצר	impregnable/ inaccessible *bə·ṣû·râ*	QAL PASS PTCP FS	verb
בָּדָ֔ד בָּדָד	solitude/isolation *bā·dād*	ABS	noun

Juxtaposing "impregnable" (בְּצוּרָה) with "isolation" (בָּדָד) without the use of an intervening verb invokes intentional irony: what was once thought to be an unassailable fortress (Jerusalem) will sit empty and deserted during the judgment of exile.

10b נָוֶה מְשֻׁלָּח וְנֶעֱזָב כַּמִּדְבָּר

a dismissed residence, abandoned like the wilderness.

נָוֶה נָוֶה	residence/dwelling *nā·**we***	ABS	noun
מְשֻׁלָּח שׁלח	being sent off/dismissed *mə·šul·**lāḥ***	PUAL PTCP MS	verb
וְנֶעֱזָב עזב	and abandoned *wə·ne·ʿĕ·**zāv***	NIPH PTCP MS W/ CONJ וְ	verb
כַּמִּדְבָּר מִדְבָּר	like/as the wilderness *kam·mid·**bār***	ABS W/ PREP כְּ + DEF. ART.	noun

Isaiah piles up more words and phrases to stress the abandoned, deserted nature of the once-great city Jerusalem. Reusing שׁלח ("send off"; previously used in v. 8) but connecting it with a "residence" (נָוֶה), something not normally or easily moved, also invokes a strong image of the power of the exile.

10c שָׁם יִרְעֶה עֵגֶל

There the calf will graze

שָׁם שָׁם	there ***šām***	---	adv
יִרְעֶה רעה	he will pasture/graze *yir·**ʿe***	QAL IMPF 3MS	verb
עֵגֶל עֵגֶל	calf ***ʿē**·gel*	ABS	noun

10d	וְשָׁם יִרְבַּץ וְכִלָּה סְעִפֶיהָ׃

and there he will lie down and put an end to its branches.

וְשָׁם שָׁם	and there *wə·šām*	--- W/ CONJ וְ	adv
יִרְבַּץ רבץ	he will lie down *yir·bāṣ*	QAL IMPF 3MS	verb
וְכִלָּה כלה	and (he) will complete finish/end *wə·kil·lâ*	PIEL WEQATAL 3MS	verb
סְעִפֶיהָ׃ סָעִיף	her branches *sə·ʿi·fɛ̂·hā*	CST W/ 3FS SX	noun

The double use of "there" (שָׁם; cf. 10c) invites the listener to picture Jerusalem in his mind's eye. Instead of a bustling metropolis or holy place of worship, cows will graze and sleep and strip bare any fruitful vegetation (again, notice the reversal of the fruitful vine metaphor).

11a	בִּיבֹשׁ קְצִירָהּ תִּשָּׁבַרְנָה

When its branches dry up, they will be broken off.

בִּיבֹשׁ יבשׁ	to be dry *bî·vōš*	QAL INF CST W/ PREP בְּ	verb
קְצִירָהּ קָצִיר	her branches *qə·ṣî·rāh*	CST W/ 3FS SX	noun
תִּשָּׁבַרְנָה שׁבר	they will be broken *tiš·šā·var·nâ*	NIPH IMPF 3FP	verb

11b	נָשִׁים בָּאוֹת מְאִירוֹת אוֹתָהּ

Women come and use them for fire,

נָשִׁים אִשָּׁה	women/wives *nā·šîm*	ABS	noun
בָּאוֹת בוא	coming *bā·ʾôt*	QAL PTCP FP	verb

מְאִירֹ֖ות אור	brightening *mə·ʾî·rôt*	HIPH PTCP FP	verb
אֹותָ֑הּ אֵת	with her *ʾô·tāh*	--- W/ 3FS SX	particle

Israel's exilic destruction will be so thorough that even the branches left behind by the runaway cow population will be broken to bits and used as firewood. Images of abandoned residences in formerly populated city streets might come to mind as possible illustrations.

11c כִּ֣י לֹ֤א עַם־בִּינֹות֙ ה֔וּא

for they are not the smartest people.

כִּ֣י כִּי	for *kî*	---	conj
לֹ֤א לֹא	not *lōʾ*	---	particle
עַם־ עַם	people *ʿam-*	CST	noun
בִּינֹות֙ בִּינָה	understandings *bî·nôt*	ABS	noun
ה֔וּא הוּא	he *hûʾ*	---	personal pron

God states Israel's condition bluntly, to say the least. They lack discernment and qualities of wisdom if they fail to see where their sin will eventually lead them. The pronoun's place at the end of the phrase lends some emphasis to its referent—*Israel* lacks discernment.

11d עַל־כֵּן֙ לֹֽא־יְרַחֲמֶ֣נּוּ עֹשֵׂ֔הוּ

Therefore, he will not have any compassion on them,

עַל־ עַל־כֵּן	upon *ʿal-*	---	adv
כֵּן֙	thus *kēn*		

לֹא־ לא	not *lō*ʾ-	---	particle
יְרַחֲמֶנּוּ רחם	he will have compassion on him *yə·ra·ḥă·**men**·nû*	PIEL IMPF 3MS W/ 3MS SX	verb
עֹשֵׂהוּ עשׂה	he will do/make him *ʿō·**śē**·hû*	QAL PTCP MS W/ 3MS SX	verb

The God of compassion (Exod 33:19; Ps 103:13) will show no compassion on his own people. This should demonstrate to the Israelites how serious their sin and its consequences have become.

11e **וְיֹצְרוֹ לֹא יְחֻנֶּנּוּ׃**

and his creator will not show him any favor.

וְיֹצְרוֹ יצר	his creator *wə·yō·ṣə·**rô***	QAL PTCP MS W/ CONJ וְ + 3MS SX	verb
לֹא לא	not ***lō***ʾ	---	particle
יְחֻנֶּנּוּ׃ חנן	he will show him favor *yə·ḥun·**nen**·nû*	QAL IMPF 3MS W/ 3MS SX	verb

Referring to the Lord as וְיֹצְרוֹ ("his creator") throws an added punch to this passage. God is not some distant deity who decides to look away from some Joe Schmoe on the street. God *as Israel's creator* has removed his favor. This elevates the sadness and horror of the situation.

27:12–13

12a וְהָיָה בַּיּוֹם הַהוּא

wəhāyâ bayyôm hahû'

And it will come to pass in that day

12b יַחְבֹּט יְהוָה מִשִּׁבֹּלֶת הַנָּהָר עַד־נַחַל מִצְרָיִם

yaḥbōṭ YHWH miššibbōlet hannāhār 'ad-naḥal miṣrāyim

YHWH will thresh from the flowing river Euphrates all the way to the brook of Egypt.

12c וְאַתֶּם תְּלֻקְּטוּ לְאַחַד אֶחָד בְּנֵי יִשְׂרָאֵל׃

wə'attem təluqqəṭû lə'aḥad 'eḥād bənê yiśrā'ēl.

And you yourselves will be gathered one by one, O sons of Israel.

13a וְהָיָה | בַּיּוֹם הַהוּא

wəhāyâ bayyôm hahû'

And it will come to pass in that day

13b יִתָּקַע בְּשׁוֹפָר גָּדוֹל

yittāqa' bəšôfār gādôl

a great horn will be blown

13c וּבָאוּ הָאֹבְדִים בְּאֶרֶץ אַשּׁוּר

ûvā'û hā'ōvədîm bə'ereṣ 'aššûr

those who are perishing in the land of Assyria will come in

13d וְהַנִּדָּחִים בְּאֶרֶץ מִצְרָיִם

wəhanniddāḥîm bə'ereṣ miṣrāyim

and also those who are scattered in the land of Egypt

13e וְהִשְׁתַּחֲווּ לַיהוָה בְּהַר הַקֹּדֶשׁ בִּירוּשָׁלָםִ׃

wəhištaḥăwû laYHWH bəhar haqqōdeš bîrûšālāyim.

and they will bow down to YHWH on the holy mountain in Jerusalem.

12a וְהָיָה֮ בַּיּ֣וֹם הַה֗וּא

And it will come to pass in that day

וְהָיָה֮ היה	and it will be *wə·hā·**yâ***	QAL WEQATAL 3MS	verb
בַּיּ֣וֹם יוֹם	in/on the day *bay·**yôm***	ABS W/ PREP בְּ + DEF. ART.	noun
הַה֗וּא הוּא	that *ha·**hû’***	--- W/ DEF. ART.	demonstr pron

The opening phrase of this verse signals a new paragraph (along with the poetry changing to prose). But this section should not be easily divorced from the previous, as it conceptually pictures the end of exile and regathering of God’s people.

12b יַחְבֹּ֧ט יְהוָ֛ה מִשִּׁבֹּ֥לֶת הַנָּהָ֖ר עַד־נַ֣חַל מִצְרָ֑יִם

YHWH will thresh from the flowing river Euphrates all the way to the brook of Egypt.

יַחְבֹּ֧ט חבט	(he) will beat out *yaḥ·**bōṭ***	QAL IMPF 3MS	verb
יְהוָ֛ה יהוה	the Lord *YHWH*	ABS	noun
מִשִּׁבֹּ֥לֶת שִׁבֹּ֫לֶת	from a flowing stream *miš·šib·**bō**·let*	CST W/ PREP מִן	noun
הַנָּהָ֖ר נָהָר	the river *han·nā·**hār***	ABS W/ DEF. ART.	noun
עַד־ עַד	until/as far as *‘ad-*	---	prep
נַ֣חַל נַ֫חַל	torrent/brook ***na**·ḥal*	CST	noun
מִצְרָ֑יִם מִצְרַ֫יִם	Egypt *miṣ·**rā**·yim*	ABS	noun

The verb חבט ("thresh/beat out") invokes imagery of farmers threshing their crops. Threshing was a process of separating the good grain from the useless husks. Here, from the highest northeast region (Assyria) to the lowest southwestern region (Egypt), God will gather together the remnant of repentant exiles and return them to their homeland of Canaan.

12c **וְאַתֶּם תְּלֻקְּטוּ לְאַחַד אֶחָד בְּנֵי יִשְׂרָאֵל׃**

And you yourselves will be gathered one by one, O sons of Israel.

וְאַתֶּם אַתֶּם	and you *wə·ʾat·**tem***	--- W/ CONJ וְ	personal pron
תְּלֻקְּטוּ לקט	you will be gathered *tə·luq·qə·**ṭû***	PUAL IMPF 2MP	verb
לְאַחַד אֶחָד	to one *lə·ʾa·**ḥad***	CST W/ PREP לְ	cardinal number
אֶחָד אֶחָד	one *ʾe·**ḥād***	ABS	cardinal number
בְּנֵי בֵּן	sons *bə·**nê***	CST	noun
יִשְׂרָאֵל׃ יִשְׂרָאֵל	Israel *yiś·rā·**ʾēl***	ABS	noun

The plural pronoun אַתֶּם ("you") is grammatically unnecessary and thus brings extra attention to the Israelites, the objects of the gleaning activity of the Lord.

13a **וְהָיָה | בַּיּוֹם הַהוּא**

And it will come to pass in that day

וְהָיָה | היה	and it will be *wə·hā·**yâ***	QAL WEQATAL 3MS	verb
בַּיּוֹם יוֹם	in/on the day *bay·**yôm***	ABS W/ PREP בְּ + DEF. ART.	noun
הַהוּא הוּא	that *ha·**hûʾ***	--- W/ DEF. ART.	demonstr pron

Verses 12 and 13 both open with the same three words, likely indicating they speak of the exact same time frame.

13b	יִתָּקַע֙ בְּשׁוֹפָ֣ר גָּד֔וֹל
	a great horn will be blown

יִתָּקַע֙	(it) will be blown	NIPH IMPF 3MS	verb
תקע	*yit·tā·**qa**ʿ*		
בְּשׁוֹפָ֣ר	horn/trumpet	ABS W/ PREP בְּ	noun
שׁוֹפָר	*bə·šô·**fār***		
גָּד֔וֹל	great	MS ATTR	adj
גָּדוֹל	*gā·**dôl***		

Though there are several New Testament passages that speak of a trumpet sounding to usher in the return of Jesus and the final resurrection (1 Cor 15:52; 1 Thess 4:16; cf. Rev 1:10; 4:1; 8:13; 9:14), this may simply be metaphorical for a victorious summoning of the exiled Israelites back to their homeland. If Matt 24:31 intentionally alludes to Isa 27:13, this may give weight to the possibility that the return from exile typifies the final resurrection and that the fulfillment of this text ultimately takes place at the return of Christ.

13c	וּבָ֡אוּ הָאֹבְדִים֩ בְּאֶ֣רֶץ אַשּׁ֗וּר
	those who are perishing in the land of Assyria will come in

וּבָ֡אוּ	and (they) will come in	QAL WEQATAL 3CP	verb
בוא	*û·**vā**·ʾû*		
הָאֹבְדִים֩	those perishing	QAL PTCP MP W/ DEF. ART.	verb
אבד	*hā·ʾō·və·**dîm***		
בְּאֶ֣רֶץ	in land	CST W/ PREP בְּ	noun
אֶרֶץ	*bə·ʾ**e**·reṣ*		
אַשּׁ֗וּר	Assyria	ABS	noun
אַשּׁוּר	*ʾaš·**šûr***		

The participial form of **אבד** ("those perishing") makes the picture more vivid than if a noun were used. The people are actively perishing in the foreign land when the trumpet sounds. One might picture a drowning child who hears the whistle of a lifeguard that signals impending rescue.

13d	וְהַנִּדָּחִים בְּאֶרֶץ מִצְרָיִם

and also those who are scattered in the land of Egypt

וְהַנִּדָּחִים נדח	and those banished/ scattered *wə·han·nid·dā·**ḥîm***	NIPH PTCP MP W/ CONJ וְ + DEF. ART.	verb
בְּאֶרֶץ אֶרֶץ	in land *bə·'**e**·reṣ*	CST W/ PREP בְּ	noun
מִצְרָיִם מִצְרַיִם	Egypt *miṣ·**rā**·yim*	ABS	noun

13e	וְהִשְׁתַּחֲוּוּ לַיהוָה בְּהַר הַקֹּדֶשׁ בִּירוּשָׁלִָם׃

and they will bow down to YHWH
on the holy mountain in Jerusalem.

וְהִשְׁתַּחֲוּוּ שחה	and they will bow down/worship *wə·hiš·ta·ḥă·**wû***	HITHPALEL WEQATAL 3CP	verb
לַיהוָה יהוה	to the Lord *la·YHWH*	ABS W/ PREP לְ	noun
בְּהַר הַר	on mountain *bə·**har***	CST W/ PREP בְּ	noun
הַקֹּדֶשׁ קֹדֶשׁ	holy *haq·**qō**·deš*	ABS W/ DEF. ART.	noun
בִּירוּשָׁלִָם׃ יְרוּשָׁלַםִ	in Jerusalem *bî·rû·šā·**lā**·yim*	ABS W/ PREP בְּ	noun

From Text to Sermon

- ***Big Idea.*** God provides atonement and his people respond with holiness.

- ***Avenues for Illustration and Application.*** Preachers will want to take extra caution when talking about the mythology behind the Leviathan. Even when treating the creature mythologically, the Bible does not affirm that Lotan, Tiamat, Rahab, or other similar gods exist; rather, it uses these cultural myths to affirm the omnipotence of the Lord.

  One might illustrate this concept by using examples from popular culture. For example, in 1998, disaster-movie director Roland Emmerich made an American Godzilla movie. It was lambasted by critics and Japanese viewers alike. Six years later, Japan culminated fifty years of Godzilla films with an epic movie called *Godzilla: Final Wars*. Among the kaiju monsters Godzilla faces was one called Zilla, a creature that looked suspiciously like the American Godzilla. It was purposefully created with terrible computer effects to further mock the American version, and in the battle, Zilla gets pulverized in less than a minute. It was Japan's way of sticking it to the American version and saying, "Our monster is better than yours!" This is similar to what the Bible does with these pagan gods. The Lord can cut off the head of the greatest forces of evil, the Leviathan—"Our God is better than yours!"

  Church members will likely take interest in the Leviathan discussion (after all, who doesn't want to talk about giant sea monsters on a Sunday morning?), but preachers will want to carefully bring the discussion back to theology and application. Two simple applications for this first verse help do this: (1) God's dominance over evil relieves our anxieties. God will conquer the forces of evil one day. The Lord is not weak. The picture of God as a divine warrior, wielding a giant sword, fighting sea serpents and dragons epically shows us that with *this* God on our side, what do we have to fear? (2) God's dominance over evil motivates believers to praise him. Preachers can consider using Ps 148:7 to highlight this application: "Praise the Lord from the earth, you great sea creatures (תַּנִּין) and all deeps" (ESV). Even the greatest creatures of creation should recognize the one who is greater than they. May all believers do the same.

  Isaiah 27 does not only allow for giant monster illustrations, but it has a richness in metaphor that gives preachers many opportunities to illustrate using the prompts from the biblical text. Verse 8 uses a strong wind from God's breath to describe the removal of Israelites into exile.

Geographical locations that see frequent windstorms, hurricanes, or tornadoes will have no problem seeing Isaiah's point. Verses 10–11 give the picture of a once-bustling city now deserted and inhabited only by wild animals. One might recall the many postapocalyptic movies or TV shows where the camera inevitably lingers over the abandoned city with newspapers blowing in the street, cars abandoned, animals roaming, and vines creeping in. Verses 12–13 give a particularly strong metaphor of God threshing Israel from the nations, gathering her people together. This idea may need more explanation than the others, since most people today are unfamiliar with the process of threshing, but a few minutes spent explaining the process can bring to light the force of God's words.

New Testament Connections. If YHWH punishing the Leviathan in Isa 27:1 represents God defeating the forces of evil, it builds on the protevangelium in Gen 3:15—the seed of the woman will crush the head of the serpent. Isaiah 27 becomes another echo of Gen 3, an echo that extends into Rev 12 when Michael and his angels fight the great and ancient dragon/serpent. The dragon faces final defeat in Rev 20 after one last ditch effort to deceive the nations. Isaiah stands at the nexus of what came before and what the future holds for the Leviathan called Satan.

On a more positive note, the activity and initiative of God's treatment of the vineyard aligns with God's activity and initiative in the application of the gospel. The text emphatically highlights God's care as the sole reason the vine produces anything. "*I*, the LORD, am its keeper; *every moment I* water it . . . *I* keep it night and day" (27:3). This is entirely a divine work, begun by God and continually sustained by God. The New Testament views a cooperation between God's divine initiative in our salvation and our human responsibility to respond appropriately to his activity (cf. Phil 2:12–13).

It is difficult to preach Isa 27 without having first preached Isa 5, or at least without first helping the congregation understand the background of Isa 5. Each text pictures a different reaction and result to God's grace, illustrated in this chart:

Isa 5:	God's grace	→	Sin	→	Judgment
Isa 27:	God's grace	→	Fruitfulness	→	Blessing

What changed between these two events, other than the timing? One takes place before the exile, the other takes place after. The text points to the judgment of exile as a means of bringing the Israelites to repentance and ultimately, atonement (27:9). By bringing Isa 5 and 27 together, preachers can give the fullest picture of the gospel at work in the Israelites by showing how atonement changes one's reaction to the grace of God:

Isa 5:	God's grace	→	Sin	→	Judgment
			ATONEMENT		
Isa 27:	God's grace	→	Fruitfulness	→	Blessing

Though the New Testament never uses the word "atone" or "atonement," it expands the theology into a rich tapestry of other terms for what God does for us in Christ, including propitiation (Rom 3:25), reconciliation (Rom 5:10), redemption (Eph 1:7), forgiveness (Col 1:14), purification (1 Pet 1:22), justification (Rom 5:1), and salvation (Rom 10:9). All these blessings come when our sins are atoned for.

WOES UPON THE LEADERSHIP

We expect leaders to live up to a certain standard of morality and propriety. We hold pastors to a higher standard of morality than the average layperson. We expect police officers to uphold the law both in and out of uniform. We want managers who show up earlier than everyone and leave later than everyone, setting the example through hard work. But human leaders let us down. They did in Isaiah's day. Prophet, priest, and king all fell into the sin of drunkenness and apathetically rejected the words of God. Isaiah's message to these sinful leaders mixes humor and horror, wit and judgment. With some knowledge of Hebrew, preachers can help the church enjoy the text in a way that English translations simply cannot offer.

LARGER LITERARY CONTEXT › 28:1–29

28:1–4

1a ה֗וֹי עֲטֶ֤רֶת גֵּאוּת֙ שִׁכֹּרֵ֣י אֶפְרַ֔יִם

hôy ʿăṭeret gēʾût šikkōrê ʾefrayim

Alas! The majestic "crown" of the drunks of Ephraim,

1b וְצִ֥יץ נֹבֵ֖ל צְבִ֣י תִפְאַרְתּ֑וֹ

wəṣîṣ nōvēl ṣəvî tifartô

and the wilting flower of his glorious "beauty,"

1c אֲשֶׁ֛ר עַל־רֹ֥אשׁ גֵּֽיא־שְׁמָנִ֖ים

ʾăšer ʿal-rôš gêʾ-šəmānîm

which sits upon the head of the rich valley,

1d הֲל֥וּמֵי יָֽיִן׃

hălûmê yāyin.

of those smitten by wine!

2a הִנֵּ֨ה חָזָ֤ק וְאַמִּץ֙ לַאדֹנָ֔י

hinnē ḥāzāq wəʾammiṣ laʾădōnāy

Behold! My Lord is strong and mighty,

2b כְּזֶ֥רֶם בָּרָ֖ד שַׂ֣עַר קָ֑טֶב

kəzerem bārād śaʿar qāṭev

as a downpour of hail, a storm of destruction,

2c כְּ֠זֶרֶם מַ֣יִם כַּבִּירִ֥ים שֹׁטְפִ֛ים

kəzerem mayim kabbîrîm šōṭəfîm

as a downpour of mighty, overflowing waters,

2d הִנִּ֥יחַ לָאָ֖רֶץ בְּיָֽד׃

hinnîaḥ lāʾāreṣ bəyād.

he cast down to the earth with his hand.

3a בְּרַגְלַיִם תֵּרָמַסְנָה
bərag**la**yim tērā**mas**nâ

They will be trampled underfoot,

3b עֲטֶרֶת גֵּאוּת שִׁכּוֹרֵי אֶפְרָיִם׃
ʿăṭeret gēʾ**ût** šikkô**rê** ʾef**rā**yim.

the majestic "crown" of the drunks of Ephraim.

4a וְהָיְתָה צִיצַת נֹבֵל צְבִי תִפְאַרְתּוֹ
wə**hā**yətâ ṣî**ṣat** nō**vēl** ṣə**vî** tifar**tô**

And the wilting flower of his glorious "beauty,"

4b אֲשֶׁר עַל־רֹאשׁ גֵּיא שְׁמָנִים
ʾă**šer** ʿal-**rôš** **gêʾ** šəmā**nîm**

which sits upon the head of the rich valley,

4c כְּבִכּוּרָהּ בְּטֶרֶם קַיִץ
kəvikkû**rāh** bəṭerem **qa**yiṣ

just like the early ripe fig before the summer fruit,

4d אֲשֶׁר יִרְאֶה הָרֹאֶה אוֹתָהּ
ʾă**šer** yirʾ**e** hārōʾe ʾô**tāh**

which, when someone takes a look at it,

4e בְּעוֹדָהּ בְּכַפּוֹ יִבְלָעֶנָּה׃
bəʿô**dāh** bəḵap**pô** yivlāʿ**en**nâ.

he gobbles it up the moment it touches his hand.

1a	הוֹי עֲטֶרֶת גֵּאוּת שִׁכֹּרֵי אֶפְרַיִם

Alas! The majestic "crown" of the drunks of Ephraim,

הוֹי הוֹי	alas!/woe! *hôy*	---	particle
עֲטֶרֶת עֲטָרָה	crown *ʿă·ṭe·ret*	CST	noun
גֵּאוּת גֵּאוּת	majestic *gē·ʾût*	CST	noun
שִׁכֹּרֵי שִׁכֹּר	drunkards of *šik·kō·rê*	MP SUBST	adj
אֶפְרַיִם אֶפְרַיִם	Ephraim *ʾef·ra·yim*	ABS	noun

The word הוֹי ("Alas!/Woe!") signals a new unit in the book of Isaiah that spans chs. 28–35 and is characterized by the usage of this word (28:1; 29:1, 15; 30:1; 31:1; 33:1). The word appears often in Isaiah (21x) and other prophetic contexts (Jer 11x; Ezek 3x; Minor Prophets 15x; only elsewhere in 1 Kgs 13:30). The word can signal a warning, a coming judgment, or a simple word of summons (cf. Harmon 1997:1032). The focus of this judgment oracle is upon the "drunks of Ephraim," with Ephraim standing for the Northern Kingdom. By using a substantival adjective (שִׁכֹּרֵי, "drunkards"), the Hebrew characterizes the people of Israel by their sin of drunkenness. It may be politically incorrect to call someone a "drunk" today, but ancient prophets had no such qualms.

1b	וְצִיץ נֹבֵל צְבִי תִפְאַרְתּוֹ

and the wilting flower of his glorious "beauty,"

וְצִיץ צִיץ	and flower/blossom *wə·ṣîṣ*	ABS W/ CONJ וְ	noun
נֹבֵל נבל	drooping/withered *nō·vēl*	QAL PTCP MS	verb
צְבִי צְבִי	beauty/glory *ṣə·vî*	CST	noun
תִפְאַרְתּוֹ תִּפְאָרָה	his beauty *tif·ʾar·tô*	CST W/ 3MS SX	noun

Many have noted that Samaria, being the capitol of the Northern Kingdom, was located on a hill overlooking a rich and fertile valley, which likely provides the background for Isaiah's mockery and metaphor. What the Samaritans/Ephraimites believed to be their "crown of beauty" was really a wilting flower due to the drunks in the valley.

1c	אֲשֶׁר עַל־רֹאשׁ גֵּיא־שְׁמָנִים

which sits upon the head of the rich valley,

אֲשֶׁר אֲשֶׁר	which *'ă·šer*	---	relative pron
עַל־ עַל	upon *'al-*	---	prep
רֹאשׁ ראשׁ	head *rôš*	CST	noun
גֵּיא־ גַּיְא	valley *gê'-*	CST	noun
שְׁמָנִים שֶׁמֶן	fat/oil *šə·mā·**nîm***	ABS	noun

The construct גֵּיא־שְׁמָנִים ("valley of fat/oil") speaks of the richness of the land, as fat and oil were only abundant for those who were wealthy and for land that was productive. If using a Bible version that translates "fat" (e.g., KJV), preachers may want to carefully contextualize the phraseology, as many moderns have an aversion to fat/oily foods.

1d	הֲלוּמֵי יָיִן׃

of those smitten by wine!

הֲלוּמֵי הלם	those smitten *hă·**lû**·mê*	QAL PASS (CST) PTCP MP	verb
יָיִן׃ יַיִן	wine ***yā**·yin*	ABS	noun

Preachers should note the passive nature of the phrase here. The drunk is not in control; rather, the wine "smites" the drinker. The verb הלם is a strong word, other times used of smashing idols into smithereens (Ps 74:6). When wine enslaves, the drinker truly becomes "hammered" by wine.

2a	הִנֵּ֨ה חָזָ֤ק וְאַמִּץ֙ לַֽאדֹנָ֔י

Behold! My Lord is strong and mighty,

הִנֵּה הִנֵּה	behold! *hin·nē*	---	particle
חָזָק חָזָק	strong/mighty *ḥā·zāq*	MS PRED	adj
וְאַמִּץ אַמִּיץ	and mighty/strong *wə·ʾam·miṣ*	MS PRED W/ CONJ וְ	adj
לַאדֹנָי אָדוֹן	to my Lord *la·ʾă·dō·nāy*	ABS W/ PREP לְ	noun

Following the opening "woe" of v. 1, הִנֵּה ("behold!") continues to grab the attention of listeners and readers, inviting them to imagine the storm metaphor. Following the text, preachers will want to shift the sermon's focus here to magnify the strength of God and his judgment rather than focus on a sad description of the drunk.

2b	כְּזֶ֥רֶם בָּרָ֖ד שַׂ֣עַר קָ֑טֶב

as a downpour of hail, a storm of destruction,

כְּזֶרֶם זֶרֶם	as rainstorm/downpour *kə·ze·rem*	CST W/ PREP כְּ	noun
בָּרָד בָּרָד	hail *bā·rād*	ABS	noun
שַׂעַר שַׂעַר	storm *śa·ʿar*	CST	noun
קָטֶב קֶטֶב	destruction *qā·ṭev*	ABS	noun

2c	כְּ֠זֶרֶם מַ֣יִם כַּבִּירִ֣ים שֹׁטְפִ֑ים

as a downpour of mighty, overflowing waters,

כְּזֶרֶם זֶרֶם	as rainstorm/downpour *kə·ze·rem*	CST W/ PREP כְּ	noun

מַ֫יִם	waters	ABS	noun
מַ֫יִם	*__ma__·yim*		
כַּבִּירִ֑ים	mighty/powerful	MP ATTR	adj
כַּבִּיר	*kab·bî·__rîm__*		
שֹׁטְפִ֑ים	overflowing	QAL PTCP MP	verb
שׁטף	*šō·ṭə·__fîm__*		

Note how Isaiah piles up phrases to intensify the terror of the mighty storm. Preachers should remind their listeners that ancient Israelites were far from the modern, protected conveniences of sturdy houses and sloping roofs, which means that storms such as these were as potentially deadly as they were powerful.

2d הִנִּ֥יחַ לָאָ֖רֶץ בְּיָֽד׃

he cast down to the earth with his hand.

הִנִּ֥יחַ	he cast	HIPH PF 3MS	verb
נוח	*hin·__nî__·aḥ*		
לָאָ֖רֶץ	to earth	ABS W/ PREP לְ + DEF. ART.	noun
אֶ֫רֶץ	*lā·__ʾā__·reṣ*		
בְּיָֽד׃	by/with hand	ABS W/ PREP בְּ	noun
יָד	*bə·__yād__*		

Isaiah highlights the omnipotence of God here, as he has power enough to control great thunderstorms as easily as one cups a handful of water from the kitchen faucet.

3a בְּרַגְלַ֖יִם תֵּֽרָמַ֑סְנָה

They will be trampled underfoot,

בְּרַגְלַ֖יִם	with/under foot	ABS W/ PREP בְּ	noun
רֶ֫גֶל	*bə·rag·__la__·yim*		
תֵּֽרָמַ֑סְנָה	they will be trampled	NIPH IMPF 3FP	verb
רמס	*tē·rā·__mas__·nâ*		

This more literal description points to what the storm imagery in v. 2 signifies: the Assyrian army was positioned to enter and trample on Samaria.

Preachers might consider reading passages like 2 Kgs 17:5–7, which describes the actual invasion.

3b	עֲטֶרֶת גֵּאוּת שִׁכּוֹרֵי אֶפְרָיִם׃
	the majestic "crown" of the drunks of Ephraim.

עֲטֶרֶת עֲטָרָה	crown *ʿă·ṭe·ret*	CST	noun
גֵּאוּת גֵּאוּת	majestic *gē·ʾ**ût***	CST	noun
שִׁכּוֹרֵי שִׁכֹּר	drunkards *šik·kô·**rê***	MP SUBST	adj
אֶפְרָיִם׃ אֶפְרַיִם	Ephraim *ʾef·**rā**·yim*	ABS	noun

This phrase is identical to the phrase in 1a. See comments in 4b for significance.

4a	וְהָיְתָה צִיצַת נֹבֵל צְבִי תִפְאַרְתּוֹ
	And the wilting flower of his glorious "beauty,"

וְהָיְתָה היה	and it will be *wə·**hā**·yə·tâ*	QAL WEQATAL 3FS	verb
צִיצַת צִיצַת	flower/blossom *ṣî·**ṣat***	ABS	noun
נֹבֵל נבל	drooping/withered *nō·**vēl***	QAL PTCP MS	verb
צְבִי צְבִי	beauty/glory *ṣə·**vî***	CST	noun
תִּפְאַרְתּוֹ תִּפְאָרָה	his beauty *tif·ʾar·**tô***	CST W/ 3MS SX	noun

This phrase is nearly identical to the phrase in 1b. See comments in 4b for significance.

4b	אֲשֶׁר עַל־רֹאשׁ גֵּיא שְׁמָנִים

which sits upon the head of the rich valley,

אֲשֶׁר אֲשֶׁר	which *ʾă·šer*	---	relative pron
עַל־ עַל	upon *ʿal-*	---	prep
רֹאשׁ רֹאשׁ	head *rôš*	CST	noun
גֵּיא גַּיְא	valley *gê*ʾ	CST	noun
שְׁמָנִים שֶׁמֶן	fat/oil *šə·mā·nîm*	ABS	noun

This phrase is identical to the phrase in v. 1c. What was once the glory of the northern Israelites—their rich agriculture—will turn into stomping grounds for the Assyrians when they invade. By bringing back the derisive imagery from v. 1, Isaiah explicitly connects the drunken, arrogant pride of the Israelites with their coming judgment.

4c	כְּבִכּוּרָהּ בְּטֶרֶם קַיִץ

just like the early ripe fig before the summer fruit,

כְּבִכּוּרָהּ בִּכּוּרָה	as its early ripe fig *kə·vik·kû·rāh*	ABS W/ PREP כְּ + 3FS SX	noun
בְּטֶרֶם טֶרֶם	before *bə·ṭe·rem*	--- W/ PREP בְּ	adv
קַיִץ קַיִץ	summer/summer fruit *qa·yiṣ*	ABS	noun

The preposition כְּ invites comparison between the way an early ripe fig is picked and quickly gobbled down and the way the Assyrians will desolate the lush landscape of northern Israel.

4d	אֲשֶׁר יִרְאֶה הָרֹאֶה אוֹתָהּ

which, when someone takes a look at it,

אֲשֶׁר אֲשֶׁר	which *ʾă·šer*	---	relative pron
יִרְאֶה ראה	he will see *yir·ʾe*	QAL IMPF 3MS	verb
הָרֹאֶה ראה	seeing *hā·rō·ʾe*	QAL PTCP MS W/ DEF. ART.	verb
אוֹתָהּ אֵת	with it *ʾô·tāh*	--- W/ 3FS SX	particle

The imperfect + participle of ראה ("to see") adds vividness and emphasizes the greed of the fig-eater. His eyes impulsively control his stomach.

4e	בְּעוֹדָהּ בְּכַפּוֹ יִבְלָעֶנָּה׃

he gobbles it up the moment it touches his hand.

בְּעוֹדָהּ עוֹד	while still it *bə·ʿô·dāh*	--- W/ PREP בְּ + 3FS SX	adv
בְּכַפּוֹ כַּף	in his palm *bə·kap·pô*	CST W/ PREP בְּ + 3MS SX	noun
יִבְלָעֶנָּה׃ בלע	he swallows it *yiv·lā·ʿen·nâ*	QAL IMPF 3MS W/ 3FS SX	verb

The Hebrew here pictures an impossible scenario, and the absurdity of it is exactly the point. It is quite impossible to swallow something that is still in your hand, but such is the impulsive greed of the fig-eater/Assyrians!

28:5–6

5a בַּיּ֣וֹם הַה֗וּא יִֽהְיֶה֙ יְהוָ֣ה צְבָא֔וֹת

bayyôm hahû' yihye YHWH ṣəvā'ôt

In that day, YHWH of hosts will be

5b לַעֲטֶ֣רֶת צְבִ֔י וְלִצְפִירַ֖ת תִּפְאָרָ֑ה

la'ăṭeret ṣəvî wəliṣfîrat tif'ārâ

a crown of glory and a wreath of beauty

5c לִשְׁאָ֖ר עַמּֽוֹ׃

liš'ār 'ammô.

for the remnant of his people,

6a וּלְר֖וּחַ מִשְׁפָּ֑ט לַיּוֹשֵׁב֙ עַל־הַמִּשְׁפָּ֔ט

ûlərûaḥ mišpāṭ layyôšēv 'al-hammišpāṭ

and a spirit of justice for those who preside over justice,

6b וְלִ֨גְבוּרָ֔ה מְשִׁיבֵ֥י מִלְחָמָ֖ה שָֽׁעְרָה׃

wəligvûrâ məšîvê milḥāmâ šā'ərâ.

and power for those who defend the gate during battle.

5a בַּיּ֣וֹם הַה֗וּא יִֽהְיֶה֙ יְהוָ֣ה צְבָא֔וֹת

In that day, YHWH of hosts will be

בַּיּ֣וֹם יוֹם	in (the) day *bay·yôm*	ABS W/ PREP בְּ + DEF. ART.	noun
הַה֗וּא הוּא	that *ha·hû'*	--- W/ DEF. ART.	demonstr pron
יִֽהְיֶה֙ היה	(he) will be *yih·ye*	QAL IMPF 3MS	verb

יְהוָה יהוה	the LORD *YHWH*	ABS	noun
צְבָאוֹת צָבָא	hosts/armies *ṣə · vā · ʾ**ôt***	ABS	noun

Once again, preachers will need to carefully explain the meaning of "in that day," as well as the text will allow. Cf. comments at 27:2a.

5b **לַעֲטֶרֶת צְבִי וְלִצְפִירַת תִּפְאָרָה**

a crown of glory and a wreath of beauty

לַעֲטֶרֶת עֲטָרָה	for a crown *la · ʿă · **ṭe** · ret*	CST W/ PREP לְ	noun
צְבִי צְבִי	beauty/glory *ṣə · **vî***	ABS	noun
וְלִצְפִירַת צְפִירָה	and for a wreath/crown *wə · liṣ · fî · **rat***	CST W/ CONJ וְ + PREP לְ	noun
תִּפְאָרָה תִּפְאָרָה	beauty *tif · ʾā · **râ***	ABS	noun

Isaiah ironically flips the imagery of the crowned drunkards in order to underscore that the true glory of God's people is God himself. What the Israelites thought was their boast and glory ended up stripped and destroyed by the Assyrians. But God allowed them to lose their beauty in order to show his people that *he* is their true crown and glory. God's judgment has a redemptive purpose. Isaiah later further transforms this picture in 62:3–4a. There, the people once again become the crown of beauty in the hand of the Lord. Do not miss the progression of Fall–Redemption–Restoration: the Israelites arrogantly boast in their own glory, so the Lord brings in Assyria to remove their source of pride (Fall); God reveals himself as their true source of glory (Redemption); God restores the Israelites to their land, where he makes them glorious like himself (Restoration).

5c	לִשְׁאָ֖ר עַמּֽוֹ׃

for the remnant of his people,

לִשְׁאָ֖ר שְׁאָר	for remnant/rest/remainder *liš·'ār*	CST W/ PREP לְ	noun
עַמּֽוֹ׃ עַם	his people *'am·mô*	CST W/ 3MS SX	noun

The preposition לְ seems to work in a different manner than the previous two in this verse. The first two mark the predicate nominatives with the verb היה, while this phrase marks the indirect object, indicating the goal of the Lord's work in the people. (see Waltke & O'Connor 1990:209).

6a	וּלְר֖וּחַ מִשְׁפָּ֑ט לַיּוֹשֵׁב֙ עַל־הַמִּשְׁפָּ֔ט

and a spirit of justice for those who preside over justice,

וּלְר֖וּחַ רוּחַ	and for spirit *û·lə·rû·aḥ*	CST W/ CONJ וְ + PREP לְ	noun
מִשְׁפָּ֑ט מִשְׁפָּט	judgment/justice *miš·pāṭ*	ABS	noun
לַיּוֹשֵׁב֙ ישׁב	to those sitting/dwelling *lay·yô·šēv*	QAL PTCP MS W/ PREP לְ + DEF. ART.	verb
עַל־ עַל	over/upon *'al-*	---	prep
הַמִּשְׁפָּ֔ט מִשְׁפָּט	the judgment/justice *ham·miš·pāṭ*	ABS W/ DEF. ART.	noun

"Those who preside over justice" (לַיּוֹשֵׁב עַל־הַמִּשְׁפָּט) likely describes the judges and magistrates of the land who oversee legal rulings. It might even describe other leaders who have the authority to maintain justice. Whatever their identity, God gives them the wisdom they need to make decisions with proper discernment, which removes all boasting in their own abilities or strength (cf. 6b; Jer 9:23–24).

6b **וְלִ֝גְבוּרָ֗ה מְשִׁיבֵ֥י מִלְחָ֣מָה שָֽׁעְרָה׃**

and power for those who defend the gate during battle.

וְלִ֝גְבוּרָ֗ה גְּבוּרָה	and for strength/might *wə · lig · vû · **râ***	ABS W/ CONJ וְ + PREP לְ	noun
מְשִׁיבֵ֥י שׁוּב	those who bring/ turn back *mə · šî · **vê***	HI (CST) PTCP MP	verb
מִלְחָ֣מָה מִלְחָמָה	battle/war *mil · ḥā · **mâ***	ABS	noun
שָֽׁעְרָה׃ שַׁ֫עַר	gate *__šā__ · ʿə · râ*	ABS W/ LOCATIVE ה	noun

28:7–8

7a וְגַם־אֵ֫לֶּה בַּיַּ֣יִן שָׁג֔וּ
*wəgam-ʾ**ē**lle bay**ya**yin šā**gû***

Even these people wander about because of wine

7b וּבַשֵּׁכָ֖ר תָּע֑וּ
*ûvaššē**ḵār** tā**ʿû***

and because of strong drink they stagger;

7c כֹּהֵ֤ן וְנָבִיא֙ שָׁג֣וּ בַשֵּׁכָ֔ר
*kō**hēn** wənā**vî**ʾ šā**gû** vaššē**ḵar***

priest and prophet wander about because of strong drink,

7d נִבְלְע֣וּ מִן־הַיַּ֗יִן
*nivlə**ʿû** min-hay**ya**yin*

they are swallowed up from the wine;

7e תָּעוּ֙ מִן־הַשֵּׁכָ֔ר
*tā**ʿû** min-haššē**ḵār***

they stagger because of the strong drink;

7f שָׁגוּ֙ בָּֽרֹאֶ֔ה
*šā**gû** bārō**ʾe***

they wander about while having prophetic visions;

7g פָּ֖קוּ פְּלִילִיָּֽה׃
*pā**qû** pəlîliy**yâ**.*

they wobble when making judicial judgments.

8a כִּ֚י כָּל־שֻׁלְחָנ֔וֹת מָלְא֖וּ קִ֣יא צֹאָ֑ה
kî** kol-šulḥā**nôt** mālə**ʾû** **qî**ʾ ṣō**ʾâ

For all their tables are filled with crappy vomit,

8b בְּלִ֥י מָקֽוֹם׃

bəlî māqôm.

without a clean plate in sight.

7a	וְגַם־אֵ֙לֶּה֙ בַּיַּ֣יִן שָׁג֔וּ

Even these people wander about because of wine

וְגַם־ גַּם	and also/even *wə·gam-*	--- W/ CONJ וְ	adv
אֵ֙לֶּה֙ אֵלֶּה	these *ʾēl·le*	---	demonstr pron
בַּיַּ֣יִן יַיִן	with wine *bay·ya·yin*	ABS W/ PREP בְּ + DEF. ART.	noun
שָׁג֔וּ שׁגה	they go astray/err *šā·gû*	QAL PF 3CP	verb

"Even these" (וְגַם־אֵלֶּה) points forward to the priest and prophet in 7c. It is surprising enough that God's people in northern Israel stagger about in drunken stupor; how much more of a surprise to find out that those who are supposed to be spiritual leaders in Israel do the same! Preachers should capitalize on this shocking image.

7b	וּבַשֵּׁכָ֖ר תָּע֑וּ

and because of strong drink they stagger;

וּבַשֵּׁכָ֖ר שֵׁכָר	and with strong drink *û·vaš·šē·ḵār*	ABS W/ CONJ וְ + PREP בְּ + DEF. ART.	noun
תָּע֑וּ תעה	they stagger *tā·ʿû*	QAL PF 3CP	verb

Isaiah highlights the impact of the leaders' alcoholism by piling up synonymous nouns for beer and synonymous verbs for drunken stagger (he uses "strong drink" 3x, "wine" 2x, "reel" 3x, "stagger" 2x, and also "swallowed" and "stumble"). The Hebrew reads with a kind of staccato cadence which can be captured in the following rough translation (see Oswalt 1986:510 for a similar translation highlighting the repetitive language):

> Wine—Reel
> Beer—Stagger
> Reel—Beer
> Swallowed—Wine
> Stagger—Beer
> Reel—Vision
> Stumble—Judgment

The only words that "interrupt" this machine-gun effect are "priest and prophet" (7c), a surprise twist on who is given to this sin.

7c כֹּהֵ֤ן וְנָבִיא֙ שָׁג֣וּ בַשֵּׁכָ֔ר

priest and prophet wander about because of strong drink,

כֹּהֵ֤ן כֹּהֵן	priest *kō·**hēn***	ABS	noun
וְנָבִיא֙ נָבִיא	and prophet *wə·nā·**vîʾ***	ABS W/ CONJ וְ	noun
שָׁג֣וּ שׁגה	they go astray/err *šā·**gû***	QAL PF 3CP	verb
בַשֵּׁכָ֔ר שֵׁכָר	with strong drink *vaš·šē·**ḵar***	ABS W/ PREP בְּ + DEF. ART.	noun

Preachers should not make too strong a distinction between the synonyms used for strong drink, beer, wine, etc. All denote alcoholic beverages, even if the proof or contents vary between them. Some distinction can be found between the verbs used in this verse, but because of the parallel effect, preachers should use caution when trying to emphasize these distinctions, sometimes at the peril of the poetic impact.

7d נִבְלְעוּ מִן־הַיַּיִן

they are swallowed up from the wine;

נִבְלְעוּ בלע	they are swallowed up *niv·lə·**ʿû***	NIPH PF 3CP	verb
מִן־ מִן	from *min-*	---	prep
הַיַּיִן יַיִן	the wine *hay·**ya**·yin*	ABS W/ DEF. ART.	noun

Do not miss Isaiah's irony: what the drunk consumes actually consumes the drunk!

7e תָּעוּ מִן־הַשֵּׁכָר

they stagger because of the strong drink;

תָּעוּ תעה	they stagger *tā·**ʿû***	QAL PF 3CP	verb
מִן־ מִן	from *min-*	---	prep
הַשֵּׁכָר שֵׁכָר	the strong drink *haš·šē·**ḵār***	ABS W/ DEF. ART.	noun

7f שָׁגוּ בָּרֹאֶה

they wander about while having prophetic visions;

שָׁגוּ שׁגה	they go astray/err *šā·**gû***	QAL PF 3CP	verb
בָּרֹאֶה רֹאֶה	with the vision/seer *bā·rō·**ʾe***	ABS W/ PREP בְּ + DEF. ART.	noun

This phrase alludes to the activity of the prophets, whereas the following phrase (7g) alludes to the activity of the priests. Both have allowed alcohol to impair their spiritual responsibilities, to their shame and to the people's detriment.

7g	פָּקוּ פְּלִילִיָּה׃

they wobble when making judicial judgments.

פָּקוּ פוק	they reel/wobble/totter *pā·qû*	QAL PF 3CP	verb
פְּלִילִיָּה׃ פְּלִילִיָּה	decision/judgment *pə·lî·liy·yâ*	ABS	noun

The verb פוק ("wobble") is only used once elsewhere in the Hebrew Bible, Jer 10:4, where it describes idols that totter if the craftsman fails to nail them down. Here in Isaiah, the verb describes the drunk's decision-making, which is as unstable as a wobbly decoration on the mantel.

8a	כִּי כָּל־שֻׁלְחָנוֹת מָלְאוּ קִיא צֹאָה

For all their tables are filled with crappy vomit,

כִּי כִּי	for *kî*	---	conj
כָּל־ כֹּל	all *kol-*	CST	noun
שֻׁלְחָנוֹת שֻׁלְחָן	tables *šul·ḥā·nôt*	ABS	noun
מָלְאוּ מלא	(they) are filled *mā·lə·'û*	QAL PF 3CP	verb
קִיא קִיא	vomit *qî'*	ABS	noun
צֹאָה צֹאָה	excrement/filth *ṣō·'â*	ABS	noun

The translation here is strong, reflecting the language of the Hebrew. The noun קִיא describes vomit, as in the infamous proverb, "as a dog returns to his vomit, so a fool repeats his folly" (Prov 26:11), and צֹאָה is the word used in Deut 23:14 [13] for human excrement. Combined, these two words form a vile picture of the end result of the people's drunken party. Here they sit, people supposed to lead Israel, their tables covered in their own vomit and filth, so drunk that they cannot control themselves, nor even stand to use the restroom. Those who are supposed to give the people spiritual food have their own physical food covered in bodily fluids. It presents a grim picture of the effects of sin, and preachers might want to lean into the offensive language and allow the repulsive imagery to impact the listeners as it should.

8b	בְּלִ֥י מָקֽוֹם׃		
	without a clean plate in sight.		
בְּלִ֥י בְּלִי	without *bə·lî*	---	particle
מָקֽוֹם׃ מָקוֹם	place *mā·qôm*	ABS	noun

Our translation is idiomatic, as the Hebrew literally reads, "without a place." The meaning likely points to the lack of clean places at the table, as it is so covered with vomit and excrement.

28:9–10

9a אֶת־מִי יוֹרֶה דֵעָה

*ʾet-**mî** yô**re** dēʿ**â***

To whom will he teach knowledge?

9b וְאֶת־מִי יָבִין שְׁמוּעָה

*wəʾet-**mî** yā**vîn** šəmûʿ**â***

And to whom will he impart news?

9c גְּמוּלֵי מֵחָלָב

*gəmû**lê** mēḥā**lāv***

Those just weaned from milk?

9d עַתִּיקֵי מִשָּׁדָיִם׃

*ʿat**tîqê** miššodā**yim**.*

Those just plucked from their mother's breast?

10a כִּי צַו לָצָו צַו לָצָו

*kî **ṣaw** lāṣāw **ṣaw** lāṣāw*

For it is command after command, command after command,

10b קַו לָקָו קַו לָקָו

***qaw** lāqāw **qaw** lāqāw*

line after line, line after line,

10c זְעֵיר שָׁם זְעֵיר שָׁם׃

*zəʿ**êr** **šām** zəʿ**êr** **šām**.*

some here, some there.

9a	אֶת־מִ֚י יוֹרֶ֣ה דֵעָ֔ה		
	To whom will he teach knowledge?		
אֶת־ / אֵת	*(direct object marker)* / *ʾet-*	---	particle
מִ֚י / מִי	who?/whom? / ***mî***	---	interr pron
יוֹרֶ֣ה / ירה	he will instruct/teach / *yô·**re***	HIPH IMPF 3MS	verb
דֵעָ֔ה / דֵּעָה	knowledge / *dē·**ʿâ***	ABS	noun

Just as the tables are absent any clean places due to the overflow of sin's effects, so the Lord is absent anyone sober enough to assimilate any knowledge or wisdom he wishes to impart. The sad reality of Israel's situation continues to worsen.

9b	וְאֶת־מִ֖י יָבִ֣ין שְׁמוּעָ֑ה		
	And to whom will he impart news?		
וְאֶת־ / אֵת	and *(direct object marker)* / *wə·ʾet-*	--- / W/ CONJ וְ	particle
מִ֖י / מִי	to who?/whom? / ***mî***	---	interr pron
יָבִ֣ין / בין	he will make understand / *yā·**vîn***	HIPH IMPF 3MS	verb
שְׁמוּעָ֑ה / שְׁמוּעָה	news/report / *šə·mû·**ʿâ***	ABS	noun

The word שְׁמוּעָה ("news/report") lacks a definite article and is nondescript. It can refer to any kind of oracle, word, report, command, etc., that the Lord wishes to impart through prophet or priest to the Israelites.

9c	גְּמוּלֵ֣י מֵחָלָ֔ב

Those just weaned from milk?

Hebrew	Gloss	Parsing	POS
גְּמוּלֵ֣י גמל	those weaned *gə·mû·**lê***	QAL PASS (CST) PTCP MP	verb
מֵחָלָ֔ב חָלָב	from milk *mē·ḥā·**lāv***	ABS W/ PREP מִן	noun

Interpreters understand this phrase and the next (9d) in two different ways: as an interrogative (so translated) or as an exclamatory statement in answer to the questions in 9a–b. If the latter, Isaiah emphatically laments that the problem in Israel has become so bad that only those "innocent" infants remain unstained by alcohol. If the statements are interrogatives, the point is still similar, but just made with a different (sarcastic) tone.

9d	עַתִּיקֵ֖י מִשָּׁדָֽיִם׃

Those just plucked from their mother's breast?

Hebrew	Gloss	Parsing	POS
עַתִּיקֵ֖י עַתִּיק	those removed *ʿat·tî·**qê***	MP CST	adj
מִשָּׁדָֽיִם׃ שַׁד	from breast *miš·šo·dā·**yim***	ABS W/ PREP מִן	noun

10a	כִּ֣י צַ֤ו לָצָו֙ צַ֣ו לָצָ֔ו

For it is command after command, command after command,

Hebrew	Gloss	Parsing	POS
כִּ֣י כִּי	for ***kî***	---	conj
צַ֤ו צַו	command ***ṣaw***	ABS	noun
לָצָו֙ צַו	to the command *lā·**ṣāw***	ABS W/ PREP לְ + DEF. ART.	noun
צַ֣ו צַו	command ***ṣaw***	ABS	noun
לָצָ֔ו צַו	to the command *lā·**ṣāw***	ABS W/ PREP לְ + DEF. ART.	noun

Though interpretive difficulties abound, most commentators agree that in some way, Isaiah mocks the intelligence and spiritual ability of the sinful Israelites. Interpretive challenges in these verses center on two main issues: (1) the implied speaker(s) of vv. 9–10; (2) the meaning of the rhyming words צַו and קַו. More detailed discussion than the aims of this commentary allow can be found elsewhere (see esp. Jodar 2022:459–71; Smith 2007:481–82; Wegner 2021:224).

For the issue of who speaks in vv. 9–10, readers may want to compare different Bible versions, such as the NLT, which sees vv. 9–10 coming from the voice of the offended drunken Israelites, and the NET, which understands the verses to continue the words of the prophet. The rhyming words צַו and קַו may relate to the words previously used in v. 8 for "crap" (צֹאָה) and "vomit" (קִיא), perhaps as some kind of mocking baby-talk (like poo-poo and yuck-yuck). Isaiah may be mocking the ungodly, drunken leaders by mimicking the sounds a baby would make when learning how to talk. Others think the prophet mimics the efforts of a drunken man trying to form a coherent sentence. Either way, the words are as absurd as they are damning. Preachers versed in Hebrew will want to read the original language out loud to get the full (and fun) effect. After discussing the meaning of the text, they may want to provide a summarizing translation of their findings. When I preached through this text, I gave this loose, amplified translation: "God can't communicate to you people! You're like a bunch of spiritual babies, diapers filled with poo-poo, high-chairs filled with yuck-yuck!" One must carefully walk the balance beam between the silly sounds of the text and the grim reality behind its meaning.

10b קַ֣ו לָקָ֔ו קַ֥ו לָקָ֖ו

line after line, line after line,

קַ֣ו / קַו	line / *qaw*	ABS	noun
לָקָ֔ו / קַו	to the line / *lā·qāw*	ABS W/ PREP לְ + DEF. ART.	noun
קַ֥ו / קַו	line / *qaw*	ABS	noun
לָקָ֖ו / קַו	to the line / *lā·qāw*	ABS W/ PREP לְ + DEF. ART.	noun

10c זְעֵיר שָׁם זְעֵיר שָׁם׃

some here, some there.

זְעֵיר	little	ABS	noun
זְעֵיר	*zə·ʿêr*		
שָׁם	there/here	---	adv
שָׁם	*šām*		
זְעֵיר	little	ABS	noun
זְעֵיר	*zə·ʿêr*		
שָׁם׃	there/here	---	adv
שָׁם	*šām*		

28:11–13

11a כִּ֚י בְּלַעֲגֵ֣י שָׂפָ֔ה

kî bəlaʿăgê śāfâ

For by lisping lips

11b וּבְלָשׁ֖וֹן אַחֶ֑רֶת

ûvəlāšôn ʾaḥeret

and by foreign speech

11c יְדַבֵּ֖ר אֶל־הָעָ֥ם הַזֶּֽה׃

yədabbēr ʾel-hāʿām hazze.

he will speak to this people,

12a אֲשֶׁ֣ר׀ אָמַ֣ר אֲלֵיהֶ֗ם

ʾăšer ʾāmar ʾălêhem

to whom he said,

12b זֹ֤את הַמְּנוּחָה֙

zōʾt hammənûḥâ

“Here’s what rest is:

12c הָנִ֣יחוּ לֶֽעָיֵ֔ף

hānîḥû leʿāyēf

Give rest to the weary!

12d וְזֹ֖את הַמַּרְגֵּעָ֑ה

wəzōʾt hammargēʿâ

Yes, this is tranquility.”

12e וְלֹ֥א אָב֖וּא שְׁמֽוֹעַ׃

wəlōʾ ʾāvûʾ šəmôaʿ.

But they were not willing to listen.

13a וְהָיָה לָהֶם דְּבַר־יְהוָה

wəhāyâ lāhem dəvar-YHWH

So the word of YHWH will be to them

13b צַו לָצָו צַו לָצָו

ṣaw lāṣāw ṣaw lāṣāw

"command after command, command after command,

13c קַו לָקָו קַו לָקָו

qaw lāqāw qaw lāqāw

line after line, line after line,

13d זְעֵיר שָׁם זְעֵיר שָׁם

zəʿêr šām zəʿêr šām

some here, some there"—

13e לְמַעַן יֵלְכוּ וְכָשְׁלוּ אָחוֹר

ləmaʿan yēləḵû wəḵāšəlû ʾāḥôr

so that they may go and totter backward.

13f וְנִשְׁבָּרוּ וְנוֹקְשׁוּ וְנִלְכָּדוּ׃

wənišbārû wənôqəšû wənilkādû.

Thus they will be broken and ensnared and captured.

11a	כִּי בְּלַעֲגֵי שָׂפָה		
	For by lisping lips		
כִּי / כִּי	for / *kî*	---	conj
בְּלַעֲגֵי / לַעַג	by mockings/ stammerings / *bə·la·ʿă·gê*	CST W/ PREP בְּ	noun

שָׂפָה שָׂפָה	lip/speech *śā·fâ*	ABS	noun

Anyone who has travelled to a foreign country without taking time to adequately learn the language can relate (on some level) to Isaiah's words. The prophet does not mock people with speech impediments here; rather, he takes the previous statements a step further by noting that if the Israelite leaders would not listen to God, God would speak to them (on some level!) through the confusing speech of the Assyrians during exile. Notice how Isaiah begins this verse with כִּי ("for"), signaling to the reader that he is coming around to the point of his taunting syllables from vv. 9–10.

11b וּבְלָשׁ֖וֹן אַחֶ֑רֶת

and by foreign speech

וּבְלָשׁ֖וֹן לָשׁוֹן	and by tongue *û·və·lā·šôn*	ABS W/ CONJ וְ + PREP בְּ	noun
אַחֶ֑רֶת אַחֵר	another *ʾa·ḥe·ret*	FS ATTR	adj

11c יְדַבֵּ֖ר אֶל־הָעָ֥ם הַזֶּֽה׃

he will speak to this people,

יְדַבֵּ֖ר דבר	he will speak *yə·dab·bēr*	PIEL IMPF 3MS	verb
אֶל־ אֶל	to *ʾel-*	---	prep
הָעָ֥ם עַם	the people *hā·ʿām*	ABS W/ DEF. ART.	noun
הַזֶּֽה׃ זֶה	the this *haz·ze*	--- W/ DEF. ART.	demonstr pron

There may be some slight derisive tones in the phrase, "to *this people*" (אֶל־הָעָם הַזֶּה). "This" refers back to the drunken, spiritually infantile Israelite leaders in the previous verses.

12a	אֲשֶׁר	אָמַר אֲלֵיהֶם
	to whom he said,

אֲשֶׁר | אֲשֶׁר	who *ʾă·šer*	---	relative pron
אָמַר אמר	he said *ʾā·mar*	QAL PF 3MS	verb
אֲלֵיהֶם אֶל	to them *ʾă·lê·hem*	--- W/ 3MP SX	prep

12b	זֹאת הַמְּנוּחָה
	"Here's what rest is:

זֹאת זאת	this *zōʾt*	---	demonstr pron
הַמְּנוּחָה מְנוּחָה	the rest *ham·mə·nû·ḥâ*	ABS W/ DEF. ART.	noun

The shift to the topic of rest may seem jarring, but it fits with the point of the Lord's comments. God tried to communicate to the Israelites (including offering rest and its implied protections and enjoyment with it), but they refused to listen and instead imbibed in hedonistic pleasures.

12c	הָנִיחוּ לֶעָיֵף
	Give rest to the weary!

הָנִיחוּ נוח	give rest *hā·nî·ḥû*	HIPH IMPV MP	verb
לֶעָיֵף עָיֵף	to the faint/weary *le·ʿā·yēf*	MS SUBST W/ PREP לְ + DEF. ART.	adj

12d	וְזֹ֖את הַמַּרְגֵּעָ֑ה

Yes, this is tranquility."

וְזֹ֖את זאת	and this *wə·zō't*	--- W/ CONJ וְ	demonstr pron
הַמַּרְגֵּעָ֑ה מַרְגֵּעָה	the rest/repose *ham·mar·gē·'â*	ABS W/ DEF. ART.	noun

Note that Isaiah uses three different terms for "rest" in this verse, none of which is the most familiar "sabbath rest" (שַׁבָּת). The words used here denote God's comfortable resting place (מְנוּחָה), a safe place to settle (נוּחַ), and a sleepful repose (מַרְגֵּעָה).

12e	וְלֹ֥א אָב֖וּא שְׁמֽוֹעַ׃

But they were not willing to listen.

וְלֹ֥א לֹא	and not *wə·lō'*	--- W/ CONJ וְ	particle
אָב֖וּא אבה	they were willing *'ā·vû'*	QAL PF 3CP	verb
שְׁמֽוֹעַ׃ שׁמע	to hear/listen *šə·mô·a'*	QAL INF CST	verb

After the three synonymous invitations to rest, the contrastive וְלֹא ("but . . . not") jars the reader. After all, what weary person wouldn't want to rest? Preachers can draw out this juxtaposition of thoughts by using the illustration of a toddler stubbornly refusing a cozy nap from a mother who knows best.

13a	וְהָיָ֨ה לָהֶ֜ם דְּבַר־יְהוָ֗ה

So the word of YHWH will be to them

וְהָיָ֨ה היה	and (it) will be *wə·hā·yâ*	QAL WEQATAL 3MS	verb
לָהֶ֜ם לְ	to them *lā·hem*	--- W/ 3MP SX	prep

דְּבַר־	word	CST	noun
דָּבָר	*də·var-*		
יְהוָה	the Lord	ABS	noun
יהוה	*YHWH*		

13b	צַ֤ו לָצָו֙ צַ֣ו לָצָ֔ו

"command after command, command after command,

צַ֤ו	command	ABS	noun
צַו	*ṣaw*		
לָצָו֙	to command	ABS W/ PREP לְ + DEF. ART.	noun
צַו	*lā·ṣāw*		
צַ֣ו	command	ABS	noun
צַו	*ṣaw*		
לָצָ֔ו	to command	ABS W/ PREP לְ + DEF. ART.	noun
צַו	*lā·ṣāw*		

Isaiah reprises the comically damning language of v. 10, but throws in an additional twist at the end (see 13e–f). Because the Israelites have rejected God's original words inviting rest, he will give them new words to listen to—from the mouths of the Assyrians.

13c	קַ֥ו לָקָ֖ו קַ֣ו לָקָ֑ו

line after line, line after line,

קַ֥ו	line	ABS	noun
קַו	*qaw*		
לָקָ֖ו	to line	ABS W/ PREP לְ + DEF. ART.	noun
קַו	*lā·qāw*		
קַ֣ו	line	ABS	noun
קַו	*qaw*		
לָקָ֑ו	to line	ABS W/ PREP לְ + DEF. ART.	noun
קַו	*lā·qāw*		

13d זְעֵיר שָׁם זְעֵיר שָׁם

some here, some there"—

זְעֵיר זְעֵיר	little *zə·ʿ**êr***	ABS	noun
שָׁם שָׁם	there/here ***šām***	---	adv
זְעֵיר זְעֵיר	little *zə·ʿ**êr***	ABS	noun
שָׁם שָׁם	there/here ***šām***	---	adv

13e לְמַעַן יֵלְכוּ וְכָשְׁלוּ אָחוֹר

so that they may go and totter backward.

לְמַעַן לְמַעַן	in order that *lə·**ma**·ʿan*	---	prep
יֵלְכוּ הלך	they will walk/go *yē·lə·**ḵû***	QAL IMPF 3MP	verb
וְכָשְׁלוּ כשל	and they will stumble/ totter *wə·ḵā·šə·**lû***	QAL WEQATAL 3CP	verb
אָחוֹר אָחוֹר	behind/back *ʾā·**ḥôr***	ABS	noun

Interpreters will need to decide whether לְמַעַן indicates result ("as a result"—as a consequence of the people rejecting God's words, the people stumble) or whether it indicates purpose ("in order that"—God's words sovereignly cause the people's stumbling). Either way, the ultimate result is that the people will fall—both literally and spiritually—from their drunkenness.

13f	וְנִשְׁבְּרוּ וְנוֹקְשׁוּ וְנִלְכָּדוּ׃		
	Thus they will be broken and ensnared and captured.		
וְנִשְׁבְּרוּ שׁבר	and they will be broken *wə·niš·**bā**·rû*	NIPH WEQATAL 3CP	verb
וְנוֹקְשׁוּ יקשׁ	and (they will be) ensnared/caught *wə·nô·qə·**šû***	NIPH WEQATAL 3CP	verb
וְנִלְכָּדוּ׃ לכד	and (they will be) captured *wə·nil·**kā**·dû*	NIPH WEQATAL 3CP	verb

Preachers can highlight the staccato impact of the three verbs here, demonstrating a progression of judgment. Sin leads to death (Rom 6:23), as metaphorically illustrated by the capture of an animal by a hunter.

From Text to Sermon

Big Idea. Godly leadership seeks sober-minded spirituality.

Avenues for Illustration and Application. The main sin that controls much of Isa 28 is the sin of drunkenness. But in particular, Isaiah focuses on the drunkenness of the *spiritual leaders* of Israel—the priests and prophets. The preacher's application, then, should follow the same vein, not only addressing the issue of alcoholism (and by extension, other substance abuse addictions), but addressing the deeper problems of ungodly leadership.

Preachers can develop some of the metaphors in the text for useful illustrations. One unfortunately does not need to spend much time explaining what drunken foolishness looks like, as all too many congregants have (or continue to) participate in such events, whether at college frat parties in the past or under the dim lights of the bar or with relatives and friends during holidays. Too many people know exactly the kind of behavior Isaiah depicts, even if they have not experienced it to the extent that he describes.

The first-ripe fig metaphor in v. 4 could be another example to develop. Compare the text to an eager child picking and chomping on an apple in a pick-it-yourself orchard. Or perhaps consider the seemingly insatiable hunger of a teenager at a buffet. These familiar examples might bring the image in the text (first-ripe figs) to a twenty-first-century audience.

The manner in which Isaiah describes God's control of nature's most powerful storms in v. 2 also invites consideration. Hailstorms and thunderstorms and other natural phenomena evoke scenes of power and terror, especially for ancient Near Eastern peoples whose crops and homes could be irreparably damaged by such weather. Displaying a few images from the news might help illustrate the overwhelming power of God's omnipotence.

A preacher with fluency in a foreign language—or perhaps a parishioner who is willing to lend a tongue—can replicate the experience of hearing another language by sharing a story or reading some text. Hearing foreign languages can be disorienting, uncomfortable, even scary for some people, and putting the congregation through a moment or so of it to highlight the terror coming upon the Israelites might have some memorable impact.

New Testament Connections. Isaiah 28 beautifully reveals the gospel and our future restoration in several ways. As the commentary has shown, the text takes the readers on a journey that shows Israel's fall, judgment, and eventual restoration (cf. Isa 62:3–4). Likewise, our own life story often travels those same paths, as we begin a life filled with hedonistic, selfish pursuits, relying on our own strengths and abilities. Often God must remove our source of strength through dramatic means before we recognize our true need for Christ. Only then does the Lord transform us into a new creation, gloriously restored.

When emphasizing the need for sober-minded spirituality in Israel's leaders, modern preachers can easily demonstrate that God has the same high standards and concerns for New Testament spiritual leaders (pastors/elders/overseers and deacons). Using passages like 1 Tim 3:1–7, 8–13; Titus 1:6–9; and 1 Pet 5:1–4, preachers can show that the majority of qualifications for the New Testament church's leadership are *spiritual* qualifications, not requirements to be business savvy, to have a certain level of education, or to be proficient at Excel spreadsheets. Pedigree, tenure, or net worth have nothing to do with leadership qualifications. What the church needs is more godly leaders who have integrity, are above reproach, and are faithful to their spouses, rather than more CEOs and media personalities.

Finally, the apostle Paul does some interesting things with Isaiah's strange speech (or, as Paul calls it, "tongues") in 1 Cor 14, especially vv. 20–25. Paul even quotes Isa 28:11–12 in 1 Cor 14:21. Knowing the background of Isaiah makes reading Paul especially delightful, as he appears to play with many of the prophet's themes in his letter. In Isaiah, God spoke in "tongues" to his own people, to their judgment. In Corinthians, believers speak in "tongues" in the presence of unbelievers, to their judgment. The passage is worthy of a more complete exploration and discussion. For a great starting point, see Garland 2003:644–54.

A KING WILL REIGN

The world yearns for righteous rulers. In America, every four years the republic has another opportunity to vote in a new leader. In some countries, rulers take office for life. In all situations, the people desire a leader who will execute justice, keep order in the land, and consider the needs of the weak and downtrodden. No human leader can perfectly live up to this expectation, but Isaiah prophesies of a ruler to come who will do all of this and far more. He will reign with such righteousness and equity that his subjects will enjoy perfect justice—for better or worse. Isaiah 32 offers a glimpse into a better tomorrow that promises a world that transcends the imperfect frustrations of our day.

LARGER LITERARY CONTEXT › 32:1–20

1a הֵ֣ן לְצֶ֖דֶק יִמְלָךְ־מֶ֑לֶךְ

__hēn__ lə__ṣe__deq yimlok̲-__me__lek̲

Look—a king will reign according to righteousness,

1b וּלְשָׂרִ֖ים לְמִשְׁפָּ֥ט יָשֹֽׂרוּ׃

ûləśā__rîm__ ləmiš__pāṭ__ yāśō__rû__.

and rulers will rule according to justice.

2a וְהָֽיָה־אִ֥ישׁ כְּמַֽחֲבֵא־ר֖וּחַ

wəhāyâ-__ʾîš__ kəmaḥăvēʾ-__rû__aḥ

Each one will be like a hiding place from the gale

2b וְסֵ֣תֶר זָ֑רֶם

wə__sē__ter __zā__rem

and a shelter from the storm,

2c כְּפַלְגֵי־מַ֣יִם בְּצָי֔וֹן

kəfalgê-__ma__yim bəṣā__yôn__

like a stream of water in a desert,

2d כְּצֵ֥ל סֶֽלַע־כָּבֵ֖ד בְּאֶ֥רֶץ עֲיֵפָֽה׃

kə__ṣēl__ __se__laʿ-kā__vēd__ bəʾ__e__reṣ ʿăyē__fâ__.

like a shadow from a huge rock in an exhausted land.

1a	הֵ֥ן לְצֶ֖דֶק יִמְלָךְ־מֶ֑לֶךְ		

Look—a king will reign according to righteousness,

הֵ֥ן הֵן	behold *hēn*	---	particle
לְצֶ֖דֶק צֶ֫דֶק	to righteousness *lə·ṣe·deq*	ABS W/ PREP לְ	noun
יִמְלָךְ־ מלך	he will reign *yim·lok-*	QAL IMPF 3MS	verb
מֶ֑לֶךְ מֶ֫לֶךְ	king *me·lek*	ABS	noun

Readers and preachers face the interpretive challenge of identifying this "king" who will reign. The most obvious and probable guess is the Messiah. Other Isaianic passages characterize his rule with justice and righteousness (e.g., 9:7; 11:3–5; 42:1–4; 53:11). The rest of the chapter contrasts this king's rule (32:15–20) with the complacency of the people (32:9–14). No king but the Messiah can bring such everlasting peace and righteousness in the land.

1b	וּלְשָׂרִ֖ים לְמִשְׁפָּ֥ט יָשֹֽׂרוּ׃		

and rulers will rule according to justice.

וּלְשָׂרִ֖ים שַׂר	and to chiefs/rulers/princes *û·lə·śā·rîm*	ABS W/ CONJ וְ PREP לְ	noun
לְמִשְׁפָּ֥ט מִשְׁפָּט	to judgment/justice *lə·miš·pāṭ*	ABS W/ PREP לְ	noun
יָשֹֽׂרוּ׃ שׂרר	(they) will rule *yā·śō·rû*	QAL IMPF 3MP	verb

Isaiah skillfully plays with the alliteration between וּלְשָׂרִים ("rulers") and יָשֹׂרוּ ("they will rule"). "Justice" (מִשְׁפָּט) and "righteousness" (צֶדֶק) are frequently paired throughout Scripture (e.g., 2 Sam 8:15; Ps 119:121; Prov 8:20; Isa 5:7). The לְ prefix indicates that the king/rulers will not rule and judge according to their own whims or an invented standard of their own but according to God's objective standards of justice and righteousness. For similar prophecies of believers ruling with the Messiah (perhaps in a future age), see Dan 7:27; 1 Cor 6:2; 2 Tim 2:11–12a; Rev 5:10; 20:4.

2a	וְהָיָה־אִישׁ כְּמַחֲבֵא־רוּחַ		
	Each one will be like a hiding place from the gale		
וְהָיָה־ היה	and it will be *wə·hā·yâ-*	QAL WEQATAL 3MS	verb
אִישׁ אִישׁ	man *ʾîš*	ABS	noun
כְּמַחֲבֵא־ מַחֲבֵא	like a hiding place *kə·ma·ḥă·vē-*	CST W/ PREP כְּ	noun
רוּחַ רוּחַ	wind/spirit *rû·aḥ*	ABS	noun

"Each one" (אִישׁ) refers specifically to the "rulers" (שָׂרִים) of v. 1b. In v. 2, Isaiah delivers four similes, each (besides the second) identified with a כְּ prefix. Here, the first simile values the rulers for their protection from blistering and potentially deadly winds. Isaiah does not specify what these winds signify (other than a danger to the exposed individual), so preachers may give several examples of ways rulers can protect their people (see below).

2b	וְסֵתֶר זָרֶם		
	and a shelter from the storm,		
וְסֵתֶר סֵתֶר	and a covering/hiding place *wə·sē·ter*	CST W/ CONJ וְ	noun
זָרֶם זֶרֶם	rain/downpour/rainstorm *zā·rem*	ABS	noun

Though this line does not begin with a כְּ prefix, the conjunctive וְ indicates it gives another simile, highlighting how these future rulers will protect their people. The first and second similes are quite similar in meaning, which perhaps explains the וְ linking them grammatically rather than the כְּ.

2c	כְּפַלְגֵי־מַ֫יִם בְּצָיוֹן		

like a stream of water in a desert,

כְּפַלְגֵי־ פֶּ֫לֶג	as a canal *kə·fal·gê-*	CST W/ PREP כְּ	noun
מַ֫יִם מַ֫יִם	waters ***ma***·*yim*	ABS	noun
בְּצָיוֹן צָיוֹן	in a dry place/waterless land *bə·ṣā·**yôn***	ABS W/ PREP בְּ	noun

The third simile shifts the imagery away from the winds/storm and compares the future rulers' goodness to the refreshment of finding water in a desert. Many in Canaan would know the experience of extreme thirst while traveling through the wilderness. It also hearkens back to the Israelites' plight in the wilderness after the exodus from Egypt (Exod 17:1–7; Num 20:2–13).

2d	כְּצֵל סֶלַע־כָּבֵד בְּאֶרֶץ עֲיֵפָה׃		

like a shadow from a huge rock in an exhausted land.

כְּצֵל צֵל	like a shadow *kə·**ṣēl***	CST W/ PREP כְּ	noun
סֶלַע־ סֶ֫לַע	rock/cliff ***se***·*la'-*	ABS	noun
כָּבֵד כָּבֵד	heavy *kā·**vēd***	MS ATTR	adj
בְּאֶרֶץ אֶ֫רֶץ	in earth *bə·'**e**·reṣ*	ABS W/ PREP בְּ	noun
עֲיֵפָה׃ עָיֵף	exhausted/weary *'ă·yē·**fâ***	FS ATTR	adj

The final simile also depicts relief for the person seeking to escape Canaan's intense heat. The adjective כָּבֵד ("heavy") emphasizes the great size of the rock, while עָיֵף ("exhausted") personifies the land by depicting the earth as a person dying of thirst. Both of these words highlight the profound contrast between the dire conditions and the total relief given by the righteous rulers.

32:3–4

3a וְלֹ֥א תִשְׁעֶ֖ינָה עֵינֵ֣י רֹאִ֑ים

wəlōʾ tišʿɛ̂nâ ʿênê rōʾîm

Then the eyes of the seeing will not be blinded,

3b וְאָזְנֵ֥י שֹׁמְעִ֖ים תִּקְשַֽׁבְנָה׃

wəʾoznê šōməʿîm tiqšavnâ.

and the ears of those who hear will listen up.

4a וּלְבַ֣ב נִמְהָרִ֔ים יָבִ֖ין לָדָ֑עַת

ûləvav nimhārîm yāvîn lādāʿat

And the hasty mind will discern knowledge

4b וּלְשׁ֣וֹן עִלְּגִ֔ים תְּמַהֵ֖ר לְדַבֵּ֥ר צָחֽוֹת׃

ûləšôn ʿilləgîm təmahēr ədabbēr ṣāḥôt.

and the speech of the stutterer
will hurry up and speak clearly.

3a וְלֹ֥א תִשְׁעֶ֖ינָה עֵינֵ֣י רֹאִ֑ים

Then the eyes of the seeing will not be blinded,

וְלֹ֥א לֹא	and no/not *wə·lōʾ*	--- W/ CONJ וְ	particle
תִשְׁעֶ֖ינָה שׁעה	they will gaze/look at *tiš·ʿɛ̂·nâ*	QAL IMPF 3FP	verb
עֵינֵ֣י עַ֫יִן	eyes *ʿê·nê*	CST	noun
רֹאִ֑ים ראה	those who see *rō·ʾîm*	QAL PTCP MP	verb

As it stands, the MT literally reads, "And the eyes of the seeing will not gaze," which contrasts with the meaning of the next line, "and the ears of those who hear will listen up." Most propose revocalizing the text as either a Qal or Hophal form of שׁעע ("be blind") rather than שׁעה ("gaze/look at"), which would result in the above translation and better agreement with the following line in 3b (Roberts 2015:409).

3b	וְאָזְנֵי שֹׁמְעִים תִּקְשַׁבְנָה׃		
	and the ears of those who hear will listen up.		
וְאָזְנֵי אֹזֶן	and ears *wə·ʾoz·**nê***	CST W/ CONJ וְ	noun
שֹׁמְעִים שׁמע	those who hear *šō·mə·**ʿîm***	QAL PTCP MP	verb
תִּקְשַׁבְנָה׃ קשׁב	(they) will listen *tiq·**šav**·nâ*	QAL IMPF 3FP	verb

4a	וּלְבַב נִמְהָרִים יָבִין לָדָעַת		
	And the hasty mind will discern knowledge		
וּלְבַב לֵבָב	and heart/mind *û·lə·**vav***	CST W/ CONJ וְ	noun
נִמְהָרִים מהר	those who are hurried *nim·hā·**rîm***	NIPH PTCP MP	verb
יָבִין בין	(it) will discern *yā·**vîn***	QAL IMPF 3MS	verb
לָדָעַת ידע	to know *lā·**dā**·ʿat*	QAL INF CST W/ PREP לְ	verb

The participle נִמְהָרִים ("hasty/hurried/rash") oftentimes denotes a hurriedness that is contrary to sound thinking and good decision-making. This verse flips the expected outcome of rash thinkers by showing that in the reign of the coming king, even the hastiest fool will have great discernment.

4b	וּלְשׁ֣וֹן עִלְּגִ֔ים תְּמַהֵ֖ר לְדַבֵּ֥ר צָחֽוֹת׃

and the speech of the stutterer
will hurry up and speak clearly.

וּלְשׁ֣וֹן לָשׁוֹן	and tongue *û·lə·**šôn***	CST W/ CONJ וְ	noun
עִלְּגִ֔ים עִלֵּג	stammerer *ʿil·lə·**gîm***	MP SUBST	adj
תְּמַהֵ֖ר מהר	(it) will hasten/quicken *tə·ma·**hēr***	PIEL IMPF 3FS	verb
לְדַבֵּ֥ר דבר	to speak *lə·dab·**bēr***	PIEL INF CST W/ PREP לְ	verb
צָחֽוֹת׃ צַח	clear(ly) *ṣā·**ḥôt***	FP SUBST	adj

Isaiah cleverly reuses מהר ("hasten/quicken"), now in a positive way (it was used negatively of rash thinking in 4a). The "hasty" thinker will grow discerning (4a), and the slow talker will "hasten" his speech (4b). The coming Messiah will reverse foolishness and misfortune to ensure perfection in his kingdom. Interpreters also may recognize the relationship between the עִלֵּג ("stammerer") here and the לָעֵג ("stammering") lips of the drunkards in Isa 28:11 (perhaps related by root via metathesis; cf. Roberts 2015:408). This chapter depicts a full reversal of the sinful condition of Israel.

32:5–8

5a לֹא־יִקָּרֵא עוֹד לְנָבָל נָדִיב

lō᾽-yiqqārē᾽ ʿôd lənāvāl nādîv

The fool will never again be called a nobleman

5b וּלְכִילַי לֹא יֵאָמֵר שׁוֹעַ׃

ûləḵîlay lō᾽ yē᾽āmēr šôaʿ.

and a rascal will never be called honorable.

6a כִּי נָבָל נְבָלָה יְדַבֵּר

kî nāvāl nəvālâ yədabbēr

For fools will speak foolishly

6b וְלִבּוֹ יַעֲשֶׂה־אָוֶן

wəlibbô yaʿăśe-᾽āwen

and his heart will create harm,

6c לַעֲשׂוֹת חֹנֶף

laʿăśôt ḥōnef

to create ungodliness,

6d וּלְדַבֵּר אֶל־יְהוָה תּוֹעָה

ûlədabbēr ᾽el-YHWH tôʿâ

and to speak perverted things about YHWH,

6e לְהָרִיק נֶפֶשׁ רָעֵב

ləhārîq nefeš rāʿēv

to keep unsatisfied the cravings of the hungry,

6f וּמַשְׁקֶה צָמֵא יַחְסִיר׃

ûmašqe ṣāmē᾽ yaḥsîr.

and he will dry up the drink of the thirsty.

7a וְכֵלַ֣י כֵּלָ֣יו רָעִ֑ים

*wǝḵē**lay** kē**lāyw** rā**ʿîm***

Now the rascal—his tools are evil;

7b ה֚וּא זִמּ֣וֹת יָעָ֔ץ

*__hû__ʾ zim**môt** yā**ʿāṣ***

he himself counsels wickedness

7c לְחַבֵּ֤ל עֲנָיִים֙ בְּאִמְרֵי־שֶׁ֔קֶר

*lǝḥab**bēl** ʿăniy**yîm** bǝʾimrê-**še**qer*

in order to destroy the poor with lying words,

7d וּבְדַבֵּ֥ר אֶבְי֖וֹן מִשְׁפָּֽט׃

*ûvǝdab**bēr** ʾev**yôn** miš**pāṭ**.*

even when the needy speaks correctly.

8a וְנָדִ֖יב נְדִיב֣וֹת יָעָ֑ץ

*wǝnā**dîv** nǝdî**vôt** yā**ʿāṣ***

But the noble man counsels noble things,

8b וְה֖וּא עַל־נְדִיב֣וֹת יָקֽוּם׃

*wǝ**hû**ʾ ʿal-nǝdî**vôt** yā**qûm**.*

and he himself will stand on noble things.

5a לֹֽא־יִקָּרֵ֥א ע֛וֹד לְנָבָ֖ל נָדִ֑יב

The fool will never again be called a nobleman

לֹֽא־ לֹא	not *lōʾ-*	---	particle
יִקָּרֵ֥א קרא	(he) will be called *yiq·qā·**rē**ʾ*	NIPH IMPF 3MS	verb

עֹ֔וד עוֹד	again *ʿôd*	---	adv
לְנָבָ֗ל נָבָל	to fool *lə·nā·vāl*	MS SUBST W/ PREP לְ	adj
נָדִ֑יב נָדִיב	noble *nā·dîv*	MS SUBST	adj

Verse 4 focused on fools becoming wise and stammerers becoming fluent; v. 5 considers the opposite side of the coin: people will no longer give foolish people the accolades of nobility, nor allow honor to rascals. Preachers should carefully explain that the term "fools" in biblical literature says very little about mental capacity, but instead speaks to *moral* capacity. The fool rejects God's ways and follows his own path to destruction (Prov 10:14; 19:3; 1 Sam 25).

5b **וּלְכִילַ֕י לֹ֥א יֵאָמֵ֖ר שֹֽׁועַ׃**

and a rascal will never be called honorable.

וּלְכִילַ֕י כִּילַי	or to a rascal/scoundrel *û·lə·ḵî·lay*	ABS W/ CONJ וְ + PREP לְ	noun
לֹ֥א לֹא	not *lōʾ*	---	particle
יֵאָמֵ֖ר אמר	it will be said *yē·ʾā·mēr*	NIPH IMPF 3MS	verb
שֹֽׁועַ׃ שׁוֹעַ	honorable/noble *šô·aʿ*	MS SUBST	adj

The noun כִּילַי ("rascal/scoundrel") is only used here and in v. 7 in the Hebrew Bible. כִּילַי is paralleled with "fool" (נָבָל) in 5a. "Honorable" (שׁוֹעַ) is its antonym. Preachers can get a sense of the character of a כִּילַי in v. 7 where the word appears again. He is one who carefully plots evil schemes in order to entrap the righteous. This can be illustrated with any number of superhero movie villains.

6a	כִּי נָבָל נְבָלָה יְדַבֵּר

For fools will speak foolishly

כִּי	for	---	conj
כִּי	*kî*		
נָבָל	fool	MS SUBST	adj
נָבָל	*nā·**vāl***		
נְבָלָה	folly/stupidity	ABS	noun
נְבָלָה	*nə·vā·**lâ***		
יְדַבֵּר	(he) will speak	PIEL IMPF 3MS	verb
דבר	*yə·dab·**bēr***		

Two characteristics (using imperfects) define the fool of v. 5. First, using wordplay, Isaiah defines the fool by his propensity to speak foolish words. Preachers might want to lean on the Proverbs for illustrations of what foolish talk sounds like (10:8, 10; 18:6–7, etc.).

6b	וְלִבּוֹ יַעֲשֶׂה־אָוֶן

and his heart will create harm,

וְלִבּוֹ	and his heart	CST W/ CONJ וְ + 3MS SX	noun
לֵב	*wə·lib·**bô***		
יַעֲשֶׂה־	(it) will do/make	QAL IMPF 3MS	verb
עשׂה	*ya·ʿă·śe-*		
אָוֶן	harm/trouble	ABS	noun
אָוֶן	*ʾ**ā**·wen*		

This phrase gives the second characteristic of the fool. The harm he makes comes from his heart, indicating that it resides in the deepest part of his being. Troublemaking represents an essential part of his character.

6c	לַעֲשׂוֹת חֹנֶף

to create ungodliness,

לַעֲשׂוֹת	to do/make	QAL INF CST W/ PREP לְ	verb
עשׂה	*la·ʿă·**śôt***		

חֹנֶף חֹ֫נֶף	godlessness *ḥō·nef*	ABS	noun

Isaiah now uses three infinitive constructs with one Hiphil imperfect to demonstrate the result (or perhaps purpose) of the fool's folly. First, Isaiah repeats the verb עשׂה ("do") from 6b. Foolish words and a heart full of trouble manufacture ungodliness.

6d **וּלְדַבֵּ֣ר אֶל־יְהוָ֣ה תּוֹעָ֔ה**

and to speak perverted things about YHWH,

וּלְדַבֵּר דבר	and to speak *û·lə·dab·**bēr***	PIEL INF CST W/ CONJ וְ + PREP לְ	verb
אֶל־ אֶל	to/about *ʾel-*	---	prep
יְהוָה יהוה	the Lord *YHWH*	ABS	noun
תּוֹעָה תּוֹעָה	error/perversion *tô·**ʿâ***	ABS	noun

Isaiah now repeats the first verb from 6a (note the chiastic verbal sequence of דבר-עשׂה-עשׂה-דבר, "speak–make–make–speak"). Fools speak untruths about the Lord. One way to discern whether or not someone is a fool is to measure their words against the absolute truths in Scripture (Ps 119:160; John 17:17).

6e **לְהָרִיק֙ נֶ֣פֶשׁ רָעֵ֔ב**

to keep unsatisfied the cravings of the hungry,

לְהָרִיק ריק	to empty out *lə·hā·**rîq***	HIPH INF CST W/ PREP לְ	verb
נֶפֶשׁ נֶ֫פֶשׁ	appetite/desire/soul ***ne**·feš*	ABS	noun
רָעֵב רָעֵב	hungry *rā·**ʿēv***	MS ATTR	adj

In the third infinitive, the fool demonstrates his foolishness by ignoring the needs of the hungry. Implied in this is the fool's ability to satisfy these cravings, but he wickedly chooses to turn a blind eye.

6f	וּמַשְׁקֶה צָמֵא יַחְסִיר׃		
	and he will dry up the drink of the thirsty.		
וּמַשְׁקֶה מַשְׁקֶה	and drink *û·maš·**qe***	ABS W/ CONJ וְ	noun
צָמֵא צָמֵא	thirsty *ṣā·**mē**ʾ*	MS SUBST	adj
יַחְסִיר׃ חסר	he will diminish/ cause to lack *yaḥ·**sîr***	HIPH IMPF 3MS	verb

This clause links to the previous not with a fourth infinitive but with a conjunctive ו. The clause thus offers a synonymous thought, exchanging food for drink. The overall picture of this fool is someone whose mouth overflows with stupidity and lies about God and whose heart overflows with such cruel wickedness that it will not even allow him to satisfy the basic needs of the destitute.

7a	וְכֵלַי כֵּלָיו רָעִים		
	Now the rascal—his tools are evil;		
וְכֵלַי כִּילַי	and rascal *wə·ḵē·**lay***	ABS W/ CONJ וְ	noun
כֵּלָיו כְּלִי	his implements/ weapons/tools *kē·**lāyw***	ABS W/ 3MS SX	noun
רָעִים רַע	evil *rā·**ʿîm***	MP PRED	adj

See v. 5b for כִּילַי ("rascal"). Note the strong assonance between וְכֵלַי ("rascal") and כֵּלָיו ("tools"). Rascals not only speak evil and ignore the destitute, but they use instruments to further their sinful causes.

7b	הֽוּא זִמּ֣וֹת יָעָ֔ץ
	he himself counsels wickedness

הֽוּא הוּא	he *hûʾ*	---	personal pron
זִמּ֣וֹת זִמָּה	wickedness *zim·**môt***	ABS	noun
יָעָ֔ץ יעץ	he advises/counsels *yā·**ʿāṣ***	QAL PF 3MS	verb

The pronoun is emphatic both by position and presence. This clause continues to heighten the sin of the fool/rascal, who not only acts wickedly himself, but encourages others to act likewise (cf. Matt 18:6).

7c	לְחַבֵּ֤ל עֲנָיִים֙ בְּאִמְרֵי־שֶׁ֔קֶר
	in order to destroy the poor with lying words,

לְחַבֵּ֤ל חבל	to ruin/destroy *lə·ḥab·**bēl***	PIEL INF CST W/ PREP לְ	verb
עֲנָיִים֙ עָנִי	poor/meek/humble *ʿă·niy·**yîm***	MP SUBST	adj
בְּאִמְרֵי־ אֵמֶר	in words *bə·ʾim·rê-*	CST W/ PREP בְּ	noun
שֶׁ֔קֶר שֶׁקֶר	deception/lie ***še**·qer*	ABS	noun

Preachers may need to illustrate how the poor can be "destroyed" (חבל) only using deceptive words. The verb was previously used in Isa 13:5 of Babylon "destroying" the people of God during the invasion, so the meaning can be quite strong. Here in 32:7, Isaiah probably thinks of lying words in a court of law. The rich and powerful can devastate the lives of the poor and socially underprivileged by false testimony and persuasive bribes.

7d	וּבְדַבֵּ֥ר אֶבְי֖וֹן מִשְׁפָּֽט׃

even when the needy speaks correctly.

וּבְדַבֵּר דבר	and in speaking *û·və·dab·bēr*	PIEL INF CST W/ CONJ וְ + PREP בְּ	verb
אֶבְיוֹן אֶבְיוֹן	needy/poor *'ev·yôn*	MS SUBST	adj
מִשְׁפָּט׃ מִשְׁפָּט	judgment *miš·pāṭ*	ABS	noun

This final clause of v. 7 adds extra emphasis on the integrity of the needy. The deceptive words of the rascal have no actual foundation in reality, but persuade to devastating effect nonetheless. The noun מִשְׁפָּט indicates that the needy speak "rightly" of their situation, in contrast to the rascal's lying tongue. Isaiah likely chooses this word in order to reflect back on the king of v. 1, who ruled with "righteousness" (מִשְׁפָּט). Here, the needy act nobly, but it results in persecution.

8a	וְנָדִ֖יב נְדִיב֣וֹת יָעָ֑ץ

But the noble man counsels noble things,

וְנָדִיב נָדִיב	and/but noble *wə·nā·dîv*	MS SUBST W/ CONJ וְ	adj
נְדִיבוֹת נְדִיבָה	noble things *nə·dî·vôt*	ABS	noun
יָעָץ יעץ	(he) advises/counsels *yā·'āṣ*	QAL PF 3MS	verb

Isaiah reuses key words from previous descriptions to contrast the rascal with the noble man. "Noble" (נָדִיב) was used in v. 5 as something the fool will no longer be called in the righteous king's future kingdom. Also in contrast to the rascal, who "counsels" (יעץ) wicked things, the noble man "counsels" noble things (note also the repetition between וְנָדִיב and נְדִיבוֹת). The effect of these literary echoes strengthens the contrast between the two individuals.

8b	וְה֕וּא עַל־נְדִיב֖וֹת יָקֽוּם׃

and he himself will stand on noble things.

וְה֕וּא הוּא	and he *wə · **hû’***	--- W/ CONJ וְ	personal pron
עַל־ עַל	on/upon *‘al-*	---	prep
נְדִיב֖וֹת נְדִיבָה	noble things *nə · dî · **vôt***	ABS	noun
יָקֽוּם׃ קוּם	he will stand *yā · **qûm***	QAL IMPF 3MS	verb

The repetition continues with נְדִיבָה ("noble things"). In a similar fashion to how Isaiah used the pronoun הוּא to front the phrase in 7b, the prophet now emphasizes the noble man—*he himself* will stand upon noble things. To stand upon something indicates a position that will not be moved and ascribes a certain amount of security to it. Preachers should note the contrast between the rascal's words that destroy the weak (7c) and the noble man standing firm in his nobility (8a–b). Though the deceptive schemes of the wicked bring down the poor for a time, their godliness will ultimately see them through any trial and prove their position secure.

From Text to Sermon

Big Idea. Noble living anticipates the Messiah's righteous rule.

Avenues for Illustration and Application. Whenever possible, preachers should lean on the text itself to generate illustrations for sermons. Isaiah packs four similes into v. 2, which describes how the future princes (and king/Messiah) will rule in the coming kingdom. The first two are similar and can be treated together (a hiding place from a gale; a shelter from a storm). Anyone who has ever been caught outside during a storm can understand the importance of a safe shelter from the rain and lightning. Preachers living near tropical climates might want to illustrate using the most recent hurricane and its devastating effects. Preachers in other contexts can use whatever deadly elements their land tends to suffer, be it tornadoes or snowstorms or something else.

The third simile Isaiah uses in v. 2 (stream of water in a desert) may not be as commonly understood. A video clip or illustration from a movie might help land the imagery (scenes from *Lawrence of Arabia*, *The Good, the Bad, and the Ugly*, or even *The Three Amigos* immediately come to mind). Even relating the feeling of playing a sport and needing that swig of Gatorade from the sideline between periods can generate the right feeling in the listening audience. The fourth simile from v. 2 (shadow from a huge rock in an exhausted land) is similar to the third, but focuses on protection from exposure to the sun rather than quenching thirst. Consider the protective effects of an umbrella on the beach (or even sunscreen!) or the cool shade of a tree on a hot day. Make sure to relate each of these to the larger reality; namely, the protection, relief, and satisfaction given by the Messiah's coming reign.

But to take these illustrations one step further, the preacher might also want to demonstrate what this looks like on a practical level. Rulers can protect people from the financial storms of life by providing tax benefits for lower-income families or championing economic policies that work for the common folk more than put additional money into the pockets of the already rich. A judge can offer cool water to the cracked lips of the accused by ruling with justice and equity, no matter what the socioeconomic background of the defendant might be. Since Isaiah does not specify what exactly each of these illustrations looks like, it gives preachers and teachers freedom to apply them in various contexts for their specific audiences.

In v. 5, Isaiah uses a word that means something very different from his context to ours: "fool." Thankfully, he illustrates exactly what this means in vv. 6 and 7. Today, "fool" can be a derisive term with connotations of mental handicaps. But in Isaiah's context, fools were *morally* inept, not *mentally* challenged. Preachers may not even need to lean on books like Proverbs to illustrate this (though Proverbs wouldn't hurt!). Picking up Isaiah's own words about fools—their hearts are full of sin, they practice ungodliness, they ignore the physical needs of the hungry and thirsty, etc.—will be enough to capture the meaning behind this word.

From here, preachers can help the congregation consider how they are living in light of the coming realities of the messianic kingdom. Do they live like fools—selfish, ungodly, ignoring social injustices and fostering wickedness in the culture? Or do they live like the noble—listening to the pleas of the needy, standing on truth and righteousness, speaking valuable and godly words? Living nobly instead of foolishly is one way believers anticipate Jesus' coming kingdom. Jesus alone perfects these traits, but we live in light of the future reality of his perfect kingdom.

New Testament Connections. The New Testament confirms the prophecies of Isa 32: believers will rule with Jesus in his future kingdom. Isaiah 32:1 sets the tone for the rest of the passage by predicting not just the coming reign of a king (which we have argued here best fits the role of the Messiah), but the future rule of princes who will reign with him. The apostle Paul points out to the Corinthians that by suing each other, they are not living in light of the reality of the future kingdom, which consists of believers taking an active role in ruling and judging (1 Cor 6:2). Paul also mentions the future reign of believers with Christ in 2 Tim 2:12. The apostle John clearly depicts this reign as earthly and future to his time (Rev 5:10; cf. 20:4). Any sermon on Isa 32 should anticipate this future reign and motivate believers today to live in light of these coming realities.

Another connection between believer and Messiah, between Old and New Testaments, emerges from the realities of Isa 32:7. Servants of God suffer, often undeservedly. The needy speaks correctly, but he still suffers persecution from the wicked scoundrel. This reality of the suffering righteous is perfected in Jesus Christ and passed on to his faithful servants (John 15:20; 1 Pet 4:13; cf. Matt 16:24; Rom 8:17; 2 Cor 1:5; Phil 3:10; etc.). Because Jesus was persecuted, his followers will be persecuted. The wicked hate the righteous; believers must realize that followers of Jesus will suffer for righteousness' sake, just like our Master. Jesus perfectly endured such suffering, leaving us an example to follow when we go through similar trials (1 Pet 2:21).

ISAIAH 37:14–20

HEZEKIAH'S PRAYER

Believers can learn a lot by listening to other mature believers pray. After Hezekiah receives a threatening letter from King Sennacherib of Assyria, the Judean king spreads it before the Lord and pours out his heart to God for protection. Hezekiah's passionate prayer exalts the one true God and couches his request in his unwavering trust in the Lord. His prayer gives a model for believers today, emphasizing the sovereignty of our creator God, praying for God's glory and reputation above all else, all while humbly presenting our requests before him.

LARGER LITERARY CONTEXT › 36:1–37:38

37:14–15

14a וַיִּקַּ֨ח חִזְקִיָּ֧הוּ אֶת־הַסְּפָרִ֛ים מִיַּ֥ד הַמַּלְאָכִ֖ים וַיִּקְרָאֵ֑הוּ

*wayyiq**qaḥ** ḥizqiy**yā**hû ʾet-hassəfā**rîm***
*miy**yad** hammalʾā**ḵîm** wayyiqrāʾ**ē**hû*

Now Hezekiah took the scroll
from the messenger's hand and he read it.

14b וַיַּ֙עַל֙ בֵּ֣ית יְהוָ֔ה

*way**ya**ʿal **bêt** YHWH*

Then he went up to YHWH's house

14c וַֽיִּפְרְשֵׂ֥הוּ חִזְקִיָּ֖הוּ לִפְנֵ֥י יְהוָֽה׃

*wayyifrə**śē**hû ḥizqiy**yā**hû lif**nê** YHWH.*

and Hezekiah spread it out before YHWH.

15a וַיִּתְפַּלֵּל֙ חִזְקִיָּ֔הוּ אֶל־יְהוָ֖ה לֵאמֹֽר׃

*wayyitpal**lēl** ḥizqiy**yā**hû ʾel-YHWH lē**ʾmōr**.*

Then Hezekiah prayed to YHWH, saying,

14a וַיִּקַּ֨ח חִזְקִיָּ֧הוּ אֶת־הַסְּפָרִ֛ים מִיַּ֥ד הַמַּלְאָכִ֖ים וַיִּקְרָאֵ֑הוּ

Now Hezekiah took the scroll
from the messenger's hand and he read it.

וַיִּקַּ֨ח לקח	and (he) took *way·yiq·**qaḥ***	QAL WAYY 3MS	verb
חִזְקִיָּ֧הוּ חִזְקִיָּ֫הוּ	Hezekiah *ḥiz·qiy·**yā**·hû*	ABS	noun
אֶת־ אֵת	*(direct object marker)* *ʾet-*	---	particle

הַסְּפָרִים סֵ֫פֶר	documents/scrolls *has·sə·fā·**rîm***	ABS W/ DEF. ART.	noun
מִיַּד יָד	from hand *miy·**yad***	CST W/ PREP מִן	noun
הַמַּלְאָכִים מַלְאָךְ	the messengers *ham·mal·'ā·**ḵîm***	ABS W/ DEF. ART.	noun
וַיִּקְרָאֵהוּ קרא	and he read/ proclaimed it *way·yiq·rā·**'ē**·hû*	QAL WAYY 3MS W/ 3MS SX	verb

As has been the case since 36:1, the *wayyiqtol* indicates that this is now prose. Though our comments here can only treat the current passage, the entire context of 36:1–37:13 is relevant to the sermon, so a summary or reading of the text will be necessary.

Though commentators tend to focus on the strange interchange between the singular and plural scroll(s), with varied plausible theories (including multiple scrolls, the plural used for the singular, and the possibility of two letters within the same scroll), preachers need not detain themselves with the *form* of the document as much as the *content*.

The verb קרא can sometimes denote "read (aloud)," as here (e.g., Exod 24:7).

14b וַיַּ֫עַל בֵּית יְהוָֹה

Then he went up to YHWH's house

וַיַּ֫עַל עלה	and he went up *way·**ya**·'al*	QAL WAYY 3MS	verb
בֵּית בַּ֫יִת	house ***bêt***	CST	noun
יְהוָֹה יהוה	the LORD *YHWH*	ABS	noun

The contrast between Hezekiah's reaction to the Assyrian threat and the earlier reaction of Ahaz (Isa 7) could not be greater. By using another *wayyiqtol* verb, Isaiah depicts Hezekiah's movement to the Lord's house (the temple) as the immediate and very next step in the reaction to the letter. Preachers would do well to encourage their congregants to consider applying the king's example to devastating or threatening news in their lives.

14c וַיִּפְרְשֵׂ֫הוּ חִזְקִיָּ֖הוּ לִפְנֵ֥י יְהוָֽה׃

and Hezekiah spread it out before YHWH.

וַיִּפְרְשֵׂ֫הוּ פרשׂ	and (he) spread it out *way·yif·rə·**śē**·hû*	QAL WAYY 3MS W/ 3MS SX	verb
חִזְקִיָּ֖הוּ חִזְקִיָּ֫הוּ	Hezekiah *ḥiz·qiy·**yā**·hû*	ABS	noun
לִפְנֵ֥י לִפְנֵי	before *lif·**nê***	---	prep
יְהוָֽה׃ יהוה	the LORD *YHWH*	ABS	noun

The suffix on וַיִּפְרְשֵׂ֫הוּ ("and he spread it out") must refer to the scroll(s) from 14a. This may be a twist on the spreading out of hands in prayer gesture seen twice in Isaiah (1:15; 65:2). The phrase לִפְנֵי יְהוָה ("before the Lord") indicates that Hezekiah's entire hopes and prayers were singularly directed towards the Lord. His hope was found in God alone to save him.

15a וַיִּתְפַּלֵּ֗ל חִזְקִיָּ֫הוּ אֶל־יְהוָ֖ה לֵאמֹֽר׃

Then Hezekiah prayed to YHWH, saying,

וַיִּתְפַּלֵּ֗ל פלל	and (he) prayed *way·yit·pal·**lēl***	HITH WAYY 3MS	verb
חִזְקִיָּ֫הוּ חִזְקִיָּ֫הוּ	Hezekiah *ḥiz·qiy·**yā**·hû*	ABS	noun
אֶל־ אֶל	to *'el-*	---	prep
יְהוָ֖ה יהוה	the LORD *YHWH*	ABS	noun
לֵאמֹֽר׃ אמר	saying *lē'·**mōr***	QAL INF CST W/ PREP לְ	verb

The preposition אֶל ("to/towards") once again points to the sole focus of Hezekiah: the Lord. He did not pray to a false god, an idol, or any patriarch, but to the Lord alone. The infinitive לֵאמֹר ("saying") indicates that what follows is the exact content of his prayer (it functions as the beginning of quotation marks).

37:16–20

16a יְהוָ֨ה צְבָא֜וֹת אֱלֹהֵ֤י יִשְׂרָאֵל֙ יֹשֵׁ֣ב הַכְּרֻבִ֔ים

*YHWH ṣəvāʾ**ôt** ʾĕlō**hê** yiśrāʾ**ēl** yō**šēv** hakkəru**vîm***

“O YHWH of Hosts, God of Israel,
who sits above the cherubim,

16b אַתָּה־ה֤וּא הָֽאֱלֹהִים֙ לְבַדְּךָ֔ לְכֹ֖ל מַמְלְכ֣וֹת הָאָ֑רֶץ

*ʾattâ-**hûʾ** hāʾĕlō**hîm** ləvaddə**ḵā** lə**ḵōl** mamlə**ḵôt** hāʾ**ā**reṣ*

you are he, you are God alone,
over all the kingdoms of the earth!

16c אַתָּ֣ה עָשִׂ֔יתָ אֶת־הַשָּׁמַ֖יִם וְאֶת־הָאָֽרֶץ׃

*ʾatt**â** ʿā**śî**tā ʾet-haššā**ma**yim wəʾet-hāʾ**ā**reṣ.*

You—you alone made the heavens and the earth!

17a הַטֵּ֨ה יְהוָ֤ה ׀ אָזְנְךָ֙ וּֽשְׁמָ֔ע

*haṭ**ṭē** YHWH ʾoznə**ḵā** ûšə**mā**ʿ*

Incline your ear, O YHWH, and listen;

17b פְּקַ֧ח יְהוָ֛ה עֵינֶ֖ךָ וּרְאֵ֑ה

*pə**qaḥ** YHWH ʿê**ne**ḵā ûrəʾ**ē***

open your eyes, O YHWH, and look;

17c וּֽשְׁמַ֗ע אֵ֚ת כָּל־דִּבְרֵ֣י סַנְחֵרִ֔יב

*ûšə**ma**ʿ ʾ**ēt** kol-div**rê** sanḥē**rîv***

and listen to all the words of Sennacherib,

17d אֲשֶׁ֣ר שָׁלַ֔ח לְחָרֵ֖ף אֱלֹהִ֥ים חָֽי׃

*ʾă**šer** šā**laḥ** ləḥā**rēf** ʾĕlō**hîm** **ḥāy**.*

which he sent to taunt the living God.

18a אָמְנָ֖ם יְהוָ֑ה

*ʾom**nām** YHWH*

Surely, O YHWH,

18b הֶחֱרִ֛יבוּ מַלְכֵ֥י אַשּׁ֛וּר אֶת־כָּל־הָאֲרָצ֖וֹת וְאֶת־אַרְצָֽם׃

heḥĕrîvû malkê ʾaššûr ʾet-kol-hāʾărāṣôt wəʾet-ʾarṣām.

the Assyrian kings have destroyed all the nations and their lands,

19a וְנָתֹ֥ן אֶת־אֱלֹהֵיהֶ֖ם בָּאֵ֑שׁ

wənātōn ʾet-ʾĕlōhêhem bāʾēš

and tossed their idol-gods into the fire.

19b כִּ֣י לֹ֤א אֱלֹהִים֙ הֵ֔מָּה

kî lōʾ ʾĕlōhîm hēmmâ

For they were not actually gods,

19c כִּ֣י אִם־מַעֲשֵׂ֧ה יְדֵי־אָדָ֛ם עֵ֥ץ וָאֶ֖בֶן

kî ʾim-maʿăśē yədê-ʾādām ʿēṣ wāʾeven

but only the product of man's hands—wood and stone.

19d וַֽיְאַבְּדֽוּם׃

wayʾabbədûm.

Therefore they destroyed them.

20a וְעַתָּה֙ יְהוָ֣ה אֱלֹהֵ֔ינוּ

wəʿattâ YHWH ʾĕlōhênû

So now, O YHWH our God,

20b הוֹשִׁיעֵ֖נוּ מִיָּד֑וֹ

hôšîʿēnû miyādô

save us from his hand,

20c וְיֵֽדְעוּ֙ כָּל־מַמְלְכ֣וֹת הָאָ֔רֶץ

wəyēdəʿû kol-mamləkôt hāʾāreṣ

so that all the kingdoms of the earth may know

20d כִּ֥י אַתָּ֛ה יְהוָ֥ה לְבַדֶּֽךָ׃

kî-ʾattâ YHWH ləvaddekā.

that you—you alone—are YHWH!"

16a יְהוָ֨ה צְבָא֜וֹת אֱלֹהֵ֤י יִשְׂרָאֵל֙ יֹשֵׁ֣ב הַכְּרֻבִ֔ים

"O YHWH of Hosts, God of Israel,
who sits above the cherubim,

יְהוָ֨ה יהוה	the Lord *YHWH*	ABS	noun
צְבָא֜וֹת צָבָא	hosts/armies *ṣə · vā · '**ôt***	ABS	noun
אֱלֹהֵ֤י אֱלֹהִים	God *'ĕ · lō · **hê***	CST	noun
יִשְׂרָאֵל֙ יִשְׂרָאֵל	Israel *yiś · rā · '**ēl***	ABS	noun
יֹשֵׁ֣ב ישׁב	who sits/dwells *yō · **šēv***	QAL PTCP MS	verb
הַכְּרֻבִ֔ים כְּרוּב	the cherubim *hak · kə · ru · **vîm***	ABS W/ DEF. ART.	noun

If Hezekiah was in or near the temple when he prayed this prayer, the comment that the Lord יֹשֵׁב הַכְּרֻבִים ("sits above the cherubim") may have been inspired by the artwork in the curtains, doors, or walls of the temple, or the carved cherubim above the mercy seat of the ark in the holy of holies (though the latter sight he was not privy to; Exod 25:18–22; 26:1, 31; 1 Kgs 6:23–35; 7:29, 36). The participle in this phrase indicates a continual sitting/dwelling—this is where the Lord chooses to be met by his people.

16b אַתָּה־ה֤וּא הָֽאֱלֹהִים֙ לְבַדְּךָ֔ לְכֹ֖ל מַמְלְכ֣וֹת הָאָ֑רֶץ

you are he, you are God alone,
over all the kingdoms of the earth!

אַתָּה־ אַתָּה	you *'at · tâ-*	---	personal pron
ה֤וּא הוּא	he ***hû'***	---	personal pron

הָֽאֱלֹהִים אֱלֹהִים	the God *hā·ʾĕ·lō·**hîm***	ABS W/ DEF. ART.	noun
לְבַדֶּךָ לְבַד	you alone *lə·vad·də·**ḵā***	--- W/ 2MS SX	adv
לְכֹל כֹּל	to all *lə·**ḵōl***	CST W/ PREP לְ	noun
מַמְלְכוֹת מַמְלָכָה	kingdoms *mam·lə·**ḵôt***	CST	noun
הָאָרֶץ אֶרֶץ	the earth *hā·**ʾā**·reṣ*	ABS W/ DEF. ART.	noun

The resumptive phrase אַתָּה־הוּא ("you are he"), tells readers that God is the incomparable and sole subject of Hezekiah's prayer. All the focus is on the Lord. The adverb לְבַדֶּךָ ("you alone") puts additional emphasis on the Lord, wholly separate from all other opponents. This phrase highlights the sovereignty of God (for a similar phrase, see Ps 86:10b).

16c	אַתָּה עָשִׂיתָ אֶת־הַשָּׁמַיִם וְאֶת־הָאָֽרֶץ׃
	You—you alone made the heavens and the earth!

אַתָּה אַתָּה	you *ʾat·**tâ***	---	personal pron
עָשִׂיתָ עשׂה	you made *ʿā·**śî**·tā*	QAL PF 2MS	verb
אֶת־ אֵת	*(direct object marker)* *ʾet-*	---	particle
הַשָּׁמַיִם שָׁמַיִם	the heavens *haš·šā·**ma**·yim*	ABS W/ DEF. ART.	noun
וְאֶת־ אֵת	and + *(direct object marker)* *wə·ʾet-*	--- W/ CONJ וְ	particle
הָאָֽרֶץ׃ אֶרֶץ	the earth *hā·**ʾā**·reṣ*	ABS W/ DEF. ART.	noun

Another emphatic אַתָּה ("you") keeps the focus entirely on the Lord. It separates him by his creative ability, making the heavens and earth (Gen 1:1). Later, Isaiah will write that creation uniquely qualifies God as God, because no one else can create from nothing (Isa 44:24). Preachers can begin building a theology of God from Hezekiah's prayer, noting that 16b focused on God's sovereignty, and 16c focuses on God as creator.

17a **הַטֵּה יְהוָה׀ אָזְנְךָ וּשְׁמָע**

Incline your ear, O YHWH, and listen;

הַטֵּה נטה	incline/turn *haṭ·ṭē*	HIPH IMPV MS	verb
יְהוָה׀ יהוה	the LORD *YHWH*	ABS	noun
אָזְנְךָ אֹזֶן	your ear *ʾoz·nə·ḵā*	CST W/ 2MS SX	noun
וּשְׁמָע שׁמע	and hear *û·šə·māʿ*	QAL IMPV MS W/ CONJ וְ	verb

Hezekiah begins a series of five imperatives. Understood in the context of prayer, interpreters should take this as strong but respectful language imploring the Lord to respond to Hezekiah's requests and act on his (and Israel's) behalf. The wording here is common in prayer; cf. Ps 17:6; 40:1; 45:10; etc.

17b **פְּקַח יְהוָה עֵינֶךָ וּרְאֵה**

open your eyes, O YHWH, and look;

פְּקַח פקח	open *pə·qaḥ*	QAL IMPV MS	verb
יְהוָה יהוה	the LORD *YHWH*	ABS	noun
עֵינֶךָ עַיִן	your eyes *ʿê·ne·ḵā*	CST W/ 2MS SX	noun
וּרְאֵה ראה	and see *û·rə·ʾē*	QAL IMPV MS W/ CONJ וְ	verb

The phrase enjoys exact parallelism with 17a. The word order has been changed in our translation for easier reading. Like 17a, these verbs are also common to biblical petitions; cf. 2 Kgs 6:17; 19:16; Dan 9:18. See also 2 Kgs 6:20; Isa 42:20.

17c	וּשְׁמַע אֵת כָּל־דִּבְרֵי סַנְחֵרִיב

and listen to all the words of Sennacherib,

וּשְׁמַע שׁמע	and hear *û·šə·**ma'***	QAL IMPV MS W/ CONJ וְ	verb
אֵת אֵת	*(direct object marker)* *'**ēt***	---	particle
כָּל־ כֹּל	all *kol-*	CST	noun
דִּבְרֵי דָּבָר	words *div·**rê***	CST	noun
סַנְחֵרִיב סַנְחֵרִיב	Sennacherib *san·ḥē·**rîv***	ABS	noun

Hezekiah repeats the verb שׁמע ("hear") from 17a and finally indicates the object of the five imperatives: he wants the Lord to incline, listen, open, look, and listen to "all the words of Sennacherib." The piling up of verbs and the synonymous parallelism heighten the request and indicate a sense of urgency in his tone.

17d	אֲשֶׁר שָׁלַח לְחָרֵף אֱלֹהִים חָי׃

which he sent to taunt the living God.

אֲשֶׁר אֲשֶׁר	which *'ă·**šer***	---	relative pron
שָׁלַח שׁלח	he sent *šā·**laḥ***	QAL PF 3MS	verb
לְחָרֵף חרף	to taunt/reproach *lə·ḥā·**rēf***	PIEL INF CST W/ PREP לְ	verb
אֱלֹהִים אֱלֹהִים	God *'ĕ·lō·**hîm***	ABS	noun
חָי׃ חַי	living ***ḥāy***	MS ATTR	adj

Hezekiah may purposefully recall the similar wording from David's encounter with Goliath (1 Sam 17:26, 36). Scripture almost always uses the verb חרף ("taunt/reproach") for enemies reviling either God or God's people. The phrase אֱלֹהִים חָי ("living God") has a slight polemical tone to it, contrasting the God who continues to have life with the so-called gods (idols) of the other nations, which have no true life or existence at all. So to taunt the living God is an exercise in utter foolishness and is quite dangerous at that.

18a	אָמְנָ֖ם יְהוָ֑ה

Surely, O YHWH,

אָמְנָ֖ם אָמְנָם	truly/surely *ʾom·**nām***	---	adv
יְהוָ֑ה יהוה	the LORD *YHWH*	ABS	noun

For the fourth time in this prayer, Hezekiah uses the Lord's personal name, YHWH. The adverb אָמְנָם ("truly/surely") draws attention to something that is undoubtedly true.

18b	הֶחֱרִ֜יבוּ מַלְכֵ֥י אַשּׁ֛וּר אֶת־כָּל־הָאֲרָצ֖וֹת וְאֶת־אַרְצָֽם׃

the Assyrian kings have destroyed all the nations and their lands,

הֶחֱרִ֜יבוּ חרב	(they) have dried up/ made desolate *he·ḥĕ·**rî**·vû*	HIPH PF 3CP	verb
מַלְכֵ֥י מֶ֫לֶךְ	kings *mal·**ḵê***	CST	noun
אַשּׁ֛וּר אַשּׁוּר	Assyria *ʾaš·**šûr***	ABS	noun
אֶת־ אֵת	*(direct object marker)* *ʾet-*	---	particle
כָּל־ כֹּל	all *kol-*	CST	noun
הָאֲרָצ֖וֹת אֶ֫רֶץ	the lands *hā·ʾă·rā·**ṣôt***	ABS W/ DEF. ART.	noun
וְאֶת־ אֵת	and + *(direct object marker)* *wə·ʾet-*	--- W/ CONJ וְ	particle

אַרְצָם׃ אֶרֶץ	and their lands *ʾar·ṣām*	CST W/ 3MP SX	noun

The Hebrew here is strange, with two consecutive uses of אֶרֶץ ("land"). Second Kings 19:14–19 offers a parallel passage to Isaiah's, which may prove helpful here. I have chosen to follow the parallel in 2 Kgs 19:17, which uses אֶת־הַגּוֹיִם ("the nations") in place of the first אֶרֶץ, which is likely Hezekiah's meaning anyway. This phrase demonstrates the magnitude of the threat Sennacherib poses to Hezekiah and Israel. The Assyrians were able to destroy every other land they set out to conquer. Without the Lord's intervention, Judah would surely also fall to Assyria's power.

19a וְנָתֹן אֶת־אֱלֹהֵיהֶם בָּאֵשׁ

and tossed their idol-gods into the fire.

וְנָתֹן נתן	and to give/set *wə·nā·tōn*	QAL INF ABS W/ CONJ וְ	verb
אֶת־ אֵת	*(direct object marker)* *ʾet-*	---	particle
אֱלֹהֵיהֶם אֱלֹהִים	their gods *ʾĕ·lō·hê·hem*	CST W/ 3MP SX	noun
בָּאֵשׁ אֵשׁ	into the fire *bā·ʾēš*	ABS W/ PREP בְּ + DEF. ART.	noun

Though Isaiah does not give credence to idols or other so-called gods (cf. 19b; 44:9–20), the cavalier and disrespectful attitude of the Assyrian kings suggested they would treat Jerusalem's holy objects in the same fashion as they did the other nations' idols/gods.

19b כִּי לֹא אֱלֹהִים הֵמָּה

For they were not actually gods,

כִּי כִּי	for *kî*	---	conj
לֹא לֹא	not/no *lōʾ*	---	particle

אֱלֹהִים אֱלֹהִים	gods *ʾĕ·lō·**hîm***	ABS	noun
הֵמָּה הֵמָּה	they/these ***hēm**·mâ*	---	personal pron

This verse clarifies Hezekiah's use of אֱלֹהִים ("gods") in 19a: make no mistake about it—these other so-called gods are not real.

19c כִּי אִם־מַעֲשֵׂה יְדֵי־אָדָם עֵץ וָאָבֶן

but only the product of man's hands—wood and stone.

כִּי אִם־ כִּי אִם־	but/except ***kî** ʾim-*	---	conj
מַעֲשֵׂה מַעֲשֶׂה	work *ma·ʿă·**śē***	CST	noun
יְדֵי־ יָד	hands *yə·**dê**-*	CST	noun
אָדָם אָדָם	man *ʾā·**dām***	ABS	noun
עֵץ עֵץ	tree/wood ***ʿēṣ***	ABS	noun
וָאָבֶן אֶבֶן	and stone *wā·**ʾe**·ven*	ABS W/ CONJ וְ	noun

Preachers should note the contrast between this phrase and Hezekiah's praise of God's creative ability in 16c: the gods of other nations are nothing more than man's creative work, but God's creative work brought the world into existence, including humans and the product of their hands. This characterization of idols is common in Deuteronomy (cf. 4:28; 28:36; 29:16 [17]; Baltzer 2001:469).

19d וַיְאַבְּדוּם׃

Therefore they destroyed them.

וַיְאַבְּדוּם׃ אבד	and they destroyed them *way·ʾab·bə·**dûm***	PIEL WAYY 3MP W/ 3MP SX	verb

The verb at the end of the sentence creates emphasis. The reason the Assyrians could destroy the gods/idols of other nations so easily is because these gods/idols were merely the product of human effort. Implicitly, in contrast, the Creator God of the universe will not be so easily burned in the fire. This aspect of God's character forms the basis of Hezekiah's request and confidence in the Lord.

20a **וְעַתָּה יְהוָה אֱלֹהֵינוּ**

So now, O YHWH our God,

וְעַתָּה עַתָּה	and now *wə·ʿat·**tâ***	--- W/ CONJ וְ	adv
יְהוָה יהוה	the Lord *YHWH*	ABS	noun
אֱלֹהֵינוּ אֱלֹהִים	our God *ʾĕ·lō·**hê**·nû*	CST W/ 1CP SX	noun

For the fifth time, Hezekiah uses God's personal, covenantal name, YHWH. He is designated "our God" (אֱלֹהֵינוּ), a powerful contrast with the weak, nonexistent gods of the fallen nations. The וְעַתָּה ("and now") signifies his prayer is coming to a conclusion.

20b **הוֹשִׁיעֵנוּ מִיָּדוֹ**

save us from his hand,

הוֹשִׁיעֵנוּ ישׁע	save us *hô·šî·**ʿē**·nû*	HIPH IMPV MS W/ 1CP SX	verb
מִיָּדוֹ יָד	from his hand *mi·yā·**dô***	CST W/ PREP מִן + 3MS SX	noun

This imperative signals the petition proper of Hezekiah's prayer: he asks God to save him and his people from the hand of Sennacherib. Preachers should encourage congregants to model their prayers on the prayers of Hezekiah: first, a recognition of God and his character, and only after, the actual request. Prayer requests should be based in the character of God.

20c	וַיֵּדְעוּ כָּל־מַמְלְכוֹת הָאָרֶץ

so that all the kingdoms of the earth may know

וַיֵּדְעוּ ידע	and (they) may know *wə·yē·də·ʻû*	QAL IMPF 3MP W/ CONJ וְ	verb
כָּל־ כֹּל	all *kol-*	CST	noun
מַמְלְכוֹת מַמְלָכָה	kingdoms *mam·lə·ḵôt*	CST	noun
הָאָרֶץ אֶרֶץ	the earth *hā·ʼā·reṣ*	ABS W/ DEF. ART.	noun

The imperfect functions here as a purposive clause: the reason that Hezekiah requests salvation from the Assyrian threat is so that all the kingdoms (including those destroyed by Sennacherib; cf. v. 18) may know that Israel's savior is YHWH alone.

20d	כִּי־אַתָּה יְהוָה לְבַדֶּךָ׃

that you—you alone—are YHWH!"

כִּי־ כִּי	that *kî-*	---	conj
אַתָּה אַתָּה	you *ʼat·tâ*	---	personal pron
יְהוָה יהוה	the LORD *YHWH*	ABS	noun
לְבַדֶּךָ׃ לְבַד	you alone *lə·vad·de·ḵā*	--- W/ 2MS SX	adv

The כִּי־ clause ushers in the dramatic conclusion of Hezekiah's prayer. For the sixth and final time Hezekiah uses YHWH's name, once more punctuated by both the personal pronoun אַתָּה ("you") and the adverb + suffix לְבַדֶּךָ ("you alone"), adding tremendous emphasis on YHWH. One might expect Hezekiah to have said, "that you, YHWH, alone *are God*," but the ellipsis here adds even more focus on YHWH as the supreme being who alone has the ability to save Judah from Assyria. Hezekiah's request, then, has an ultimate purpose that goes beyond just the salvation of God's people; the king wants God's actions to draw glory and attention to YHWH's name alone.

From Text to Sermon

Big Idea. Godly prayers lean on God's character for God's glory.

Avenues for Illustration and Application. Unlike the more poetic sections of Isaiah, this passage does not offer many ready-made metaphors or illustrations for easy preaching. However, Hezekiah's prayer is packed with deep theology and can serve as a model for believers today. Unlike many contemporary prayers, which seem to launch straight into "request mode" ("Lord, I need this . . . please heal so-and-so . . . can't you please accomplish such-and-such . . ." etc.), Hezekiah chooses first to exalt God for his uniqueness, creation, and sovereignty. These qualities each connect to his eventual request—God uniquely holds the power over all creation (unlike the Assyrian idols and so-called gods), and therefore God alone sovereignly determines which nation will conquer which nation. Hezekiah's trust is not in Judean might or power but rests solely in God's character and abilities. Preachers can draw attention to this by noting the many emphatic pronouns and grammatical constructions which emphasize the Lord in the prayer (see esp. vv. 16b–c and 20d).

Also in contrast to many modern practices, Hezekiah's ultimate request is not for Judah's survival, but for God's glory and reputation among the nations. What if we were to pray like this? Yes, ask God to heal the terminal cancer patient (based on his goodness and ability to heal all diseases), but do so for God's ultimate glory and fame, not your own. Yes, request that the Lord move in your boss's heart for that promotion and raise your family so desperately needs (based on God's desire to bless his faithful people), but do so in order to increase God's name among your unbelieving coworkers. Yes, pray for God to remove the threats of violence against your country (based on God's character of peace and love), but do so in order that the name of Jesus and his love and peace will be manifest through the situation. Teaching people to pray like Hezekiah—based on God's character, with faith in God's actions, for God's glory—will deepen their relationship and dependence upon the Lord.

In all of this, make sure not to neglect prayer in the church service! Model it yourself before, during, or after the sermon. Save time at the end of the sermon to encourage congregants to pray in small groups using Hezekiah's prayer as their model. Leave the church with practical, hands-on action steps to sweeten their time with God.

Preachers can also make use of the biblical context to highlight elements in the prayer. In order to understand the gravity of Hezekiah's (and Judah's) situation, the material in 36:1–37:13 must at least be summarized for listeners. The more a preacher magnifies the reality of Assyria's threat upon Judah, the more magnified Hezekiah's trust in God becomes (and the more magnified God himself becomes in his ability to save Judah from such a threat!). Preachers may also want to contrast Hezekiah's reaction to the letter to Ahaz's reaction to a similar threat several decades earlier (Isa 7). This may take some time setting up and reminding listeners of the previous story, but the contrast is sharp and it may be well worth the effort to make the connection.

New Testament Connections. Hezekiah's prayer may bring to mind parallels with the so-called "Lord's Prayer" in Matt 6:9–13. This is especially the case considering the similar opening to both prayers, exalting/hallowing God's name before any requests are presented. It may also call to mind some of the apostle Paul's prayers, which consistently highlight God's character and aim at God's glory (e.g., Phil 1:3–11). Though few preachers will have time to adequately cover more than one passage per sermon, they might at least mention some of these other examples of similarly structured prayers, which will strengthen the notion that believers should learn from Hezekiah's exemplary prayer.

Preachers may also want to consider the gospel-laden values of Hezekiah's prayer. The king does not come before God claiming any authority or right to have his request honored. Hezekiah has a very real picture of his place before God: God is God and Hezekiah is not. The king must fully rely on God's deliverance to be saved from the Assyrian threat. By analogy, this is the starting point of the gospel of Jesus Christ. We are sinners, fully reliant on God's grace to deliver us from the consequences of our sin (Rom 6:23). But even our own salvation (or rejection of it) ultimately brings God glory rather than making us the center of attention (9:22–23). To God be the glory for our salvation in Jesus Christ!

ISAIAH 38:1–8

HEZEKIAH'S LIFE EXTENSION

Hearing a terminal diagnosis can upend one's world and radically change one's perspective on life. The way someone reacts to such a death sentence gives an indication of where their hope lies and where their relationship with the Lord truly is. In this chapter, King Hezekiah receives a terminal diagnosis from the prophet Isaiah. Rather than simply despairing, Hezekiah turns to the Lord, who ends up granting him an extension of life. Since all people face death, this passage challenges us to consider the brevity of life and the precious time we have on earth.

LARGER LITERARY CONTEXT ▸ 38:1–22

38:1–3

1a בַּיָּמִים הָהֵם חָלָה חִזְקִיָּהוּ לָמוּת

*bayyā**mîm** hā**hēm** ḥā**lâ** ḥizqiy**yā**hû lā**mût***

In those days, Hezekiah was terminally ill,

1b וַיָּבוֹא אֵלָיו יְשַׁעְיָהוּ בֶן־אָמוֹץ הַנָּבִיא

*wayyā**vô**ʾ ʾē**lāyw** yəšaʿ**yā**hû ven-ʾā**môṣ** hannā**vî**ʾ*

and Isaiah the prophet, son of Amoz, visited him.

1c וַיֹּאמֶר אֵלָיו כֹּה־אָמַר יְהוָה

*way**yō**ʾmer ʾē**lāyw** **kō**-ʾā**mar** YHWH*

And he said to him, “Thus says YHWH:

1d צַו לְבֵיתֶךָ

***ṣaw** ləvê**te**ḵā*

‘Organize your affairs,

1e כִּי מֵת אַתָּה

kî mēt** ʾat**tâ

for you’re a dead man

1f וְלֹא תִחְיֶה׃

*wə**lō**ʾ tiḥ**ye**.*

and you will not survive.’ ”

2a וַיַּסֵּב חִזְקִיָּהוּ פָּנָיו אֶל־הַקִּיר

*wayyas**sēv** ḥizqiy**yā**hû pā**nāyw** ʾel-haq**qîr***

So Hezekiah rolled over and faced the wall

2b וַיִּתְפַּלֵּל אֶל־יְהוָה׃

*wayyitpal**lēl** ʾel-YHWH.*

and he prayed to YHWH.

3a וַיֹּאמַר אָנָּה יְהוָה זְכָר־נָא

*wayyō'**mar** 'ān**nâ** YHWH zə**kār**-**nā'***

And he prayed, "Oh please, YHWH, I beg you to remember

3b אֵת אֲשֶׁר הִתְהַלַּכְתִּי לְפָנֶיךָ בֶּאֱמֶת וּבְלֵב שָׁלֵם

'ēt 'ăšer** hithal**lak**tî ləfā**nê**kā be'ĕ**met** ûvə**lēv** šā**lēm

how I walked before you faithfully
and with wholehearted allegiance,

3c וְהַטּוֹב בְּעֵינֶיךָ עָשִׂיתִי

*wəhaṭ**ṭôv** bə'ê**nê**kā 'ā**śî**tî*

and I have done good in your sight."

3d וַיֵּבְךְּ חִזְקִיָּהוּ בְּכִי גָדוֹל׃

*way**yēvk** ḥizqiy**yā**hû bə**kî** gā**dôl**.*

Then Hezekiah sobbed uncontrollably.

1a בַּיָּמִים הָהֵם חָלָה חִזְקִיָּהוּ לָמוּת

In those days, Hezekiah was terminally ill,

בַּיָּמִים יוֹם	in the days *bay·yā·**mîm***	ABS W/ PREP בְּ + DEF. ART.	noun
הָהֵם הֵם	the them *hā·**hēm***	--- W/ DEF. ART.	demonstr pron
חָלָה חלה	(he) was sick *ḥā·**lâ***	QAL PF 3MS	verb
חִזְקִיָּהוּ חִזְקִיָּהוּ	Hezekiah *ḥiz·qiy·**yā**·hû*	ABS	noun
לָמוּת מות	to die *lā·**mût***	QAL INF CST W/ PREP לְ	verb

The stock phrase "in those days" (בַּיָּמִים הָהֵם) loosely places the story in the events of the preceding chapters. Preachers may need to help the church understand that the narrator was not as concerned with strict chronology as modern readers (see esp. 38:6, which places this story during the already resolved Assyrian invasion). The infinitive לָמוּת ("to die") indicates that Hezekiah's illness was certainly terminal. Compare 2 Chr 32:25 for the Chronicler's theological reasoning behind the king's sickness.

1b	וַיָּבוֹא אֵלָיו יְשַׁעְיָהוּ בֶּן־אָמוֹץ הַנָּבִיא
	and Isaiah the prophet, son of Amoz, visited him.

וַיָּבוֹא בוא	and (he) came *way·yā·vô'*	QAL WAYY 3MS	verb
אֵלָיו אֶל	to him *'ē·lāyw*	--- W/ 3MS SX	prep
יְשַׁעְיָהוּ יְשַׁעְיָהוּ	Isaiah *yə·ša'·yā·hû*	ABS	noun
בֶּן־ בֵּן	son *ven-*	CST	noun
אָמוֹץ אָמוֹץ	Amoz *'ā·môṣ*	ABS	noun
הַנָּבִיא נָבִיא	the prophet *han·nā·vî'*	ABS W/ DEF. ART.	noun

The reintroduction of Isaiah the prophet ("son of Amos, the prophet") may indicate the inspired narrator used a previously published or otherwise established story from elsewhere. Literarily, though, the extended phrase contributes to the gravity of the visit.

1c	וַיֹּאמֶר אֵלָיו כֹּה־אָמַר יְהוָה
	And he said to him, "Thus says YHWH:

וַיֹּאמֶר אמר	and (he) said *way·yō'·mer*	QAL WAYY 3MS	verb
אֵלָיו אֶל	to him *'ē·lāyw*	--- W/ 3MS SX	prep

כֹּה־ thus כֹּה *kō-*		---	adv
אָמַר (he) says אמר *ʾā·mar*		QAL PF 3MS	verb
יְהוָה the LORD יהוה *YHWH*		ABS	noun

The phrase "thus says YHWH" (כֹּה־אָמַר יְהוָה) is typical prophetic speech indicating an authoritative word from the Lord. Along with the prophet's extended introduction (see notes on 1b), this causes the first-time reader to believe this prophetic word will be irrevocable, thus heightening the surprise twist later when the Lord reverses his decision.

1d צַו לְבֵיתֶךָ

'Organize your affairs,

צַו command/charge צוה *ṣaw*		PIEL IMPV MS	verb
לְבֵיתֶךָ your house בַּיִת *lə·vê·te·ḵā*		CST W/ PREP לְ + 2MS SX	noun

The Hebrew here is terse and abrupt. It is as surprising to the readers as it must have been for Hezekiah. The phrase is somewhat idiomatic: "Draw up your will; organize your affairs; get your house in order" or the like.

1e כִּי מֵת אַתָּה

for you're a dead man

כִּי for כִּי *kî*		---	conj
מֵת dying מות *mēt*		QAL PTCP MS	verb
אַתָּה you אַתָּה *ʾat·tâ*		---	personal pron

The translation is purposefully brusque to match the tone of the Hebrew. The brevity borders on offensive and lacks all the tact of modern bedside manners. Though some argue that Isaiah simply states the facts and does not mean to call down judgment (Oswalt 2003:427), the theological interpretation in 2 Chr 32:25 may point in another direction. The overly terse Hebrew emphasizes the certainty of the oracle (and once more heightens the surprise at the eventual reversal).

1f	וְלֹא תִחְיֶה׃

and you will not survive.' "

וְלֹא לֹא	and not *wə·lō'*	--- W/ CONJ וְ	particle
תִחְיֶה׃ חיה	you will live *tiḥ·ye*	QAL IMPF 2MS	verb

This final phrase is the third time in one verse where we are told of the terminal nature of the illness (first "Hezekiah was terminally ill" [1a], then "you're a dead man" [1e], and now this, "you will not survive"). The doctor's report is in: the disease has progressed to stage four. He will not survive, save a miracle.

2a	וַיַּסֵּב חִזְקִיָּהוּ פָּנָיו אֶל־הַקִּיר

So Hezekiah rolled over and faced the wall

וַיַּסֵּב סבב	and (he) turned *way·yas·sēv*	HIPH WAYY 3MS	verb
חִזְקִיָּהוּ חִזְקִיָּהוּ	Hezekiah *ḥiz·qiy·yā·hû*	ABS	noun
פָּנָיו פָּנֶה	his face *pā·nāyw*	CST W/ 3MS SX	noun
אֶל־ אֶל	to/toward *'el-*	---	prep
הַקִּיר קִיר	the wall *haq·qîr*	ABS W/ DEF. ART.	noun

2b	וַיִּתְפַּלֵּל אֶל־יְהוָה׃

and he prayed to YHWH.

וַיִּתְפַּלֵּל פלל	and he prayed *way·yit·pal·**lēl***	HITH WAYY 3MS	verb
אֶל־ אֶל	to *ʾel-*	---	prep
יְהוָה׃ יהוה	the LORD *YHWH*	ABS	noun

Readers should note the two uses of אֶל־ ("to") in 2a and 2b, juxtaposed for rhetorical effect. If only the first were used (2a), it would show great despair and an attitude of resignation. But the next verb (וַיִּתְפַּלֵּל) surprises the reader, along with the second אֶל־. The news may have shocked Hezekiah, but his faith remains intact and he is not ready to give up yet. His only hope is the Lord.

3a	וַיֹּאמַר אָנָּה יְהוָה זְכָר־נָא

And he prayed, "Oh please, YHWH, I beg you to remember

וַיֹּאמַר אמר	and he said *way·yōʾ·**mar***	QAL WAYY 3MS	verb
אָנָּה אָנָּא	please/I pray *ʾān·**nâ***	---	particle
יְהוָה יהוה	the LORD *YHWH*	ABS	noun
זְכָר־ זכר	remember *zə·ḵār-*	QAL IMPV MS	verb
נָא נָא	please/I pray ***nāʾ***	---	particle

Most translations struggle to bring out the force of the double particles here. Preachers can draw attention to them by commenting on the impact of these words. Hezekiah prays with the passion and urgency of a man who pleads for his life.

3b	אֵ֣ת אֲשֶׁ֣ר הִתְהַלַּ֣כְתִּי לְפָנֶ֗יךָ בֶּֽאֱמֶת֙ וּבְלֵ֣ב שָׁלֵ֔ם

how I walked before you faithfully
and with wholehearted allegiance,

אֵ֣ת אֵת	*(direct object marker)* *ʾēt*	---	particle
אֲשֶׁ֣ר אֲשֶׁר	who/which *ʾă·šer*	---	relative pron
הִתְהַלַּ֣כְתִּי הלך	I walked *hit·hal·**la**ḵ·tî*	HITH PF 1CS	verb
לְפָנֶ֗יךָ לִפְנֵי	to your face *lə·fā·**nê**·ḵā*	--- W/ 2MS SX	prep
בֶּֽאֱמֶת֙ אֱמֶת	with/in faithfulness/ truth *be·ʾĕ·**met***	ABS W/ PREP בְּ	noun
וּבְלֵ֣ב לֵב	and with heart *û·və·**lēv***	ABS W/ CONJ וְ + PREP בְּ	noun
שָׁלֵ֔ם שָׁלֵם	whole/complete *šā·**lēm***	MS ATTR	adj

The direct object marker (אֵת) indicates that this entire phrase (and the next) signifies what Hezekiah desires for the Lord to "remember" (זכר in v. 3a). To "walk" (הלך) before the Lord is a common biblical idiom for living a godly lifestyle. Grammatically, the two prepositions בְּ ("in/with") further define Hezekiah's walk before the Lord, and the adjective שָׁלֵם ("whole/complete") further defines Hezekiah's heart. Hezekiah believes that based on his faithful life, the Lord should grant an extension to his time on earth.

3c	וְהַטּ֥וֹב בְּעֵינֶ֖יךָ עָשִׂ֑יתִי

and I have done good in your sight."

וְהַטּ֥וֹב טוֹב	and the good (thing) *wə·haṭ·**ṭôv***	MS SUBST W/ CONJ וְ + DEF. ART.	adj
בְּעֵינֶ֖יךָ עַיִן	in your eyes *bə·ʿê·**nê**·ḵā*	CST W/ PREP בְּ + 2MS SX	noun
עָשִׂ֑יתִי עשׂה	I did *ʿā·**śî**·tî*	QAL PF 1CS	verb

This phrase further qualifies Hezekiah's "walk" (הלך). The adjective טוֹב ("good") here functions substantively, denoting good deeds. Hezekiah declares in no uncertain terms that his life has been one characterized by integrity and faithfulness; therefore, the Lord should respond positively to his request.

3d וַיֵּ֥בְךְּ חִזְקִיָּ֖הוּ בְּכִ֥י גָדֽוֹל׃

Then Hezekiah sobbed uncontrollably.

וַיֵּ֥בְךְּ בכה	and (he) wept *way·yēvk*	QAL WAYY 3MS	verb
חִזְקִיָּ֖הוּ חִזְקִיָּ֫הוּ	Hezekiah *ḥiz·qiy·yā·hû*	ABS	noun
בְּכִ֥י בְּכִי	weeping *bə·ḵî*	ABS	noun
גָדֽוֹל׃ גָּדוֹל	great *gā·dôl*	MS ATTR	adj

The Hebrew text literally reads, "And Hezekiah wept—a great weeping." The brevity and passion of the prayer, the desperate body language of the broken king, and now the uncontrolled sobbing all work together to reveal Hezekiah's pitiful and hopeless condition. Preachers can lean into these features of the text to draw out the nature of Hezekiah's fate.

38:4–6

4a וַיְהִי֙ דְּבַר־יְהוָ֔ה אֶל־יְשַׁעְיָ֖הוּ לֵאמֹֽר׃

*way**hî** dəvar-YHWH **ʾel**-yəša**ʿyā**hû lē**ʾmōr**.*

So the word of YHWH came to Isaiah, saying,

5a הָל֞וֹךְ וְאָמַרְתָּ֣ אֶל־חִזְקִיָּ֗הוּ

*hā**lôḵ** wəʾāmar**tā** ʾel-ḥizqiy**yā**hû*

“Go back and say to Hezekiah,

5b כֹּה־אָמַ֤ר יְהוָה֙ אֱלֹהֵי֙ דָּוִ֣ד אָבִ֔יךָ

***kō**-ʾ**āmar** YHWH ʾělō**hê** dā**wid** ʾā**vî**ḵā*

‘Thus says YHWH, God of your father David:

5c שָׁמַ֙עְתִּי֙ אֶת־תְּפִלָּתֶ֔ךָ רָאִ֖יתִי אֶת־דִּמְעָתֶ֑ךָ

*šā**ma**ʿtî ʾet-təfillā**te**ḵā rā**ʾî**tî ʾet-dim**ʿā**teḵā*

“I heard your prayer and I saw your tears.

5d הִנְנִי֙ יוֹסִ֣ף עַל־יָמֶ֔יךָ חֲמֵ֥שׁ עֶשְׂרֵ֖ה שָׁנָֽה׃

*hin**nî** yô**sîf** ʿal-yā**mê**ḵā ḥā**mēš** ʿeś**rē** šā**nâ**.*

Behold! I will increase your life by fifteen years.

6a וּמִכַּ֤ף מֶֽלֶךְ־אַשּׁוּר֙ אַצִּ֣ילְךָ֔ וְאֵ֖ת הָעִ֣יר הַזֹּ֑את

*ûmik**kaf** me**leḵ**-ʾaš**šûr** ʾaṣ**ṣî**ləḵā wəʾ**ēt** hā**ʿîr** hazz**ō**ʾt*

I will also save you and this city
from the clutches of the Assyrian king,

6b וְגַנּוֹתִ֖י עַל־הָעִ֥יר הַזֹּֽאת׃

*wəgannô**tî** ʿal-hā**ʿîr** hazz**ō**ʾt.*

and I will defend this city.

4a וַיְהִי דְּבַר־יְהוָה אֶל־יְשַׁעְיָהוּ לֵאמֹר׃

So the word of YHWH came to Isaiah, saying,

וַיְהִי היה	and (it) was/came *way·**hî***	QAL WAYY 3MS	verb
דְּבַר־ דָּבָר	word *də·var-*	CST	noun
יְהוָה יהוה	the Lord *YHWH*	ABS	noun
אֶל־ אֶל	to ***ʾel**-*	---	prep
יְשַׁעְיָהוּ יְשַׁעְיָהוּ	Isaiah *yə·šaʿ·**yā**·hû*	ABS	noun
לֵאמֹר׃ אמר	saying *lēʾ·**mōr***	QAL INF CST W/ PREP לְ	verb

The typical prophetic language here sets up the readers to expect another oracle, this time in direct response to Hezekiah's prayer request. The last oracle was unwaveringly negative; if Hezekiah's claim to have walked faithfully with the Lord is accurate, the reader should expect this one to be much more positive. Prayer changes things.

5a הָלוֹךְ וְאָמַרְתָּ אֶל־חִזְקִיָּהוּ

"Go back and say to Hezekiah,

הָלוֹךְ הלך	walk/go *hā·**lôḵ***	QAL INF ABS	verb
וְאָמַרְתָּ אמר	and (you) say *wə·ʾā·mar·**tā***	QAL WEQATAL 2MS	verb
אֶל־ אֶל	to *ʾel-*	---	prep
חִזְקִיָּהוּ חִזְקִיָּהוּ	Hezekiah *ḥiz·qiy·**yā**·hû*	ABS	noun

Attentive readers may notice the reuse of the verb הלך ("walk/go"), echoing Hezekiah's confident assertion that he faithfully "walked" (הלך) with the Lord. Though the word has the impact here of "return/go back," the echo of Hezekiah's language connects the two events. Hezekiah's faithful "walk" has impacted Isaiah's "walk" and thus changed his future.

5b	כֹּה־אָמַר יְהוָה אֱלֹהֵי דָּוִד אָבִיךָ

'Thus says YHWH, God of your father David:

כֹּה־ כֹּה	thus *kō-*	---	adv
אָמַר אמר	says *ʾā·**mar***	QAL PF 3MS	verb
יְהוָה יהוה	the LORD *YHWH*	ABS	noun
אֱלֹהֵי אֱלֹהִים	God *ʾĕ·lō·**hê***	CST	noun
דָּוִד דָּוִד	David *dā·**wid***	ABS	noun
אָבִיךָ אָב	your father *ʾā·**vî**·ḵā*	CST W/ 2MS SX	noun

Invoking the covenant/dynastic terminology "God of your father David," the Lord indicates that the answer to Hezekiah's request primarily serves the Davidic/messianic lineage rather than serving to personally benefit Hezekiah. Compare 2 Kgs 20:6 (// Isa 37:35), which also indicates that it was for the Lord's and David's sake that Hezekiah was healed, not because of his own piety.

5c	שָׁמַעְתִּי אֶת־תְּפִלָּתֶךָ רָאִיתִי אֶת־דִּמְעָתֶךָ

"I heard your prayer and I saw your tears.

שָׁמַעְתִּי שׁמע	I heard *šā·**maʿ**·tî*	QAL PF 1CS	verb
אֶת־ אֵת	*(direct object marker)* *ʾet-*	---	particle
תְּפִלָּתֶךָ תְּפִלָּה	your prayer *tə·fil·lā·**te**·ḵā*	CST W/ 2MS SX	noun

רָאִ֫יתִי ראה	I saw *rā·**ʾî**·tî*	QAL PF 1CS	verb
אֶת־ אֵת	*(direct object marker)* *ʾet-*	---	particle
דִּמְעָתֶ֑ךָ דִּמְעָה	your tears *dim·ʿā·**te**·ḵā*	CST W/ 2MS SX	noun

Note the perfect parallelism. It would almost be considered poetry were it not for the direct object markers, which usually characterize narrative. The Lord's words directly recall Hezekiah's two primary actions: praying and crying. Neither escaped the Lord's attention.

5d הִנְנִי֙ יוֹסִ֣ף עַל־יָמֶ֔יךָ חֲמֵ֥שׁ עֶשְׂרֵ֖ה שָׁנָֽה׃

Behold! I will increase your life by fifteen years.

הִנְנִ֫י הִנֵּה	behold, I! *hin·**nî***	--- W/ 1CS SX	particle
יוֹסִ֣ף יסף	it will be increased/ added *yô·**sîf***	HIPH IMPF 3MS	verb
עַל־ עַל	upon/over *ʿal-*	---	prep
יָמֶ֫יךָ יוֹם	your days *yā·**mê**·ḵā*	CST W/ 2MS SX	noun
חֲמֵ֥שׁ חָמֵשׁ	five *ḥă·**mēš***	CST	cardinal number
עֶשְׂרֵ֖ה עָשָׂר	ten *ʿeś·**rē***	ABS	cardinal number
שָׁנָֽה׃ שָׁנָה	year *šā·**nâ***	ABS	noun

The exclamatory "behold!" (הִנֵּה) catches readers and Hezekiah by surprise. It heralds a great message of hope and invites readers to consider the circumstances through the eyes of the king.

6a	וּמִכַּ֤ף מֶֽלֶךְ־אַשּׁוּר֙ אַצִּ֣ילְךָ֔ וְאֵ֖ת הָעִ֣יר הַזֹּ֑את

I will also save you and this city
from the clutches of the Assyrian king,

וּמִכַּ֤ף כַּף	and from palm *û·mik·**kaf***	CST W/ CONJ וְ + PREP מִן	noun
מֶֽלֶךְ־ מֶ֫לֶךְ	king ***me**·lek-*	CST	noun
אַשּׁוּר֙ אַשּׁוּר	Assyria *ʾaš·**šûr***	ABS	noun
אַצִּ֣ילְךָ֔ נצל	I will snatch/deliver you *ʾaṣ·**ṣî**·lə·kā*	HIPH IMPF 1CS W/ 2MS SX	verb
וְאֵ֖ת אֵת	and *(direct object marker)* *wə·**ʾēt***	--- W/ CONJ וְ	particle
הָעִ֣יר עִיר	the city *hā·**ʿîr***	ABS W/ DEF. ART.	noun
הַזֹּ֑את זֹאת	this *haz·**zōʾt***	--- W/ DEF. ART.	demonstr pron

This entire verse adds a bonus, something additional beyond the direct request of the prophet. The language indicates that Hezekiah currently resides in the "palm" (כַּף) of the Assyrian king, like he is a small object or toy to be played with at will. But God will forcibly "snatch" (נצל) both the king and the city of Jerusalem from the palm of the Assyrian king. Both God's sovereign omnipotence and his generosity are on display here.

6b	וְגַנּוֹתִ֖י עַל־הָעִ֥יר הַזֹּֽאת׃

and I will defend this city.

וְגַנּוֹתִ֖י גנן	and I will defend *wə·gan·nô·**tî***	QAL WEQATAL 1CS	verb
עַל־ עַל	over/upon *ʿal-*	---	prep
הָעִ֥יר עִיר	the city *hā·**ʿîr***	ABS W/ DEF. ART.	noun
הַזֹּֽאת׃ זֹאת	this *haz·**zōʾt***	--- W/ DEF. ART.	demonstr pron

The redundancy of this phrase puts emphasis on the city of David, which coincides with the remark about God answering the prayer in view of Hezekiah descending from David's lineage (v. 5b). This is another indication that God is not answering Hezekiah's prayer solely for Hezekiah's sake, but rather for the sake of his covenantal promises to David and his offspring (2 Sam 7:8–16) and his desire to protect the holy city (cf. Isa 37:35).

7a וְזֶה־לְּךָ֥ הָא֖וֹת מֵאֵ֣ת יְהוָ֑ה

*wəze-ləkā hāʾ**ô**t mēʾ**ē**t YHWH*

And this will be YHWH's sign for you

7b אֲשֶׁר֙ יַעֲשֶׂ֣ה יְהוָ֔ה אֶת־הַדָּבָ֥ר הַזֶּ֖ה אֲשֶׁ֥ר דִּבֵּֽר׃

*ʾă**šer** yaʿă**śe** YHWH ʾet-haddā**var** haz**ze** ʾă**šer** dib**bēr**.*

that YHWH will do this thing which he promised:

8a הִנְנִ֣י מֵשִׁ֣יב אֶת־צֵ֣ל הַֽמַּעֲל֡וֹת

*hin**nî** mē**šîv** ʾet-**ṣēl** hammaʿă**lôt***

Look! I am bringing back the shadow on the steps

8b אֲשֶׁ֣ר יָרְדָה֩ בְמַעֲל֨וֹת אָחָ֤ז בַּשֶּׁ֙מֶשׁ֙

*ʾă**šer** yārə**dâ** vəmaʿă**lôt** ʾā**ḥāz** baš**še**meš*

which has gone down by the steps of Ahaz in the sun

8c אֲחֹרַנִּ֔ית עֶ֖שֶׂר מַעֲל֑וֹת

*ʾăḥōran**nît** ʿ**e**śer maʿă**lôt***

ten steps backwards."'"

8d וַתָּ֤שָׁב הַשֶּׁ֙מֶשׁ֙ עֶ֣שֶׂר מַעֲל֔וֹת בַּֽמַּעֲל֖וֹת אֲשֶׁ֥ר יָרָֽדָה׃

*wat**tā**šāv haš**še**meš ʿ**e**śer maʿă**lôt** bammaʿă**lôt** ʾă**šer** yā**rā**dâ.*

Then the sun returned ten steps
upon the stairs where it came down.

7a **וְזֶה־לְּךָ הָאוֹת מֵאֵת יְהוָה**

And this will be YHWH's sign for you

וְזֶה־ זֶה	and this *wə·ze-*	--- W/ CONJ וְ	demonstr pron
לְּךָ לְ	to you *lə·kā*	--- W/ 2MS SX	prep
הָאוֹת אוֹת	the sign *hā·ʾôt*	ABS W/ DEF. ART.	noun
מֵאֵת אֵת	from *(direct object marker)* *mē·ʾēt*	--- W/ PREP מִן	particle
יְהוָה יהוה	the Lord *YHWH*	ABS	noun

Isaiah's use of the word הָאוֹת ("the sign") should recall the earlier usage in 7:11, 14 (cf. 8:18), where another Judean king (Ahaz) had his life threatened by an Assyrian king and was given a "sign" from the Lord. Here though, this sign was not a response to the unbelief of the king, but a response to his prayers.

7b **אֲשֶׁר יַעֲשֶׂה יְהוָה אֶת־הַדָּבָר הַזֶּה אֲשֶׁר דִּבֵּר׃**

that YHWH will do this thing which he promised:

אֲשֶׁר אֲשֶׁר	that *ʾă·šer*	---	relative pron
יַעֲשֶׂה עשׂה	(he) will do *ya·ʿă·śe*	QAL IMPF 3MS	verb
יְהוָה יהוה	the Lord *YHWH*	ABS	noun
אֶת־ אֵת	*(direct object marker)* *ʾet-*	---	particle
הַדָּבָר דָּבָר	the word/thing *had·dā·var*	ABS W/ DEF. ART.	noun
הַזֶּה זֶה	the this *haz·ze*	--- W/ DEF. ART.	demonstr pron

אֲשֶׁר אֲשֶׁר	which/that *'ă·šer*	---	relative pron
דִּבֵּר׃ דבר	he spoke *dib·bēr*	PIEL PF 3MS	verb

The sign will assure Hezekiah's extended life and Jerusalem's protection.

8a **הִנְנִ֨י מֵשִׁ֜יב אֶת־צֵ֣ל הַֽמַּעֲל֗וֹת**

Look! I am bringing back the shadow on the steps

הִנְנִי הִנֵּה	Behold, I! *hin·nî*	--- W/ 1CS SX	particle
מֵשִׁיב שׁוב	bringing back *mē·šîv*	HIPH PTCP MS	verb
אֶת־ אֵת	*(direct object marker)* *'et-*	---	particle
צֵל צֵל	shadow *ṣēl*	CST	noun
הַֽמַּעֲלוֹת מַעֲלָה	the steps/stairs *ham·ma·'ă·lôt*	ABS W/ DEF. ART.	noun

Another הִנֵּה ("behold!") again invites readers to participate by imagining through their mind's eye the sign the prophet describes. The Hebrew here is notoriously challenging, but the overall sense is clear: the sun's shadow (and perhaps time itself) reverses direction, as evidenced by the steps of Ahaz.

8b **אֲשֶׁ֣ר יָֽרְדָ֩ה בְמַעֲל֨וֹת אָחָ֤ז בַּשֶּׁ֨מֶשׁ**

which has gone down by the steps of Ahaz in the sun

אֲשֶׁר אֲשֶׁר	which *'ă·šer*	---	relative pron
יָֽרְדָה ירד	it went down *yā·rə·dâ*	QAL PF 3FS	verb
בְמַעֲלוֹת מַעֲלָה	by steps/stairs *və·ma·'ă·lôt*	CST W/ PREP בְּ	noun

אָחָז אָחָז	Ahaz *ʾā·ḥāz*	ABS	noun
בַּשֶּׁמֶשׁ שֶׁמֶשׁ	in the sun *baš·še·meš*	ABS W/ PREP בְּ + DEF. ART.	noun

The mention of the "steps of Ahaz" provides another link (in addition to the "sign") with Isa 7. The "sign" for Ahaz was a child (7:14). Now, the "sign" for Ahaz's child Hezekiah would be found on the steps of Hezekiah's father Ahaz! If preachers have already preached Isa 7, they will not want to miss drawing out some of the theological irony in the text.

8c אֲחֹרַנִּית עֶשֶׂר מַעֲלוֹת

ten steps backwards." ' "

אֲחֹרַנִּית אֲחֹרַנִּית	backwards *ʾă·ḥō·ran·nît*	---	adv
עֶשֶׂר עֶשֶׂר	ten *ʿe·śer*	CST	cardinal number
מַעֲלוֹת מַעֲלָה	steps/stairs *ma·ʿă·lôt*	ABS	noun

Even though 8a would have been sufficient to describe the nature of this sign, the addition of 8c makes the meaning of the text even more clear. God will prove Hezekiah's healing and Jerusalem's protection by means of something miraculous. Preachers should be careful not to read in additional details that the text does not explicitly mention, like confidently asserting that each step indicates one hour of time. Though this may be true, there is not enough in the text to give one confidence in the matter.

8d וַתָּשָׁב הַשֶּׁמֶשׁ עֶשֶׂר מַעֲלוֹת בַּמַּעֲלוֹת אֲשֶׁר יָרָדָה׃

Then the sun returned ten steps
upon the stairs where it came down.

וַתָּשָׁב שׁוּב	and (it) returned/turned *wat·tā·šāv*	QAL WAYY 3FS	verb
הַשֶּׁמֶשׁ שֶׁמֶשׁ	the sun *haš·še·meš*	ABS W/ DEF. ART.	noun

עֶ֫שֶׂר עֶ֫שֶׂר	ten *ʿe·śer*	CST	cardinal number
מַעֲל֔וֹת מַעֲלָה	steps/stairs *ma·ʿă·**lôt***	ABS	noun
בַּֽמַּעֲל֖וֹת מַעֲלָה	on the steps/stairs *bam·ma·ʿă·**lôt***	ABS W/ PREP בְּ + DEF. ART.	noun
אֲשֶׁ֥ר אֲשֶׁר	which *ʾă·**šer***	---	relative pron
יָרָֽדָה׃ ירד	it came down *yā·**rā**·dâ*	QAL PF 3FS	verb

This final phrase borrows and repackages language from the earlier phrases in 8a–c, which has the effect of prophecy fulfillment. What Isaiah predicted is accomplished. Preachers should avoid unnecessary "scientific" speculation on how this shadow reversal could have happened, be it something astronomical, or having to do with light refraction, or otherwise. The sign was likely miraculous, which means it may not correspond with natural phenomena.

From Text to Sermon

Big Idea. God graciously answers prayers beyond expectations.

Avenues for Illustration and Application. Unlike the more poetic passages of Isaiah, which are packed with metaphors ripe for illustrations, the narrative section here does not offer many built-in opportunities to clarify the text. However, Hezekiah's situation is all-too-familiar for many people and families. Preachers will not have to stretch anyone's imagination in order to get them to consider Hezekiah's plight. In fact, preachers and teachers should take extra care to be sensitive to those in the congregation who are currently fighting a potentially terminal disease, or who have had family members who recently lost such a fight. Merely drawing a line between Hezekiah's situation and the reality of many individuals will be enough to engage audiences in the story.

Preachers can point to Hezekiah's response to show the raw emotions—and yet correct posture—of someone with a terminal diagnosis. Though Hezekiah's self-pity and frustration show through his body language and prayer, he knows his life is in the Lord's hands and prays accordingly. When facing death, people either despair or they turn to the Lord with trust; oftentimes, the reaction is a mix of both. Preachers should avoid casting judgment on those who wrestle with crushing despair, and not pretend that one can experience only hopefulness without any sort of difficulty. Even godly men like Hezekiah experience a mix of emotions.

Additionally, Hezekiah's prayer cautions preachers to take care not to promise anything miraculous for those seeking healing, for God's sovereign will alone determines the answer to our prayers, no matter how godly we might be. But the emphasis in the text on David's line and Jerusalem's protection indicates that though Hezekiah based his prayer on his own faithfulness, God's answer was based on grace, not bound by Hezekiah's integrity. Likewise, even though the prayers of righteous people are powerful and effective (Jas 5:16), this does not ensure that godly believers get *anything* they ask for.

Finally, preachers can also offer sober encouragement to consider the brevity of one's life. Hezekiah anticipated many more years but was given shocking news that upended his perspective. What if we were given such news today? Are we living in light of the oftentimes surprising imminence of death? No one is promised tomorrow; therefore, live for Christ today.

New Testament Connections. Though the text offers no explicit, direct contact with the New Testament, several avenues exist to link themes. The reality of death for all people obviously brings to mind the equal reality of the resurrection for believers. Death is not the end for any of us. Life in Christ offers a resurrection hope that extends beyond the physical grave (1 Cor 15). The passage can therefore be preached with gospel application in mind.

Additionally, many New Testament passages point to the hope a believer has beyond death. John 3:16 and Rom 6:23 may be among the most classic and memorable, but other passages such as Paul's confident assurance that death is "gain" (Phil 1:21) and his knowledge that to be absent from the body (in death) is to be present with the Lord (2 Cor 5:8) all have relevance to the theology of this passage. Even reflecting on eschatological truths, like the eventual death of death (Rev 21:4), can have great impact on the church.

Preachers can also consider the theme of effective prayer for possible New Testament connections. The connection between godly people and the effectiveness of their prayers is abundantly clear (e.g., John 9:31; Jas 5:16; 1 John 3:22; cf. Ps 34:15). Again, preachers should not make God seem like a genie in a bottle, granting wishes for those who keep up their spiritual disciplines, but they should also avoid downplaying too much the biblical assertion that God does respond to faithful believers in his great grace.

WORKS CITED

Avalos, Hector. 1992. "Zaphon, Mount." Pp. 1040–41 in vol. 6 of *The Anchor Bible Dictionary*, edited by David Noel Freedman. New York: Doubleday.

Baltzer, Klaus. 2001. *Deutero-Isaiah*. Hermeneia. Translated by Margaret Kohl and edited by Peter Machinist. Minneapolis: Fortress.

Fyall, Robert S. 2002. *Now My Eyes Have Seen You: Images of Creation and Evil in the Book of Job*. New Studies in Biblical Theology 12. Downers Grove, IL: InterVarsity Press.

Garland, David E. 2003. *1 Corinthians*. Baker Exegetical Commentary on the New Testament. Grand Rapids: Baker Academic.

Harman, Allan. 1997. "Particles." Pp. 1028–42 in vol. 4 of *New International Dictionary of Old Testament Theology and Exegesis*, edited by Willem A. VanGemeren. Grand Rapids: Zondervan.

Hagner, Donald A. 1993. *Matthew 1–13*. Word Biblical Commentary 33a. Dallas: Word.

Jodar, Etienne. 2022. "The Cryptic Saying of Isaiah 28:10, 13 and Paul's Controversy over Tongues in 1 Corinthians 14:20–25." *Themelios* 47 (3): 459–71.

Murawski, Bryan. 2021. *Preaching Difficult Texts of the Old Testament*. Peabody, MA: Hendrickson.

Ortlund, Eric. 2021. *Piercing Leviathan: God's Defeat of Evil in the Book of Job*. New Studies in Biblical Theology 56. Downers Grove, IL: InterVarsity Press.

Oswalt, John N. 1986. *The Book of Isaiah, Chapters 1–39*. New International Commentary on the Old Testament. Grand Rapids: Eerdmans.

———. 2003. *Isaiah*. NIV Application Commentary. Grand Rapids: Zondervan.

Price, James D. 1997. “צלל.” Pp. 807–10 in vol. 3 of *New International Dictionary of Old Testament Theology and Exegesis*, edited by Willem A. VanGemeren. Grand Rapids: Zondervan.

Roberts, J. J. M. 2015. *First Isaiah*. Hermeneia. Minneapolis: Fortress.

Smith, Gary V. 2007. *Isaiah 1–39*. New American Commentary 15A. Nashville: Broadman & Holman.

Waltke, Bruce K., and M. O’Connor. 1990. *An Introduction to Biblical Hebrew Syntax*. Winona Lake, IN: Eisenbrauns.

Walton, John. 1997. “עֲלוּמִים.” Pp. 415–19 in vol. 3 of *New International Dictionary of Old Testament Theology and Exegesis*, edited by Willem A. VanGemeren. Grand Rapids: Zondervan.

Wegner, Paul D. 2021. *Isaiah: An Introduction and Commentary*. Tyndale Old Testament Commentaries 20. Downers Grove, IL: InterVarsity Press.

INDEX OF BIBLICAL REFERENCES

NOTE: The primary purpose of a Scripture index in a book like this, where biblical passages are being treated directly, is not to present the reader with every biblical reference found in the book, but to offer ones that lie outside the range of each of the passages treated. Hence, this index presents references to such outside passages, plus verses from the passages treated in this book *but only when these are cross-referenced in a discussion of another verse found in these passages.*

ABOUT THE AUTHOR

Bryan Murawski (PhD, Westminster Theological Seminary) is an Associate Professor at Cairn University where he teaches courses in Old Testament, Hebrew, theology, and ministry. He also serves part-time as a pastor at Riverstone Church in Yardley, PA. His books include *Preaching Difficult Texts of the Old Testament* and *1 Peter: A Commentary for Biblical Preaching and Teaching* (with Tim Miller). His writing has been featured on websites such as The Gospel Coalition and Modern Reformation. In addition to his academic and pastoral roles, he teaches at camps and retreats. Bryan and his wife, Janice, have been married for more than sixteen years and have four children.